22836

PIERRE VERLET · MICHEL FLORISOONE
ADOLF HOFFMEISTER · FRANÇOIS TABARD

THE BOOK OF TAPESTRY

HISTORY AND TECHNIQUE

PRÉFACE BY JEAN LURÇAT

CONTENTS

PUBLISHER'S PREFACE

For many people, tapestry belongs to the past. It evokes the thousand-year-long Middle Ages and hazy memories of mythical unicorns, of gallant armour-clad knights, of the blood of martyred saints, of Christianity trembling before the vision of the Apocalypse. Or else it calls to mind some celebrated and fragile work of art hung in a museum or in an out-of-the-way European church. Yet this half-forgotten wonder is a living reality; this art is not extinct. In today's concrete houses and on the vast, denuded walls of our public buildings, tapestries—monumental tapestries—are reappearing like so many modern woolwrought frescoes.

The renaissance of the art of tapestry-making has taken place largely over the last twenty years. The revival came only after a period of decline of more than two hundred years during which the art, as old as human history, almost disappeared entirely. That it was revived at all owes most to the artists and craftsmen of France.

In 1962, the First International Biennial Tapestry Exhibition was organized at Lausanne, Switzerland. One hundred and fifty-two tapestries were submitted by seventeen different countries and the jury chose fifty-seven for exhibition. At the conclusion of the show one fact was clear: although France was in the vanguard of the recent revival—with painter Jean Lurçat and master weaver François Tabard in the very front rank—the movement was being enthusiastically pursued in other countries. Moreover, the time was at last ripe and the pioneers' tenacity had coincided with a public awakening to the need for something which would lend feeling to ultra-functional architecture and help satisfy the need for warmth and grandeur lingering in men's hearts. This something turned out to be tapestry.

The latter-day meeting of modern architecture and tapestry, however fortunate, was not merely a matter of chance. Both arts were persistently linked during the centuries-long history of European civilization. Tapestry was already well acquainted with the cold, bare walls of huge feudal castles. So, to really understand this art which is being reborn now in our own age, one must go back, far back—if not as far as tapestry's obscure origins, then at least to the remote Middle Ages, for this is the period which has tutored the artists responsible for today's resurrection.

When we set out here at Edita to create an intelligible account of this aspect of contemporary artistic life we found that, on the one hand, we had to compose a panoramic survey of tapestry as it is being made today and, on the other, to study tapestry's past to know precisely how the present came about. At present no other book deals with tapestry's history as a whole. Recently published works have been monographs usually devoted to one country only or to one historic period and their obvious defect has been to present only very fragmentary views of the subject. With this book we have filled the gap.

"Great Tapestries" is, therefore, a completely new and original work. For the first time scores of tapestries, of widely differing origins and spanning more than seven centuries of history, have been reproduced together. For the first time complete sets of tapestries, designed and woven specifically to be hung together (but now split up between different museums), have been reunited on paper. For the first time all the most celebrated havens of tapestries which hold thousands of works treasured by the Hapsburgs, the Kings of Poland and of Sweden, the Vatican and the greatest museums of Europe and America, have been metaphorically plundered to supply our illustrations. Our book is divided into four parts, the first three devoted to the history of tapestry and the fourth to the technique of weaving.

Pierre Verlet, who wrote the introduction to mediaeval tapestry, has the double responsibility of caring for the beautiful *Lady with the Unicorn* at the Musée de Cluny and the splendid *Noble Pastoral* at the Louvre. He explains how feudal lords made use of such sets as the *Heroes* (now in The Cloisters, New York) in their castle halls, and how the Church helped create and preserve world famous works like the Angers *Apocalypse*. He also describes the subjects preferred by princes and prelates for their tapestries, as well as the working methods of the designers and weavers of France and Flanders.

When Michel Florisoone wrote our second chapter he was the Director of the Gobelins National Manufactory and thus the successor of 17th-century painters Charles Le Brun (who, among other things, helped Louis XIV decorate Versailles), and Pierre Mignard. No one alive knows better than he how the Renaissance, which transformed society and the arts, also had a decisive influence on the development of tapestry. Beginning with an account of the bourgeois Flemish and princely Italian, Spanish and English workshops, he goes on to trace the main steps in the history of the Gobelins where, starting with Le Brun's famous *Story of the King*, so many masterpieces have been woven.

The revival of tapestry-making over the last twenty years has nowhere, until now, been described impartially and fully enough. Adolf Hoffmeister, who is a historian and a member of the committee of the *Centre International de Tapisseries Anciennes et Modernes* (International Center of Antique and Modern Tapestries) at Lausanne, Switzerland, interweaves a description of how this revival took place with brief discussions of the best-known French tapestry designers of today. Many of these artists—like Jean Lurçat, Jean Picart Le Doux and Marc Saint-Saëns— have tapestries on show in the most important museums in the world. Naturally the author gives an account of the French school. But he concludes with something that has never been done before—a world round-up of tapestry, which comments on the quality and characteristics of the most significant of recent works particularly those shown at the First International Biennial Tapestry Exhibition at Lausanne, in 1962.

The final chapter is by master weaver François Tabard. In his family the weaving tradition goes back to 1637 and he gives a comprehensive, step-by-step account of how tapestries are designed and woven to this day.

The art of tapestry-making has not much changed during the centuries. For a long time the famous "Bayeux tapestry" in France, illustrating the Norman Conquest of England was thought to represent an evolution of the old weaving methods. However, we know today that it is not a real tapestry at all but a masterpiece of embroidery, probably unique in the world.

Tapestry owes its resurrection in recent years mainly to Jean Lurçat who very kindly assisted us in the accomplishment of this work. We could not have found a better adviser and we are happy to say that the adviser has since become a friend of the editors.

For these reasons the reader will here find—in a single volume—a collection of texts and pictures together constituting a valuable overall guide to a living and fascinating art intimately linked to many of the most provocative moments in human history. Here, for his interest, are the dreams, the legends and the everyday occupations of our medieval forefathers, naïvely related by Gothic tapestries; the pomp, the power and the glory of kings boasted by the tapestries of Flanders, Italy and the Gobelins; and our 20th-century conquests, our joys and our anguish, and our artistic experimentation mirrored in contemporary tapestry.   J.J.

GOTHIC TAPESTRY

from the 12th to the 16th Century

PIERRE VERLET

Curator of the Musée de Cluny, Paris
Curator of the Department of Objets d'Art, Musée du Louvre, Paris

The visitor entering the great hall in the Château of Angers (France) will find himself face to face with the finest and largest tapestry sequence surviving from the Middle Ages—the Angers *Apocalypse* which was woven between 1375 and 1380. It is also one of the very oldest tapestries still in existence. When it was fresh off the looms, Gothic art had been flourishing in France for two centuries and most of the great French cathedrals were already completed. The *Apocalypse*, and other tapestries woven from that period up to the mid-16th century, belong, therefore, to art's Gothic era. And the revival of tapestry which we in our century are now witnessing claims descent, precisely, from the qualities of Gothic tapestry, namely, few—but warm and living—colours, sturdy wools and a rugged weave. Rather than deal with the *history* of Gothic tapestry from the purely chronological point of view, we propose, in the following pages, to examine the most important *aspects* of the art during the last two centuries of this long and rich period. A clearer idea will thus be given of those firmly-entrenched traditional qualities which survived during the ensuing classical period—from the 16th century to the 20th—and also of those characteristics which have been directly inherited or re-acquired by contemporary weavers and artists after four centuries of neglect. This, we hope, will enable readers to appreciate just how much tapestry today owes to the painters and weavers of the long-distant Middle Ages.

It may seem superfluous to explain that a tapestry's essential role is to cover a wall. This obvious link between wall and tapestry, however, had an unexpected and paradoxical consequence: in its evolution Gothic architecture, which grew out of man's aspiration towards God, was more favourable to secular tapestry than to religious tapestry.

THE USES OF GOTHIC TAPESTRY

It is always a surprise to realize how few Gothic tapestries on religious topics are mentioned in old texts in comparison with the many which are devoted to worldly subjects. To conclude that the former were less popular than the latter or that the Church was uninterested in religious art would be to misunderstand totally the prevailing spirit of the epoch. Yet the great abbeys and cathedrals did exert an enormous influence in the Middle Ages. Then why aren't more Gothic tapestries religious? How can the paradox be explained? The explanation in fact is architectural rather than ecclesiastical. It has to do with what kinds of wall surfaces needed to be covered.

The château was originally a fortified castle, but later the term came to be applied to any palace or large country residence. Up until the end of the Middle Ages, a château's fortress-like purpose and construction were stoutly maintained even in its residential quarters—and even in the more fancy and pretentious constructions of the Dukes of Orleans and Burgundy. Its immense bare walls were broken only by the chimney-breasts, narrow doors and sparsely scattered windows. What wonderful surfaces for displaying tapestries are offered, for example, by the Audience Chamber of the old

Popes' Palace at Avignon, or by the great hall of the Duc de Berry's château (now the Palace of Justice) at Poitiers! But no correspondingly vast tapestry sequences remain today, with the exception of the Angers *Apocalypse* (see pages 37 to 39), the *Heroes* (in The Cloisters, New York—see page 40) or the *Chartsworth Hunts* (in the Victoria and Albert Museum, London—see pages 50 to 51).

But if château walls were huge and unbroken, the walls of churches were simultaneously shrinking to make way for more and more windows. Naturally, local circumstances here and there led to certain naves having larger stretches of wall—as, for instance, in the great Chapel at Avignon, and in Angers Cathedral, where until recently the *Apocalypse* tapestries, bequeathed by King René of Anjou and Anne de Beaujeu, were displayed in summer. But, as a general rule, tapestry played only a secondary role in the decoration of churches during the Middle Ages. Tapestries customarily were relegated to the walls of the side-aisles, were hung over the stalls, or suspended between the pillars and they constituted an addition to the church's treasury. But, in general, for want of walls on which it could be shown to advantage, tapestry did not meet with the same success in churches as in secular life.

The fact that tapestries could be woven to the dimensions of the wall they were intended to decorate was a great advantage. The vast tapestry illustrating the *Story of Judas Maccabeus and of Antiochus*, which belonged to Charles V, seems to have been made to fit the great wall of the gallery of the Château of Beauté-sur-Marne—at least judging from the following entry in the inventory drawn up after the king's death: "Item, one large cloth of Arras work with the deeds and battles of Judas Maccabeus and Antiochus, stretching from one of the turrets of the gallery at Beauté to just beyond the turret at the far end of the same, and being of the same height as the said gallery."

Although this entry is a precise and exceptional example, the case referred to seems to have been fairly typical. Many of the differences in height and width between different tapestries of the same set are not due to accidents or alterations over the years. They can be explained time and again by the unequal dimensions of the castle walls or the apses of the church for which they were woven. Rheims Cathedral's *Life of the Virgin* and even the *Lady with the Unicorn* (see page 45) must also be included in the category of existing tapestries which were produced for a specific setting. So must most of those pieces designed and woven in long narrow bands and intended for hanging over the stalls in the choir of cathedrals and abbeys. The *Saint Stephen* series, ordered by a bishop of Auxerre for his cathedral and now in the Musée de Cluny, is a famous example.

But what made tapestries even more practical in the Gothic period was their extreme mobility. Because they could be easily packed up and moved about, tapestries were eagerly sought after by princes who were constantly travelling—either to do battle, to govern their lands, or to collect tribute offered by their vassals. Like everyone else, they naturally wished to carry their familiar surroundings with them. Silk hangings could be used for the same purpose, but in France they tended to be too expensive. And they withstood wear and tear far less well than tapestries. Easily folded and stowed away, tapestries were also light enough to be loaded on to waggons or pack-animals. Anne of Brittany's accounts, for instance, mention several payments made "to the driver of the beast bearing the said Lady's tapestry".

Because tapestries were so often found in a warring prince's baggage, they also began to form a rich part of the booty when he was beaten. The story of how tapestries changed hands, in fact, is often something like a shortened account of the major war of a given period. The large pieces making up the *Story of Clovis*, for instance, an account of the life of the first king of France, which were given to Rheims Cathedral in 1579 by the Cardinal de Lorraine, were originally ordered by Philip the Good of Burgundy and were used to decorate one of the rooms where the marriage of Charles the Bold and Margaret of York was celebrated in 1468. Eventually they fell into the hands of the Lorraine family when the Holy Roman Emperor Charles V (a descendant of the Dukes of Burgundy) had to abandon his baggage to François de Lorraine, Duc de Guise, at the siege of Metz in 1553.

At stopping-places or on arrival in a new residence, the tapestries were unloaded, unrolled and hung up on nails specially made and carried along for the purpose. This procedure is illustrated in the household accounts of Charles VI of France during the first year of his reign, in 1380-1381. By following the record of petty expenses occasioned by the removal and installation of the king's tapestries, we can follow the progress of the Court from Paris to Rheims. A certain Guérin Briquart "hookmaker, dwelling in Paris" is entered on October 3, for two hundred hooks, "bought from him for hanging the tapestries in the chambers of the King and my lord the Duke of Valois, at Melun". On October 17, for a thousand hooks for the chambers of the king and his suite; on November 1, for four thousand hooks during the royal halt at Igny. On November 4, for two thousand hooks "to hang the King's chambers at Rheims." The return journey can likewise be traced step by step, and the accounts include the hooks for the Palace of Paris, the Louvre, the Hôtel Saint-Pol and the Château de Vincennes, and even two iron hammers.

One can see from these details that the hanging of tapestries, even in the greatest residences, resulted each time in a different arrangement and the need for a certain amount of improvisation. Such adjustments followed from the mobile and supple character of the fabric itself and from the variable measurements of the sequences which, as already stated, were often designed for a predetermined position. Perhaps the court hookmaker was greedy for an unending flow of orders, even from the châteaux where Charles V had had a customary residence. In any event, hooks were always left in place at the prince's home so that his tapestries could be rehung rapidly. During the course of Jean Trouvelot's restorations at the Château de Châteaudun many hooks of this kind were found, which had been left in place even by the 18th-century occupants when their purpose was apparently understood.

The principal aim of tapestry, obviously, was to cover the walls of a given room completely, and to provide a homogeneous decoration which related to both the walls and the furniture. The simplest, but most rarely used, method of creating this kind of interior decoration consisted in weaving panels to fit chosen walls. But that method did not supply the equally sought-after quality of interchangeability. This led to another obvious solution: to have very large tapestries woven for halls, medium-sized pieces for private rooms and small strips for wardrobes which were often situated in towers and lined with wood panelling—in short, a basic size pattern, BIG, MEDIUM and SMALL, like those used today in making sweaters. A varied supply of tapestries could be used to the best advantage on arrival at any new residence, simply by unpacking those which best suited the walls requiring decoration.

But no prince, however rich his general stock of tapestries might be, could expect to have a wide enough choice of tapestries to achieve a perfect fit everywhere he went (the vertical wall-to-wall carpeting of the time!). The servant entrusted with the work of decoration was expected to improvise. Some of the possible combinations and resources open to him are illustrated by the two following examples—taken from French miniatures from the early 15th century. The first was to make tapestry in narrow strips, presenting not scenes but decorative symbols. These could be added or cut out, as leaves are added to expandable tables. For example, in a manuscript by Christine de Pisan, now the property of the British Museum, Queen Isabeau of Bavaria, wife of Charles VI, is shown in her room surrounded by her ladies. She is sitting on a cushion placed on a bench covered with material, and her little dog is beside her. Opposite is her four-poster bed, its curtains drawn back to reveal the counterpane, the back-cloth and the canopy. And fixed to the walls with large hooks are bands of fabric bearing alternately the lilies *(fleurs-de-lys)* of France and the lozenges of Bavaria, stretching from either side of the window at the far end of the room, turning the corners and coming back along the two walls towards the onlooker. The repetition of the heraldic motif could imply either silk or woollen hangings—but they are most probably tapestries. Isabeau possessed works of this kind and among the tapestries of the royal treasury, scattered by the English during their occupation of Paris in the 100 Years' War, can be noted "a green bedroom set from Brittany in two parts, marked YY"—thought to denote the queen's monogram (in the Middle Ages the name Isabeau was spelt with "Y": Ysabeau.) Fragments of tapestry from this period, with a background of lilies and the crowned L's of the Dukes of Anjou, have been preserved in the museums of Angers and Nantes, and correspond to this same type of easy-to-use heraldic tapestry. In the same connection we may mention those ordered from Paris in 1442 by René of Anjou for his Accounts Chamber: "four large pieces of tapestry, eight bench-cushions and two square cushions, all with the arms of Anjou".

Another idea was to treat tapestries like a kind of removable wallpaper and simply bend them around corners on coming to the end of a wall. This system is seen in the Duc de Berry's famous miniatures *Les Très Riches Heures* (Book of Hours), preserved at Chantilly. On the page corresponding to January, Duc Jean de Berry can be seen at table, seated in front of a great hearth with a wicker fire-screen behind him. Over his head is a dais with his coat-of-arms and emblems—the bear and the swan. And, fixed with un-equally-spaced nails, a tapestry depicting a battle scene, with inscriptions in the upper part, decorates the whole wall. This miniature shows the casual, almost careless manner, in which these works were handled at the time— works whose beauty and rarity today command our greatest respect. Starting on the left-hand wall, just after a dresser, the tapestry turns the corner and unfolds along the rear wall which contains the fire-place. To leave the mantelpiece free, the lower part of the tapestry has been pushed up into great lumpy folds which are thoroughly noticeable. The back-cloth of the dais has also received the same treatment.

In the Middle Ages, "door-pieces" (called *portières*) existed—small tapestries specially woven to hang over doors. But more often than not, if a tapestry was too large for the available space, it was ruthlessly cut, either to fit around doorways or to adapt to a better position. This misfortune befell one of the Middle Ages' most famous works, the *Battle of Roosebecke*, ordered by Philip the Bold of Burgundy from Michel Bernard of Arras in 1387; it was divided into three parts in the early 15th century and some time later these were again cut in two.

The complete decoration of a hall with tapestry gradually began to entail matching the furniture to the wall hangings. Of course, in the early days, furniture and mural decorations were not designed to match each other. For example, in the inventory made in 1328 after the death of Clémence of Hungary, widow of Louis X (called "the Headstrong"), various still entirely separate items are mentioned—some seats "with daisies" on the one hand, and "a set of eight tapestries, with a hunting motif, to decorate a room" on the other.

But only a hundred years later, in the early 15th century, the inventory of the Duc de Berry's tapestries shows that a decorative evolution had by then taken place. It mentions a "swan room" made up of a back-cloth, canopy, counterpane and three bed-curtains, a tapestry to cover a bench, two large cushions and four small ones, and finally "a large tapestry" and "six other tapestries" of varying sizes, matching the rest of the furnishings. Further, among those tapestries owned by Charles VI are noted: "The canopy and

14

back-cloth of a *Tournai room*, in gold and silk, with six tapestries belonging to the said room, five large and one small."

Similarly, the accounts, instructions and inventories of the Dukes of Burgundy are full of entries dealing with tapestries, and two of these are quoted here. The first mentions "a rich chamber of high-warp tapestry, of Arras thread, called the *little children's room*, with a canopy, back-cloth and bed-spread all worked in gold and silk... the said back-cloth and bed-spread strewn with trees, grasses and little children; and at the top with rambling roses on a red background". The second, a payment made in 1464 to Pasquier Grenier "tapestry merchant dwelling in Tournai" describes "a *chamber* of tapestry worked in wool and silk threads, containing six cushions, one bench-cloth and nine other pieces, namely, one large bed-spread, one canopy, one back-cloth, a cot cover and a back-cloth for the said cot, and four wall hangings, all covered with shrubs and verdure, and all over these pieces are shown adult figures such as servants, peasants, and woodcutters, ploughing and working in various manners, the said nine pieces, bench-cloth and cushions containing 350 ells".

Quite elaborate décors could be obtained because these tapestries were so movable—especially when they were joined by pieces of cloth prepared for the furniture itself. It was easy to change both wall hangings and furnishings, not only to accompany a prince on his travels but also to suit his changes of mood. The rich were thus able to renew their interior decoration constantly, and the not-so-rich had an ornament which could easily be put in place according to the season or to suit the needs of any especially festive occasions.

This was particularly true of church tapestries which, in the same way as in private homes, could be hung up in winter to keep out the cold a little. When hung over the choir-stalls of a church, they certainly formed a kind of screen which muffled the chill draughts coming from the vaults and side-aisles. This practice led to the weaving of long panels which are found in both France and the German-speaking countries. Such panels are still used in the old Chaise-Dieu abbey, where the *Life of Christ* series was presented by Abbot Jacques de Sennect in the early 16th century and hung in the choir for the first time in 1518.

One of the most charming devices ever to have been invented by the weavers of the Gothic age is known as "mille-fleurs" (thousand flowers), in which the tapestry's background is sprinkled all over with hundreds of flower motifs (see pages 46 to 47). The origin of the idea may have been the desire to have a gay floral decoration permanently to hand, but woven in durable wool. In the French countryside, during "Fête-Dieu" (Corpus Christi) religious processions, the custom still exists of fixing bouquets of flowers on to sheets of bunting to decorate the streets. The Middle Ages flowered tapestries may have been simply a permanent transcription of these fast-wilting decorations.

A protection against the cold, a decoration for great occasions and a magnificent pictorial reserve, these were the functions of Gothic tapestry—in each
case facilitated by its mobility. The subjects represented will be dealt with
later. But it is not hard to imagine also the joyous effect of these beautiful
tapestries when they were hung in unaccustomed places. The brilliance of
their colours and the richness of their designs were undoubtedly appreciated
on ceremonial church occasions, for instance, by clergy and laity alike.
Both groups clamoured for the tapestries of Paris, Arras or elsewhere.

Any attempt at classification is bound to be somewhat arbitrary. Nevertheless some of the main themes and preoccupations of Gothic tapestry are
clear enough. It is useful to put them under subject headings because the
method not only helps in enumerating some of the principal works still in
existence, but allows organized speculation about certain masterpieces which
have now unfortunately disappeared.

We have already talked about the relatively small number of religious
tapestries, compared with those intended for secular buildings, in Gothic
times at least. The proportion, of course, does not apply to what still exists
today, for a fairly large number of tapestries have survived simply because
they were kept safely in their churches, where they were less often used and
less vulnerable to changes of fashion. Some, indeed, have been in the same
church for centuries. The most outstanding example is undoubtedly fur-
nished by Halberstadt Cathedral which, ever since 1205, has owned at least
three ancient tapestries or fragments of tapestry, two of them on religious
topics. Another notable case is that of the two parts of *Saint Piat* and *Saint
Eleuthère* (see page 41), reunited during the 19th-century restorations,
which have been the property of Tournai Cathedral since 1402. An old
inscription gives this date and the name of their donor, Toussaint Prier,
chaplain of the Duke of Burgundy and canon of the cathedral. Many
other pieces, complete or otherwise, have remained since the Middle Ages in
the churches of France: the *Apocalypse* (see pages 37 to 39) and *Saint
Maurille* at Angers, *Saint Peter* at Beauvais, *Saint Florent* at Saumur, *Saint
Gervase* at Le Mans, the previously-mentioned *Life of the Virgin* at Rheims
and the *Life of Christ* at the Chaise-Dieu.
Such subjects, mostly linked to the cult of local saints, were the result of
special orders. We can often trace the date or the name of the donor: a
bishop of Beauvais in 1460, for instance, the chapter of the cathedral for the
patron saint of Angers in the same year, an abbot of Saint Florent's in
Saumur in 1524, and a canon of Le Mans who ordered the series on *Saint
Gervase* and *Saint Protais* in 1509.
Many more such examples exist, among them: the *Saint-Stephen* series (now
in the Musée de Cluny) presented by a bishop of Auxerre to Saint Stephen's
Cathedral in the late 15th century; an eleven-piece set on *Saint Anatolius*
(three surviving pieces are on show in the Louvre Museum), completed at

Bruges in 1501 for the canons of Saint Anatolius' church at Salins; and the *Saint-Remy* sequence, commissioned some time before 1531 for Saint Remy's abbey at Rheims by Archbishop Robert de Lenoncourt who at the same time ordered the *Life of the Virgin*, already mentioned, for his cathedral.

Broader subjects of more general interest, however, must have had the greatest influence on the development of Gothic tapestry. We can imagine the impetus given to painters, weavers and fellow princes by the magnificence of a famous prince's lavish order. The beauty of such a work of art as Louis I of Anjou's *Apocalypse* (whose origin will be examined later in connection with "cartoons" and composition), could not fail to attract the attention of the Valois princes. It is not surprising to find an *Apocalypse* mentioned in the inventory of Duc Jean de Berry, although it is smaller than the one of Anjou. We shall also refer later to the part played by patrons, but it is well to consider at this stage the repercussions of such an order as the one for *Gideon* "the richest tapestry ever to have graced a king's court". The designs (or cartoons as they are called) for this eight-piece sequence were painted at Arras by Baudouin de Bailleul and the weaving was carried out at Tournai; the preparation of such a vast work inevitably had a pronounced effect on the development of tapestry in the mid-15th century. When, a few years later, Philip the Good of Burgundy commissioned from Pasquier Grenier the "six large tapestries for a church, richly made and worked with wool, silk, gold and silver" constituting the now lost *Story of the Passion*, it is all but certain that the other tapestries on the same theme at Saragossa, the Vatican, Brussels, and Angers were, if not replicas or repetitions of this fine work, at least strongly influenced by it.

Generally speaking, subjects taken from the New Testament were more popular than those from the Old. For one thing, they were more easily identifiable, and for another they were more often referred to in the Church's teachings. The different scenes from the Passion, the *Calvary* in particular, could be used for voluminous tapestries, whereas the scenes showing the *Descent from the Cross*, the *Entombment* and the *Resurrection* were better suited to the kind of long, narrow panels customarily placed at the front of the altar. Two tapestries of this kind remain, one in the Victoria and Albert Museum, the other, the *Resurrection*, in the Musée de Cluny. Both are finely woven in gold and silver and were certainly produced at Arras in the first half of the 15th century. The *Entombment* (now in Toledo Museum, Spain), completed a little later, is very much like them in style and technique as well as content.

As subjects, the *Life of Christ* and *Life of the Virgin* frequently have overlapping scenes and each has inspired many tapestries. The *Annunciation*, done in the first half of the 15th century and now hung in the Metropolitan Museum, and the *Three Kings* (see page 48) which forms part of the historical collections of Berne Museum and bears the coat-of-arms of Georges de Saluces, Bishop of Lausanne (d. 1461), can be considered as isolated works

17

or as fragments of larger sequences. Further examples are the fourteen-piece *Life of Christ* bearing the English coat-of-arms and dated 1511, which has been in the cathedral of Aix-en-Provence since the mid-17th century, and a *Life of the Virgin* in five parts, ordered in 1474 by Cardinal Jean Rolin for the church of Notre-Dame, Beaune, where it can still be seen. Waves of similar inspiration led to the illustration of Christ's miracles or parables. One such tapestry is the golden-threaded *Feeding of the Five Thousand* (now in the Louvre), another is the *Prodigal Son*. Several drawings of the latter were made by Gaignières at the time of Louis XIV, and a large fragment showing the beginning of the story is now in the Musée de Cluny.

However, the Old Testament did hold its own to a certain extent, for it was, after all, an inexhaustible source of stories and characters; *Jephthah* in Saragossa Cathedral, *Judith* in Sens Cathedral and *Susannah* in the Musée Marmottan, Paris, are among the best results. Charles VI possessed a "famous woollen tapestry, made after the fashion of Arras, wherein are shown several wise men, such as Solomon, Jason, Absalom and others". The bloody *Story of Esther* seems to have been woven many times after the subject was made fashionable by an order placed with Pasquier Grenier in 1462 by Philip the Good for "six tapestries... wrought with the story of King Ahasuerus and Queen Esther". Complete pieces or fragments can be found in Saragossa, in the Poldi-Pezzoli Museum (Milan), in Minneapolis Museum, Nancy's Musée Lorrain and the Louvre. All date from the second half of the 15th or the early 16th century.

Another favourite mediaeval device was the inclusion, in the same work, of parallel scenes from the Old and New Testaments. Among the Crown tapestries existing in Charles VI's time were "two large tapestries of the Old Testament and the New, called the *Passions*, of gold thread and Arras thread". The *Life of Christ* and *Life of the Virgin* already mentioned were composed like this and so, too, were hangings ordered about 1470 by the Bishop of Tournai, Guillaume Fillastre, for his Abbey of Saint-Bertin. (Two fragments are now in the museum at Saint-Omer.) Another double-barrelled biblical tapestry, dating from 1485, contrasts the *Rock of Moses* with the *Purifying Well* and includes the *Virgin in Glory*.

The *Seven Sacraments* could also be accompanied by reminders of their Old-Testament prefigurations. Around 1475 a sequence on this double theme was woven and presented to St. Quentin's church, Tournai, by Pasquier Grenier. A few fragments remain of this tapestry or of replicas; the most important belong to the Metropolitan Museum.

Reverence for relics of the Passion naturally led to the illustration of *Instruments of the Passion*, which are either depicted on a flowered background (as in the tapestry bearing the arms of Don Enrique of Spain, in The Cloisters, New York, and in the three pieces with the arms of Pierre de Rohan in the Cathedral of Angers); or else depicted in conjunction with *Saint Gregory's Mass* in Nuremberg's Germanic Museum.

The cult of the Holy Sacrament was also interwoven into tapestry, particularly in the *Miracles of the Eucharist*. One example done in Germany in the early 15th century is now on view in the Bavarian National Museum. Another sequence, the hangings of the old Abbey of Ronceray, is today split up between Paris, Boston, the Château of Langeais and Leeds Castle. Symbolism, which occupied a natural place in the mediaeval mind, understandably played a prominent role in tapestry-making, especially in Brussels around the turn of the 15th century. There was, for example, the tapestry of St. Francis's Basilica at Assisi showing Franciscan Saints and Popes, including Sixtus IV (1471-1484) with his coat-of-arms. Another series is devoted to an illustrated verse of the *Credo* and a fine piece of it, given by a queen of Spain, can be seen in the Vatican Galleries. One more such work, the *Redemption*, is now divided up between Haarzuylens, Hampton Court, Narbonne Cathedral, Worcester Museum in the United States, the Victoria and Albert Museum, the Louvre, etc.

But the richness of religious iconography should not lead to under-estimating the importance of historical subjects, though in truth Gothic tapestry-makers looked on biblical events *as* history, and secular and biblical history are often linked. Many biblical scenes concerning the life of Christ could rank among historical works. Where, for example, should one classify the *Story of Titus or the Vengeance of Our Lord* which relates the destruction of Jerusalem?

Naturally the history of heroic antiquity was very popular, especially the *War of Troy* which 15th-century cartoon-designers and weavers never seemed to grow tired of. In 1396 the Parisian Jacques Dourdin completed a series on *Hector of Troy* for Philip the Bold of Burgundy, who presented it—perhaps as heroic inspiration—to the Grand Master of the Order of Teutonic Knights. In 1472 the town of Bruges gave Charles the Bold of Burgundy a tapestry on the *Destruction of Troy* by Pasquier Grenier. Not surprisingly, several Trojan tapestries still remain today—at Zamora Cathedral *(The Abduction of Helen)*, the Victoria and Albert Museum *(Penthesilea, Pyrrhus)*, and the Metropolitan Museum *(Hector, Priam)*—as well as preparatory drawings which can be seen in the Louvre and the Ambrosian Library.

Emperors and notable classic conquerors were also trapped in the webs of woven cloth. In the Doria Museum, Rome, are two pieces thought to be part of the *Story of Alexander* set ordered from Pasquier Grenier in 1459 by Philip the Good, and two more fragments can be seen in the Petit Palais Museum, Paris. Together with the four-piece *Story of Caesar* in Berne's Historical Museum (see pages 52-53), which probably belonged to Charles the Bold himself, these tapestries come under a characteristic category, in which history and legend, ancient epic and mediaeval romance are combined and exploited in such a way as to vaunt the luxury of a particular court or lord, in this case the court of Burgundy. For Philip the Good—who created the Order of the Golden Fleece with its sumptuous costumes—and for the nobles of his court, scenes from antiquity and especially the lives of Alexander and Caesar, were simply "mirrors" of their own chivalry and heroism. The same idea is visible behind the various tapestries which make use of historical and epic narratives to stress the link between the French royal house of Valois and its predecessors, the Merovingian kings and Carolingian emperors. In 1389, the future Duke of Orleans and brother to the king, commissioned from Arras "a tapestry with gold threads devoted to the *Story of Charlemagne*". Madame Crick-Kuntziger (one of the foremost experts on Flemish tapestry) has identified two parts of this work, of which one is now in Brussels and the other in Florence, both belonging to the *Battle of Roncevaux*. These tremendous battle scenes and historical episodes were splendid propaganda to assert the ancient lineage of the Valois *fleur-de-lys* which eventually became the lilies of all France. This same urge for self-glorification can be clearly seen behind the *Story of the Great King Clovis*, ordered by the Dukes of Burgundy and held in high esteem by them. Of the original six parts, two remain in the treasury of Rheims Cathedral, where they have been for nearly five hundred years.

Even recent events, provided they were sufficiently glamorous, were seized upon and immortalized in wool by these extroverted and warlike princes. Philip the Bold of Burgundy simultaneously commissioned a *Story of Bertrand du Guesclin* (battling French general in the 100 Years' War) from the Parisian tapestry-maker Pierre de Beaumetz and a *Battle of Roosebecke* (a victory of Charles VI of France over the Flemish in 1382) from Michel Bernard of Arras. Charles VI was the proud possessor of the *Jousts of Saint Denis* by Nicolas Bataille and Jacques Dourdin of Paris, and Charles VII owned a tapestry about the Battle of Formigny (one of the decisive battles of the 100 Years' War, won by the Connétable de Richemont's armies over the occupying English troops in 1450).

Heroes of bygone days, both fictitious and historical, dressed in 15th-century clothes and often wearing magnificent suits of armour, gave wall decoration a bizarre but sumptuous look. A *Story of Hercules*, for example, was probably woven between 1476 and 1488 for the Cardinal de Bourbon; and the priceless *Perseus delivering Andromeda*, so similar in style to what is probably the most famous tapestry of all time—*the Lady with the Unicorn*— was created around the same period.

Another theme which met with resounding success was the *Nine Heroes*. The inventory drawn up after Charles V's death mentions "two tapestries on the Nine Heroes," and it is more or less certain that the fragments so skilfully brought together and presented to the Cloisters Museum by Mr. James Rorimer were once the property of Duc Jean de Berry. These remnants, originally belonging to a set of three pieces, each of which was devoted to three Heroes, now depict two great figures from the Old Testament (Joshua and David), two from Antiquity (Caesar and Alexander) and one from Christianity (King Arthur; see page 40). In addition, nineteen small surrounding figures remain (out of the original twenty-four or thirty-six) together with the upper part corresponding to six of the main characters. The story of these precious remnants is curious. The *King Arthur* panel, with six small figures, from the Clarence McKay collection, was the first to enter the Museum. The rest, with the exception of a little standard-bearer, donated in 1948, were acquired in 1947 after having been discovered in the small Château of Martinvast near Cherbourg, where they were being used by the unwitting owners as window curtains.

Right through into the 16th century, the *Nine Heroes* were still going strong in the tapestry productions of the province of La Marche and probably at Felletin, too. Produced in an entirely different spirit from the earlier pieces and done in a rather heavy-handed manner, they still retained the Gothic style. One of the surviving sets, in three pieces, is now in the Kulturan Museum at Lund, Sweden.

It had to happen, of course. The logical consequence of the *Heroes* was a series devoted to *Heroines*. Several tapestries on this topic belonged to Charles VI, including one on *Penthesilea*, the queen of the Amazons. An isolated figure representing this husky lady, rather incongruously set against a dainty background of flowerets, is on view at the Château of Angers. It is thought to date from the late 15th century. The same idea of *Illustrious Women* was embodied in a ten-piece set originally housed in a Burgundian château but almost completely destroyed by fire in the 18th century. Eight small and very lovely fragments now remain in Boston Museum, three from the section on *Penelope* (in which the panel showing Ulysses' wife sitting at her loom is amazingly similar to the *Lady with the Unicorn*), two more from the *Cimbrian Women* suite, and three with the coat-of-arms of Cardinal Ferry de Clugny who was Canon of Autun and Bishop of Tournai (d. 1483).

Rich and fabulous scenes were plentiful in these exotic-style historic tapestries, especially in such things as *Portuguese Conquests*, travels in the Indies, and the *Story of Carrabarra*, one piece of which remains in the Stockholm National Museum. The fantastic *Savages' Ball* to be found in the church of Nantilly-les-Saumur might well stem from the same source but it could just as easily represent some bizarre contemporary court scene. Two more examples which spring to mind are Charles V's "tapestries with wild men" and the idea was often repeated in Switzerland and Germany during the 15th century, with or without the addition of outlandish animals (Basle Historical Museum).

Many other tapestries bear the stamp of literature, history or travel but do not fall into any particular category. The mediaeval verse-chronicle, apart from supplying historical matter, was also a rich source of purely romantic tapestry subjects. In 1385, the Parisian weaver Jacques Dourdin delivered "two tapestries worked with gold after the fashion of Arras". One represented the story of *Jourdain de Blaye*. Another tapestry, also inspired by this tale, is now displayed in Padua's Civic Museum. Both were based on an epic poem belonging to a cycle on national heroes. The theme is that timeless favourite of the matchless hero who, faced with innumerable difficulties and dangers finally overcomes them all to conclude his quest, win his lady and so live happily ever after. Another tapestry born of the influence of literature was *The Story of the Swan Knight*, commissioned by Philip the Good from the weaver Pasquier Grenier in 1462. The legend of the Swan Knight was extremely popular in the Middle Ages, being a mixture of the usual fantastic adventures and memories of deeds that actually happened during the First Crusade. This poem, incidentally, inspired Richard Wagner's opera "Lohengrin".

In high favour during the Middle Ages were morality plays—short stories illustrating the proper way to live, and allegories—in which abstract things or characteristics are represented by people or animals. This fashion naturally found its way into tapestry, and a glance at the list of Charles VI's possessions reveals "a woollen tapestry of Good Renown" and others on "the Orchard of Youth", "the Goddess of Love", "Friendship", "Goodness and Beauty", "the Seven Deadly Sins", and so on. In all these allegorical works the same method of using figures to personify certain qualities can be seen. A modern projection of the idea is the representation of Justice by a female figure, blindfold, with a pair of scales in one hand and a sword in the other.

Sometimes the morality theme grew to large proportions and gave works such as the *Clemency of Trajan* and the *Communion of Herkenbald*, now in the Historical Museum, Berne. The first of these relates a picturesque, if implausible, legend concerning the great Roman emperor Trajan. Petitioned for justice by a widow whose son has been slain, he immediately gives the order for the murderer to be executed. Centuries later, the Pope, Saint Gregory, sends for Trajan's remains. And wonder of wonders, the tongue (i.e. the organ responsible for justice being done) is seen to have withstood the corruption of time, and to have remained intact.

The second of the two tapestries, only a little less gruesome, is based on an old Brussels legend. Herkenbald, a judge, is lying desperately ill when he hears that his nephew has raped a young girl. This crime is punishable by death and Herkenbald, faithful to his duty, forces himself to kill the offender with his own hand. After this, the bishop refuses to give him Communion, maintaining that he is guilty of murder. But, because Herkenbald has acted justly and as required by his office, he receives the Communion miraculously from Heaven.

A special place must be reserved for allegorical sequences. The most celebrated of these is the *Lady with the Unicorn*, which was acquired by the Musée de Cluny from the Château de Boussac at the end of the 19th century. It is generally agreed today that the five senses—Sight, Hearing, Smell, Taste and Touch—are represented in five of the pieces of this famous set; the sixth, with its motto "to my sole desire", is probably a reference to the betrothal of Jean de Chabannes and Claude Le Viste, whose arms appear on each piece of the set, supported by a lion and a unicorn. The whole work, with its beautiful red backgrounds, its wealth and accuracy of detail, the sober elegance of its composition and the mystery in which it is shrouded, is unquestionably one of the greatest masterpieces of Gothic tapestry.

The second notable allegorical sequence is *The Triumphs*, inspired by a work of the 14th-century Italian poet and inventor of the sonnet, Francis Petrarch. On each of the six tapestries making up the set, a quatrain explains the step-by-step allegory in which first of all love triumphs over reason, then chastity triumphs over love, then death over chastity, then glory over death, time over glory and finally eternity over time completes the series. Part of the set is in the Viennese Kunsthistorisches Museum and the rest is in the Metropolitan Museum. Although these tapestries are neither as rich, precise or decorous as the *Lady with the Unicorn*, their flowered backgrounds, lovely scenery and sense of balance nevertheless give them remarkable charm which is enhanced by the delicate blending of their colours.

Works about work, of course, never ran out of subject matter. It happens that the very earliest surviving tapestry produced in the Christian West was dedicated to the *Occupations of the Months*. It is in the Oslo Decorative Arts Museum and came from a Norwegian church. In it *April* is represented by a man standing on a red ground dotted with shrubs, birds and lozenges; *May* is summed up by a mounted warrior, on a blue background sprinkled with rosettes.

Other subjects, as picturesque as they are varied, include *Shepherds* (in the Gobelins Museum), *Woodcutters* (Musée des Arts Décoratifs, Paris, with a piece showing the arms of Chancellor Rolin), *Husbandmen* (in the Louvre), *Grape-pickers and Vine-growers* (Musée de Cluny), and a *Lord dispensing Justice* in front of his castle or paying his vineyard workers (in the Decorative Arts Museum, Copenhagen).

Despite the fact that the tapestries in which they appear are often about mundane subjects, a distinctive aura of poetry clings to the figures enacting the everyday lives of lords and peasants as they are presented in Gothic tapestry, though the characters are placed either on a very nearly lifelike setting or else transported to flower-scattered backgrounds.

It was often said of the nobility of the time that they would rather hunt than eat. This weakness for hunting is naturally reflected in tapestry, notably in the *Departure for the Hunt* (Musée de Cluny; see page 57), and the large four-piece *Hunts* for many years kept at Chatsworth (see pages 50-51), the famous estate of the Dukes of Devonshire. The four *Hunt* scenes show hawking and duck-hunting; boar- and bear-hunting; otter-, swan- and bear-hunting; and deer- and duck-hunting. Cutting and re-arrangement over the years may have altered the original appearance of these pieces, but they none the less form an outstandingly well-organized integral composition. They were no doubt woven at Arras and Tournai, either for the Court of Burgundy or, according to the English tapestry expert Mr. Wingfield Digby, for René of Anjou whose daughter Marguerite married Henry VI of England in 1444.

Fact was often laced with fantasy in Gothic tapestry. This created odd mixtures for instance subjects midway between real hunting and pure legend. Among the two best-known is one called *Hunting the Elephant*, bequeathed to the Louvre by Madame Marquet de Vasselot, which shows, in the background, a fight between an elephant and a unicorn. Much of its beauty is due to the softness and strangeness of its colours, and its green-sturned-blue accentuate the unreal quality pervading the whole work. The second is the famous series in The Cloisters, called *Hunting the Unicorn* (see pages 54-55). An inventory of the La Rochefoucauld family, dating from 1728, mentions this "well-worn" five-piece tapestry as decorating the finest room in the Château de Verteuil. Today, it comprises five large pieces and one smaller piece (from the Morgan and Rockefeller collections) plus two fragments (acquired separately by the Museum). The tapestry's beauty is undiminished by the fact that, like the *Lady with the Unicorn*, it was restored in the late 19th century. Today it is in a magnificent condition. But the subject is enigmatic. Is the lady portrayed really Anne of Brittany? Can the *Captive Unicorn* on its delicate flowered background be counted as part of the actual hunting series, with its various depths of field and forest interiors? These are only two of the riddles which still remain unanswered at the present time.

Similarities of style have been noted between this work and the beautiful *Rustic Scenes* in Washington's Corcoran Gallery of Art. The pursuit of the unicorn, treated in an entirely different manner, is also the theme of certain German tapestries in which the cult of the Virgin Mary is sometimes involved.

For a rich lord, the most decorative form of self-praise, of course, were tapestries showing "life" in his court. *The Offering of the Heart* (see page 42) which is placed as a symbol at the entrance to the Musée de Cluny; the strange and precious *lords* and *ladies* on the panels acquired by the Musée des Arts Décoratifs, Paris, through the Peyre bequest; the magnificent *Cavaliers* fragment to be found in the church of Nantilly, and even less polished works such as the *Card Players* in Basle's Historical Museum, are some of the very earliest works to have come down from the Middle Ages. Later and still finer tapestries include a *Concert* taking place near a fountain on a back-ground of flowers (Gobelins Museum), another *Concert* where the singer is said to be Pierre de Rohan accompanied at the organ by his wife Marguerite d'Armagnac (Château d'Angers; see page 47), the six parts of *Aristocratic Life* (see pages 56-57), the three-piece *Noble Pastoral* generously bequeathed to the Louvre by the Larcade family (see page 46), and two tapestries with a red background from the former Martin Le Roy collection. The perfection of these pieces, dating from around 1500, is due in large measure to the simplicity and tranquillity of both subjects and composition.

The same qualities of soberness, softness and refinement glow through three panels which have been named *The Giving of Roses* (see page 44). The backgrounds are in bands of red, white and green or green, white and red, covered with rambling roses, and the main figures (three, four and eight) are grouped more or less in couples. Placed at varying heights and nearly all looking to the left, they are walking, conversing or holding flowers. Noble and elegant in style, this sequence was probably of royal origin around the time of Charles VII, and is unquestionably one of the masterpieces of the Gothic era. However, it must be admitted that any criticism is bound to be subjective, especially when we read the comments made some fifty years ago by that great connoisseur of the history of tapestry, Jules Guiffrey: *"The Giving of Roses"*, he wrote, "is strange rather than pleasing. The weavers of old seem to have stopped at no audacity. Who would dare produce such a work today?"

Pictorial work formed the backbone of Gothic tapestry. But no study of Gothic tapestry should overlook "heraldic" works, in which escutcheons and emblems make up the subject instead of merely supplying a decorative mark of ownership in supplement to the main theme. A special chapter in Charles V's inventory is devoted to this kind of tapestry. Usually, a monogram or a coat-of-arms is repeated on a background which can be plain or striped, covered with lozenges or ornaments, animals or popinjays, trees or flowers. The crest, however, sometimes also forms the centre of the panel. The famous tapestries in the Hospice in Beaune (Burgundy) are simply a repetition of a motto, a monogram, a bird on a dead branch and a few heraldic shields. The fragments of one of the oldest surviving tapestries of this kind are now divided between the Metropolitan Museum, the Rijksmuseum in Amsterdam and the Boston Museum. They appear to date from the end of the 14th century and show two animals, rampant, supporting the arms of Beaufort and Comminges set in a lozenged background, girt around with battlements. Another example is the exquisite tapestry, belonging to the *Winged Stags* set, which is now in the Seine-Maritine Musée des Antiquités, Rouen. It was woven in the reign of Charles VII and not surprisingly shows two winged stags. The first of these is wearing around its neck the crown of France, from which hangs the royal shield bearing three *fleur-de-lys*. The second is carrying a banner. This kind of subject was by no means rare and it also appears in a miniature by Jean Fouquet in which a ceremonial setting of Charles VII's parliament is shown taking place in a room hung with two red, white and green striped tapestries emblazoned with winged stags supporting the arms of France.

HOW TAPESTRIES WERE COMPOSED

The theme chosen for a tapestry is bound to influence its composition. The arrangement of patterns of coats-of-arms or of a few glamorized human figures requires a different approach from the one needed to tell a great historical story or present a tremendous battle scene. There seem to have been two divergent trends in Gothic tapestry. One of them appears to scorn perspective, favouring the sober representation of a few elegant and studiously-placed figures, and resembling the arts of miniaturism, sculpture, fresco and stained-glass windows.

The other trend, nearer to the art of oil-painting, sought above all to achieve an effect of richness by using great numbers of figures, confused if necessary, and clever landscape effects. To be sure that these discernible trends represented formally constituted schools or styles we would, of course, need far more than our present hypothetical knowledge of the working methods of mediaeval cartoon-painters and weavers. But the difference in results is clearly visible.

It is difficult not to admire the simplicity of the earliest Gothic tapestries—or at least of those that have, one way or another, managed to come down to us. The early remnants preserved at Oslo and at Halberstadt all show the same characteristically plain background which throws a few monumental figures into relief. They have the same occasional decorations—floral or animal, geometrical or architectural—and show the same influence exerted by the art of miniaturism. Such characteristics are also found in the Angers *Apocalypse* on whose preparation fairly full documentation exists.

This grandiose work of art germinated originally from miniature-illuminated manuscripts. It should be remembered that today's too-frequently applied distinction between "major" and "minor" arts was non-existent in the Middle Ages. Some of the masterpieces of 13th- or 14th-century sculpture were produced by craftsmen working in ivory or gold. Miniaturism made its appearance even in stained-glass windows. It is not surprising, therefore, that these various arts should be found triumphantly mingled in a tapestry as vast and important as the *Apocalypse*.

The first models were provided by various illuminated manuscripts on the Apocalypse (now in Paris, Cambrai, Metz and elsewhere). At least one of these was borrowed from the king's library and is mentioned shortly afterwards in the inventory as having been entrusted to "My lord of Anjou for the weaving of his fine tapestry". These preparatory models were no doubt the counterpart of the sketches used today as bases from which to choose scenes to be elaborated, as well as for the overall composition.

The next stage—payments made to the cartoonist—is recorded in the accounts of the Dukes of Anjou. The artist was a court painter, Hennequin de Bruges who, in 1378, signed a receipt for "the portraits and patterns . . . for the said tapestries of the story of the Apocalypse". The cartoon, a detailed diagram made to the full size of the future tapestry, and usually with complete instructions concerning the colours to be used, was and is an essential adjunct to tapestry-weaving.

Cartoon-painters must have been persons of some consequence. At any rate this seems a logical assumption when we consider that they were sometimes attached, for long periods of time, to the households of great princes. This

26

was the case for Hennequin de Bruges who was first appointed as court painter to Charles V, then given the honorary title of "valet de chambre". In this way his protector could bestow occasional favours on him and at the same time have him constantly at his service. Now Charles V ordered great numbers of tapestries, all designed, naturally, by Hennequin de Bruges. We have few specimens of this artist's work today because his tapestries have either disappeared or have remained unidentified but it can reasonably be supposed that the style of so high-placed a painter had a great influence on French tapestry of the period.

Furthermore, the influence of a painter in favour at the court of a certain prince could bring about the development of a style peculiar to the region. For example, when Duke Philip the Good of Burgundy placed large orders in his northern realm of Flanders, the resulting Arras tapestries were quite different from those of France. The names of some of the cartoon-painters responsible are known, such as Guillaume au Vaissel and Baudouin de Bailleul who gave many cartoons to the Arras weavers. Many other names, however, were forgotten or were never recorded, but sometimes we can recognize in a certain tapestry the style of a known master. For instance, the *Three Kings* (see page 48) has been attributed to the Maître de Sainte Gudule; *Saint Piat and Saint Eleuthère* (see page 41) is claimed to have similarities of style with the work of Jan van Eyck (1390-1441), the father of Flemish painting; and in certain tapestries woven by Jacques Daret many experts see the genius of one of the greatest of all 15th-century Flemish painters—who is, alas, only known to us as the Maître de Flémalle.

If little is known about the painters, even less is sure about the cartoons. They were probably painted on the spot, under the patron's eyes, but they also could have been painted in one country while the tapestry was woven in another. However, two general trends of composition discernibly took shape. First, in the domains of the French kings, the composition was always of the greatest simplicity, consisting of a very few figures standing out from a plain or a flower-sprinkled background. We do not know how the painter set about designing the cartoons for these flowered ("mille-fleurs") tapestries. Did he supply a complete cartoon to the size of the future tapestry with every single background flower planted in? Or did he simply design the main figures and accessory objects, leaving the weaver to do the gardening? This second alternative would explain certain repetitions of minor figures, animals and flowers noted in different tapestries. Among these calm tapestries, simple in style and arrangement, which flourished in the heart of France, two examples are outstanding: the *Apocalypse* and the *Lady with the Unicorn*.

The second trend, in complete and utter contrast, grew up in the lands of the Dukes of Burgundy. These swashbuckling princes were, from father to son, lovers of lavish living and glamorous occasions. Their lives were turbulent and every minute was filled to the brim. Conservative tapestries would clearly not do for the Dukes! Their décor must be as exuberant as their own personalities. So, under their stimulus, Flemish cartoonpainters began to produce lively compositions, well filled with figures and trees, each cut up into several separate compartments or scenes by means of motifs borrowed from architecture—colonnades, flying buttresses, battlements, etc. This fullness of composition can already be seen in the *Saint Piat and Saint Eleuthère* tapestry (see page 41). Flemish works began literally to teem with figures, each scene of each tapestry being completely framed, rather like a picture, by its own private architectural-type surround. Identical compositions and architectural "frames" are even found in entirely different tapestries, such as the *Triumph of Christ* (Musée Royaux d'Art et d'Histoire, Brussels), and *Story of Jephthah* (Louvre).

The next stage was almost inevitable. One fine day each scene became a separate tapestry complete with its architectural surround which was transformed into a border. And the Brussels weavers seem to have been the first to adopt the system of setting their subjectmatter between two bands of simulated moulding, the whole surrounded by a thick border composed of clumps of flowers. This development was to have heavy consequences for the traditional Gothic style, because tapestries began more and more to resemble paintings. And when Pope Leo X ordered cartoons for the *Acts of the Apostles* mentioned above from Raphaël, the artist naturally produced a typically Renaissance-style pictorial composition.

Other influential patrons, such as Francis I of France and the Emperor Charles V, followed the new pictorial trend, thereby ultimately killing Gothic tapestry. Gone was the demand for the dream-world designs of Gothic days, with their flower-strewn backgrounds, their skies scattered with stylized clouds, their woven captions at top or bottom explaining the subject. Tapestry had emerged from its "mille-fleurs" phase and was entering the Renaissance era.

Is there a link between the early Coptic tapestries (very small in size if we may judge from those surviving today) and the first "illustrative" tapestries of the mediaeval West? If so, by what means was the technique of weft and warp handed down from generation to generation and from country to country? Again, particularly in the texts collected by Mr. Jean Hubert dating from the Carolingian period and around the year 1000, how can we distinguish between true woven tapestries and those made of decorated or embroidered linen, such as the embroidered work known as *Queen Matilda's Tapestry* at Bayeux? How convenient it would be if some far-seeing scribe of ancient days had anticipated 20th-century curiosity and recorded all the answers to these questions! Unhappily, documentary evidence is non-existent and we have no means of tracing the origins of tapestry in the West. All we can definitely state is that high- and low-warp looms existed in France during the 12th and 13th centuries.

TRADITIONAL
TECHNIQUES OF
TAPESTRY-WEAVING

Very few raw materials are needed for the production of tapestry. In the Middle Ages the chief requirement, wool, was produced in every rural district and was easily obtainable in large towns like Paris. A register of goods sold in Paris at the end of the 13th century mentions, under the heading "tapestry-makers, felt-makers and makers of felt hats": "woollen thread from Anjou, Poitou and elsewhere, to make tapestries." A century later, in the *Apocalypse* set, the Parisian weaver Nicolas Bataille used wool both for the warp threads (the basic "up-and-down" structure of the tapestry) and for the weft (the coloured threads which, interwoven across the warp, form the tapestry's design).

It is probable that during the 14th century the Arras weavers stole a march on their Parisian rivals by using not only gold and silk threads but also a much finer thread of wool. The Parisians retaliated by using the same materials. After Charles V's death in 1380, his inventory mentions several "tapestries . . . of Arras thread," without noting the origin of the works. But we do know that Charles VI's order, some years later, for the *Jousts of Saint Denis* "figured in gold and of fine Arras thread" was made in Paris. The distinction between the quality of the thread and the place of manufacture is also evident in the inventory of Charles VI's tapestries sold or dispersed by the English between 1422 and 1437. The terms "Arras thread" or "gold thread and Arras thread" are never confused with "fashioned in Arras"; and among the numerous "Arras" tapestries, whether "on wool," "with gold on wool" or "of gold, silk and wool," can even be found one specifically woven "of Paris thread."

The mixing of silk with wool gave a finer and richer work, of the kind referred to in Charles V's inventory as "a very beautiful green chamber, decorated with silk-woven tapestry, on a green background covered with leaves of different kinds...". It will be recalled, too, that the *Story of Gideon*, ordered by Philip the Good from Tournai in 1448, was woven of wool and silk with gold in the yellow parts and silver in the white parts.

Together with silk, gold threads (or silver gilt) and silver threads were in fact frequently used for especially rich and delicate work, and the expression "Cyprus gold" often occurs. Although metallic threads were used by the Parisian weavers too, this kind of workmanship was the speciality of Arras which acquired a reputation for the greater beauty of its products. Two precious sachets for holy relics, probably woven with metallic thread and dating from the early 14th century, are in existence. One of them, discovered by Monseigneur Lestocquoy and now on view in the Diocesan Museum of Arras, is adorned on either side by a shield with a rampant lion. The second belongs to the Cleveland Museum and bears the arms of France and of Castille. Both are of fine tapestry embellished with gold. Another magnificent specimen is the altar frontal called the *Triple Coronation* which is part of the treasury of Sens Cathedral, not far from Paris. We know nothing definite concerning its origin but it was probably ordered in the third quarter of the 15th century by Cardinal de Bourbon, Archbishop of Lyons and nephew of Philip the Good. Gold and silver, silk and wool are exquisitely intertwined in a work whose exceptionally fine weaving gives it a precision and subtlety that matches the most skilful painting.

Only a small number of colours—between fifteen and twenty—were used in Gothic tapestry. According to Guiffrey, the Angers *Apocalypse* required no more than twelve to fifteen. These natural colours have now lost something of their original brightness. The yellows and browns especially, obtained from bark and roots, have faded with age; but the greens, purples and particularly the reds and blues (produced with madder and pastel) are still warm and harmonious.

The development of the craft at Arras can be partly explained by the facilities offered by the nearby Flemish lands for the preparation and dyeing of wool. Some interesting contemporary texts about these subjects have been quoted by two top-ranking Belgian experts in the history of the Middle Ages, Georges Espinas and Henri Pirenne. Early in the 13th century, Guillaume Le Breton wrote about the craftsmen in the town of Ypres: "Ypra colorandis gens prudentissima lanis." (The people of Ypres colour wool with skill and care.) And in 1375, Louis de Male, Count of Flanders, took an interest in pastel's "quotation"—by taxing it.

Weavers were distinguished according to the type of loom they used. Low-warp, or "treadle" weavers, so called because of the pedal mechanism they used to separate the warp threads, belonged to a different category from the high-warp workers of Arras and Tournai in the north of France. The Parisian toll records for the years 1292 and 1313 mention the word "tapicier" (tapestry-maker) which is used to denote the profession of the contributor or as a surname following his Christian name. In 1303, a note was added to the Parisian weavers' Statutes concerning an agreement concluded with "another manner of 'tapicier' who are called highwarp workers," indicating not merely the existence but perhaps also the recent introduction of the vertical loom.

It is always dangerous to assert categorically that a tapestry was woven on a high-warp or a low-warp loom simply by looking at it. But it is clear that when working on a low-warp loom it was impossible to check the design and colour properly. As a result the high-warp loom, which was slower and less mobile but more accurate, was usually reserved for more expensive works. This in turn affected both the grain of the weave and, eventually, even the place of manufacture. A text dating from 1408 mentions a low-warp tapestry which was "of a thick thread, on a grassy green background". And an arbitration concerning tapestries delivered by Pasquier Grenier, of Tournai, to Jehan Peliche "a low-warp weaver from Puy in Auvergne" in 1449, stresses that these were not "as fine as they should be".

The average number of warp threads to the inch in Gothic tapestries is 13 to 15 (about 5 or 6 to the centimetre). Yet the use of silk, and especially of gold thread, went hand in hand with the development of a finer weave. The richest of the gold-flecked tapestries ordered by the Dukes of Burgundy from Arras and Tournai are no longer in existence. But from the rare surviving pieces—such as the *Verdure* with the arms of Burgundy, at Berne, with its 18 threads to the inch (7 to the centimetre) and the panel of the Cardinal de Bourbon's *Triple Coronation* in Sens Cathedral with 28 threads to the inch (11 to the centimetre)—we can imagine the fineness of the tapestries woven for these princes and ordered, in the main, from high-warp weavers. By contrast, a series such as the *Heroes*, which was certainly produced by a low-warp workshop, probably at Felletin, is characterized by the coarseness of the warp—which only had an average of 10½ threads to the inch (4 to the centimetre).

If more were known about working methods and particularly of the division between high-warp and low-warp weaving, this would in turn shed more light on the study of centers of production. We imagine that the vertical loom, less manœuvrable than the horizontal loom and harder to set up, but more suitable for large-scale tapestries, was used more often in the big towns, whose role will be referred to in the section dealing with patronage. A high-warp loom is shown, with the Virgin weaving, in the *Annunciation* scene of the *Très Riches Heures* miniatures, composed in 1409 for the Duc de Berry and now in the Bibliothèque Nationale (Paris).

The low-warp loom, on the other hand was less cumbersome. Penelope is seen sitting at a loom of this type in the fragment of the *Illustrious Women* set now at Boston Museum in the United States.

If a lord, a bishop or an abbot wished to have his premises decorated by a tapestry woven on the spot, it was quite a simple matter to call in a low-warp weaver. The loom was not very heavy and could be easily transported; wool could be procured and even dyed in the vicinity; and the cartoons—if not already included in the weaver's material—could be ordered from a local artist. The possibility (put forward by the French historian Jules Guiffrey) that individual nomadic weavers existed, could answer many of the still unresolved questions about Gothic tapestry-making and would certainly explain the lack of precise information regarding the town (or towns) where the numerous "mille-fleurs" tapestries were woven.

It is ascertainable from contemporary documents that in the Middle Ages and even up to the 16th and 17th centuries, weavers moved around quite freely as required by circumstances. In 1385, the Duc de Berry, who usually ordered tapestries from Paris and Arras, brought to Bourges a number of weavers who are thought by some to have woven the *Heroes* in this town. It has likewise been speculated that the Duke of Anjou's *Apocalypse* might have been produced by Nicolas Bataille at Angers and not at Paris. Other low-warp weavers were called to Hesdin by the Duke of Burgundy, to Saint-Michel by the Duke of Lorraine, to Navarre by the Queen of Navarre, to Avignon by the Pope and to Rennes by the Duke of Brittany.

If one tries to plot a map (as was done during the 1946 exhibition of French tapestry at the Musée d'Art Moderne, Paris) showing as far as possible the origin of the principal "mille-fleurs" tapestries woven around the turn of the 15th century, it is surprising to see how these works seem to be grouped. Broadly speaking, they appear to have originated along the Loire valley with a certain margin to the north and the south. In no text is there any trace of one or two important centers, such as might reasonably have grown up in Tours or Blois. The scattering of the workshops may correspond to the spacing of the noble residences, it being remembered that this valley was often at that period the home of the royal court. It is a great temptation to explain the different geographic origins, coupled with the unity of style of these tapestries, by the wanderings of the same small groups of weavers, summoned hither and thither from château to château, from cathedral to abbey, according to the progress of the constructional work. The theory is logical but no documentary proof exists.

As far as we can reconstitute mediaeval weavers' working methods, two characteristics are generally agreed upon. One is complete mastery of their craft; the other precise concern for, and control of, colour.

From the Oslo *Months* (between the 11th and 13th centuries) and the Angers *Apocalypse* (late 14th century) to the *Lady with the Unicorn* (early 16th century), colour joins and contour shading are handled with astonishing skill. By means of these joins (which necessarily circumscribe individual features and areas of relief) the weavers achieved quite grandiose effects, which have been accentuated by the stretching and "fabric fatigue" produced by the passage of time. Hands, faces, books; every detail is outlined, apparently effortlessly, by this simple process and the result has surprising vibrancy. It is hard to find terms in which to describe the solidity of the relief effects obtained by this technique of flat patches of colour, which has no parallel in any other art. The simplest-seeming works so achieved are also the greatest, and their soberness and dignity are carried through from the *Apocalypse* to the *Giving of the Roses* and the "mille-fleurs" tapestries. Today, as we have already noted, much of the original colour has disappeared. But even dimmed or ruined, it still commands our admiration. Once flame-like, these mediaeval tones now glow like steadily-burning embers. Their masterful distribution, their sober warmth, their lingering beauty, make a tremendous impact which nobody who has seen them will forget.

But here a question must be asked—to what extent was the weaver responsible? It was possible for the cartoonist to demand a faithful rendering of his colours, to mark on his "patterns" the exact shade required, to supervise the dyeing of the wool and check the work on the loom. This might indeed have been the method in force in firmly-directed workshops. But was it prevalent in the majority of cases? Probably not. A few years ago, by a stroke of luck, we were able to acquire for the Musée de Cluny a tapestry representing *Honour*. The museum already possessed another fragment on this same theme and the two were minutely compared. Both date from the early 16th century but nevertheless bear the Gothic stamp. Both were probably woven in northern France, or in the southern Netherlands. Both were executed from the same cartoon. But what a world of difference between them! Variations in the design, hinting that the weaver took a rather free-and-easy attitude towards his model; variations above all in the use of colours—even though it is most likely that different exposure to light had, over the years, affected the colours of one more than those of the other. One thing is certain, however. Such variations point to a wide degree of latitude left to the individual weavers—and to a great difference of imagination among them.

HOW PATRONS HELPED
In the foregoing pages mention has often been made of Charles V or of the Dukes of Burgundy. It should not, in fact, be forgotten that princes throughout the Middle Ages regarded tapestry as an important item of luxury. The art was quick to respond to this noble or royal stimulus which largely explains the development and prosperity of tapestry-making. The encouragement given to contemporary tapestry by the State, the great banks and large commercial undertakings; the patronage accorded in the 17th century by Charles I to Mortlake, by Louis XIV to the Gobelins, by the Electors of Bavaria, Saxony and Brandenburg in their own domains, are simply a continuation of what was almost a general rule in the Middle Ages. It was above all the "princes of the blood" who made the greatest contribution to the flowering of Gothic tapestry.

Charles V's acquisitions were probably the first to show the great variety of decorative potential offered by pictorial tapestries, heraldic tapestries and later by complete sets for furnishing particular rooms. Nicolas Bataille, burgher of Paris and Charles VI's chief supplier in the early part of his reign, had previously worked for Duke Louis I of Anjou who attached him to his personal retinue with the title of "valet de chambre." One of the Duke's first orders was for the high-warp *Story of Hercules*, completed before the great Angers *Apocalypse*.

Jacques Dourdin, who may have been Bataille's partner before succeeding him, worked for Charles VI, for Queen Isabeau and for the Duke of Orleans. And the Parisian weavers' loss of ground to Arras in the early 15th century is surely accounted for by the weakening of royal power and the simultaneously increasing Burgundian patronage.

The role of Countess Mahaut of Artois, great-niece of the saintly King Louis IX, may have been decisive in the birth of tapestry at Arras, the capital of Artois. Mahaut was an intelligent and energetic woman, known to have been interested in tapestry, and quite capable of introducing the craft to her domain. However the Arras bourgeoisie might equally well have taken an interest in the industry without any urging. One thing is sure: an industry in full bloom, as tapestry-making was in Paris during the

14th century, will quite naturally throw off shoots provided a suitable climate is found, and there is no reason why the trade should not have been brought from its native Paris and implanted in the North by the combined efforts of Mahaut and the Arras bourgeoisie. The new workshops took root and soon began to show every sign of promise. In 1315 the Parisian weaver Jehan de Condé sold Countess Mahaut "one tapestry with little animals," but at the same time Mahaut was also purchasing tapestries from Arras. Her accounts mention, in 1311, a "woollen cloth decorated with various figures," which she presented to Enguerrand de Marigny, and in 1313, "five wrought high-warp cloths" bought from Isabelle Caurrée, also known as Isabelle de Hallennes.

However, it was not until the rich days of the great Burgundian Dukes that the Arras industry really began to blossom. Philip the Bold and his descendants John the Fearless, Philip the Good and Charles the Bold, all with the same insatiable love of ostentation, usually followed the same canny economic policy by ordering their richest tapestries from workshops operating in their own states. Philip the Bold, like his brothers of Anjou and Berry, was also a customer of Parisian Nicolas Bataille. But in 1387, shortly after having inherited Artois and its capital of Arras from his father-in-law Louis de Male, Philip sealed the commercial future of the town by ordering the great *Battle of Roosebecke*. This marked the real beginning of several centuries of tapestry-making there. For a prince owning vast tracts of land peppered with huge castles which were almost completely unfurnished during his absences, there was nothing so tempting as the accumulation of these brilliant fabrics with their marvellous stories, sometimes inspired by antiquity, sometimes by his own military feats. Wool, silk and gold fused into a warm and luxurious decoration which was yet supple enough to be moved at will and re-hung on any chosen wall. Fortune decreed that the first of the Dukes of Burgundy, faithful to Valois traditions, should understand the role of tapestry and should pass on that understanding to his descendants.

Contemporary scholars seem to enjoy arguing over the origin of tapestries from these bygone days, one putting forward Arras, another Tournai or Bruges or Brussels as the center of manufacture and scouring France or Belgium (according to their own personal origin) for texts in support of their claims. The Duke of Burgundy was not over-patriotic about such things. Although Tournai belonged to the King of France and Brussels to the Emperor and he himself was frequently at odds with both, he not only sought prosperity for his domains but the greatest possible beauty in his tapestries. If the quality of Arras work fell off, he would order from Tournai or elsewhere. In 1456, shortly after the weaving of *Gideon* at Tournai, this policy brought Philip the Good a complaint from the aldermen of Arras that "merchants and high-warp weavers ... have gone to dwell in other towns, such as Valenciennes, Tournai and Bergues."

The patronage of the 15th-century French kings and their courtiers, although less appreciable and less known than that of Burgundy, nevertheless played a part in the development of tapestry-making. A good example is Charles VII and works like the *Giving of Roses* (see page 44) quite probably intended for the Château of Loches. The court of Moulins also had an as yet undetermined influence on late mediaeval tapestry. Around the turn of the 15th century the fondness of French kings for their Loire châteaux, like Amboise and Blois, stimulated the construction of new châteaux in this area and undoubtedly encouraged the establishment—even if only temporary—of tapestry workshops to fulfil the needs of the great lords of the court—Rohan, La Rochefoucauld, Chabannes, Bohier and so on. But this did not prevent Francis I from turning to Brussels a little later for the *Scipio* series when he found the models and weaving of Brussels more to his liking. Freedom of choice is after all one of the rights of a patron...

The patronage of the Church was also considerable. Subjects, of course, were bound to be limited, as they had to be drawn either from the Bible or from the lives of the Saints, and, as was noted earlier, there was less available wall-space in churches than in châteaux. But undoubtedly the Church played a part from the very earliest days. In 12th- and 13th-century Western Europe there existed a technique, even a style, which owed its wide dissemination to the interest of the great abbeys. Wherever an abbey existed, so also the existence of the craft has almost invariably been traced. Such rare tapestries as those of Halberstadt and Oslo should not be considered as isolated cases or as the ancestors of later works, but rather as part of a movement which was fostered and spread by the Church.

Orders for tapestries, sometimes to be woven on the spot, were also placed in the 15th and 16th centuries by certain monasteries in Switzerland, Germany and Alsace. And although tapestries with a religious motif seem to occupy a secondary place in the enormous output of the 15th century, we should consider not only the magnificence of those pieces remaining today, but also the nobility and influence of churchmen who commissioned them. Some of these, like the Cardinal de Bourbon, Cardinal Rolin and Cardinal d'Amboise were closely connected to the noblest families in the realm.

To improve our knowledge and understanding of Gothic tapestry, we must pursue to the utmost limit the study of what now remains, taking into account repairs carried out over the centuries, which make the task singularly difficult. These research efforts should not stop at the examination of the various known tapestry centers, but should try to look into the history of the wandering groups of weavers, attempt to reconstruct the work of painters and throw light on the personality of the patrons. We must find other means than mere hypothesis and speculation by which to rescue these fabulous works and their creators out of the state of semi-anonymity in which they now reside.

THE ANGERS APOCALYPSE: 3RD SCENE, BY NICOLAS BATAILLE — 8 FT. 2½ IN. × 4 FT. 11 IN. — FRANCE, LATE 14TH CENTURY

Château d'Angers

"And I turned to see the voice that spake with me. And being turned, I saw seven golden candlesticks; and in the midst of the seven candlesticks one like unto the Son of man, clothed with a garment down to the foot, and girt about the paps with a golden girdle. His head and his hairs were white like wool, as white as snow, and his eyes as a flame of fire; and his feet were like unto fine brass, as if they had burned in a furnace; and his voice was as the sound of many waters. And he had in his right hand seven stars; and out of his mouth went a sharp two-edged sword: and his countenance was as the sun shineth in his strength." Rev., 11, 12-16.

37

THE ANGERS APOCALYPSE: 41ST SCENE, BY NICOLAS BATAILLE — 8 FT. 2½ IN. × 4 FT. 11 IN. — FRANCE, LATE 14TH CENTURY Château d'Angers

The Angers *Apocalypse*, woven for Duke Louis I of Anjou by Nicolas Bataille, from "cartoons" (painter's diagrams) by Hennequin de Bruges. It was inspired by illuminated manuscripts illustrating Saint John the Evangelist's text, and composed of seven hangings. Each was about eighty feet long by twenty feet high. Unhappily the whole sequence is no longer complete. During the anti-clerical period following the French Revolution (1790-1840) the *Apocalypse* tapestries were put to sacrilegious uses—such as wrapping orange trees against bad weather, and padding for horse stalls. Seventy-one scenes however are still partly intact.

THE NINE HEROES:
KING ARTHUR
9 FT. 11¾ IN. × 11 FT.
6¼ IN. FLANDERS,
C. 1385
The Cloisters, New York

STORY OF SAINT PIAT AND SAINT ELEUTHÈRE — 8 FT. 10¼ IN. × 6 FT. 3 IN. — ARRAS, 1402

Tournai, Cathedral

In 1402, Canon Toussaint Prier, chaplain to Duke Philip the Good of Burgundy, presented a magnificent tapestry sequence to Notre-Dame de Tournai, as a choir-stall decoration. It was roughly six feet high and sixty-five feet long. Of its original eighteen scenes, only fourteen still remain today. Six of these are devoted to Saint Piat, 3rd-century apostle in the Tournai district, and the other eight to Saint Eleuthère, the first bishop of Tournai in the 6th century. The seventh scene (above, left) represents a mass christening ceremony after a conversion of heathens; the eighth (above, right) shows Saint Eleuthère leaving for Rome after being elected bishop by the townsfolk of Tournai. Proof of the tapestry's origin is given by an inscription on it which says: "These hangings were made at Arras by Pierrot Feré, in the year one thousand four hundred and two, in December, the month of grace. May all saints pray to God for the soul of Toussaint Prier." The author of the cartoons is unknown, but his art quite clearly reveals a certain realism—particularly noticeable in the buildings and communal baptismal tubs depicted—which show realistic Flemish rather than aristocratic French influence.

41

THE OFFERING OF THE HEART — 6 FT. 10¼ IN. × 8 FT. 5½ IN. — ARRAS, EARLY 15TH CENTURY   Musée de Cluny, Paris

THE SEVEN SACRAMENTS: CHRISTENING – 7 FT. 3½ IN. × 5 FT. –
TOURNAI, THIRD QUARTER OF THE 15TH CENTURY

This tapestry on the baptismal ceremony was woven by Pasquier Grenier, one of Tournai's master-weavers, and presented to the town's church of Saint Quentin in 1475. The priest, who is baptizing by immersion and not by sprinkling, is flanked on one side by the child's god-parents and on the other by the sacristan; two more church officials are looking on. As it was originally composed, the whole sequence comprised two superimposed registers, represent-ing, above, the various Old Testament prefigurations of the Sacraments and, below, the Seven Sacraments themselves. Five themes from each of the two parts are still in existence today.

43

THE GIVING OF ROSES – 11 FT. × 9 FT. 0¾ IN. – ARRAS OR TOURNAI, 1435-1440   Metropolitan Museum, New York

Nobody would guess, by looking at this serene and graceful scene, that it was woven in the midst of the horrors of the 100 Years' War, nor does it reveal the many cares besetting Charles VII of France. But the costumes are in fact those worn during his reign and the background colours of red, white and green are the king's own colours. The vertical bands must have had a special heraldic meaning, since they were also used to decorate the room at Vendôme (as shown in a miniature by Jean Fouquet) where a sitting of Charles' Parliament was held in 1458.

THE LADY WITH THE UNICORN: SIGHT — 12 FT. 1¾ IN. × 10 FT. 6 IN. — FRANCE, EARLY 16TH CENTURY   Musée de Cluny, Paris

The meaning of this tapestry is as mysterious as its composition and colours are beautiful. It is thought to be an allegory of Sight, four other parts of the same set of hangings being devoted to allegories on Hearing, Smell, Taste and Touch. The sixth part of the set, bearing the caption "To my sole desire," is a tribute to the young woman portrayed. But the most enigmatic feature of this tapestry, and certainly the most charming, is precisely this unknown lady on her pale red background. In the absence of any checkable facts we can only speculate—and admire.

THE NOBLE PASTORAL: THE PREPARATION OF WOOL – 10 FT. 1¼ IN. × 7 FT. 4½ IN. – LOIRE, EARLY 16TH CENTURY   Musée du Louvre

The pleasures and the labours of the field are represented in this exquisite set of tapestries, known as the *Noble Pastoral*, and acquired by the Louvre in 1950. Sheep-shearing and the carding of wool, fruit-picking, dancing and playing at hopscotch are illustrated, as lords and ladies, dressed with elegant simplicity, mingle with the country folk. The coats of arms shown probably belong to Thomas Nohier (d. 1523), chamberlain to the king of France, and his wife Catherine Briçonnet (d. 1526), who built the famous and handsome Château de Chenonceau.

46

THE LADY AT THE ORGAN – 8 FT. 10¼ IN. × 7 FT. 10½ IN. – FRANCE, EARLY 16TH CENTURY   Château d'Angers

In a setting of flowers and leaves, a fine example of the "mille-fleurs" (thousand flowers) style (see page 76), a graceful young woman is playing a portable organ, accompanying the song of an elegant gentleman. She is surrounded by three children. One is working the organ's bellows for her. A second, apparently indifferent to the music, is frolicking with a dog. The third is holding a cat by the tail. All the costumes are done in the graceful Italian style which was introduced into France following King Charles VIII's short-lived conquest of Naples in 1495.

47

THE THREE KINGS — 12 FT. 7½ IN. × 12 FT. 1 IN. — TOURNAI, 1440-1455   Musée d'histoire, Berne

Georges de Saluces (d. 1461), bishop of Lausanne from 1440 to 1461, donated a number of now-famous tapestries to this cathedral: one shows the *Three Kings* (above), two are on the emperor *Trajan* and two more are on *Herkenbald*. These hangings are often erroneously claimed to have been taken from Lausanne by Charles the Bold, Duke of Burgundy, and to have subsequently found their way to Berne following Charles' crushing defeat by the Bernese at Morat in 1476. It is true that the Duke was at Lausanne during the spring of 1476 and that he celebrated Easter in the cathedral of Notre-Dame, resplendent with its new tapestries. But it is hard to believe that he then carried off these tapestries with him! And in fact, a later inventory of Notre-Dame's treasures confirms that these hangings were taken as booty by the Bernese in 1537 after their conquest of what is now the Canton of Vaud and its chief town, Lausanne.

48

CATALOG
OF GOTHIC TAPESTRIES

In the Middle Ages, tapestry sets consisting of several pieces on the same theme served two main purposes. The first of these was religious—to enrich church interiors and edify worshippers by telling biblical stories, dramatizing the lives of saints and martyrs like St. Peter and illustrating the tenets of Christian belief as laid down in the Catechism, in the same way as statues, stained-glass windows and spandrels. The second and secular use of tapestry was originally of a purely practical nature. These woolen hangings were an efficient way of keeping out the cold, and soon this custom was reinforced by the desire for ostentation and splendour. In the following pages, we have brought together the different parts of famous tapestry sequences at present split up between various museums. Thus, for the first time in centuries, these sets can be seen in their complete original form.

Hunting the Deer – 28 ft. 5 ¼ in. × 13 ft. 4 ½ in.

Hunting the Otter – 36 ft. 9 in. × 13 ft. 9 ¼ in.

Hunting Wild Birds – 26 ft. 3 in. × 14 ft. 6 in.

THE CHATSWORTH HUNTS

Chatsworth House in Derbyshire

Victoria and Albert Museum, London

The theme of hunting was not very often used in Gothic tapestry, despite the fact that this was one of the favourite pastimes of the aristocracy. With the exception of *Hunting the Unicorn* (see pages 54-55) which is above all allegorical, the only pieces existing on this subject are the *Departure for the Hunt* (see page 57), a *Hawking* scene (now in Minneapolis Museum), a *Boar-Hunting* (in the former Burrell collection, now housed in a Glasgow museum), and this set of *Hunts*, for many years kept in Chatsworth House, Derbyshire, and probably dating from the mid-15th century. Tournai and Arras have both been put forward as the town of origin but Arras seems the more likely on account of certain details of technique and of composition. For instance, in the scene on *Bear-Hunting* (below), Mme. Marthe Crick-Kuntziger has pointed out small kidney-shaped flints lying on the ground. These stones are only very rarely found in the Tournai district but they are abundant in the Artois region of which Arras is the chief town—a fact which seems to strengthen the argument for Arras. The designer of the "cartoons" is unknown but they are thought to have been inspired by the celebrated manuscript devoted to hunting composed around 1370 for Gaston de Foix, who was also known as Gaston Phébus (1331-1391). The hangings were mentioned in the first inventory of Hardwick Castle but it is impossible to tell whether they were especially woven for an English nobleman. Mr. Wigfield Digby, curator of the Victoria and Albert Museum, maintains that they were brought across the Channel by Marguerite of Anjou when she married Henry VI of England in 1444.

Hunting the Bear
33 ft. 3 ¾ in. × 13 ft. 5 in.

THE STORY
OF JULIUS CAESAR
Musée d'Histoire, Bern

The Departure of Caesar and Crassus for their Provinces; Caesar receives a Gallic Delegation   20 ft. 11 in. × 14 ft.

Caesar crosses the Rubicon, the Battle of Pharsalia   24 ft. 9½ in. × 14 ft.

"...Item: the four large tapestries which are usually hung in the choir-stalls, on which is represented the story of Caesar, with the coat-of-arms of Illens." Despite these details listed in the inventory of the treasures of Lausanne Cathedral written by two notaries in September, 1536, the origin of the tapestries remains uncertain. They are supposed to have belonged successively to Duke Philip the Bold of Burgundy, to Louis of Luxembourg, then to Guillaume de la Baume, lord of Illens, who died childless in 1490. Their subject was inspired by Julius Caesar's book on the Gallic wars. However, the suits of armour, the horses' trappings and the costumes of both ladies and courtiers come straight out of the Burgundian court and have nothing to do with antiquity. The almost bewildering profusion of detail and the architectural elements used to divide each tapestry up into separate scenes are characteristic of Flemish tapestry of the period.

Caesar's Victory over Ariovist; the Capture of Sens; Expedition to Brittany   21 ft. 7¾ in. × 13 ft. 9¼ in.

The Triumph of Caesar, Caesar's Death   24 ft. 7½ in. × 14 ft. 0¾ in.

HUNTING THE UNICORN

Metropolitan Museum of Art, New York
The Cloisters Collection

According to a very old tradition, the unicorn was part horse and part ass, with one long, pointed horn on its forehead. Its body was white, its head was red and its eyes were blue. But it was chiefly remarkable for its beautiful shape, its great agility and its pride. For this reason the unicorn was invisible to all but virgins. Rare and reputedly uncatchable, the animal was greatly in demand since its horn was supposed to have the marvellous power of counteracting poison. Wine which had been poisoned became harmless if drunk from a unicorn's horn; knife handles made from this substance exuded small beads of liquid if the meat was poisoned; and indeed, the horn itself became black if it touched any toxic matter. Naturally, such a talisman would fetch any price and was avidly sought after by kings and noblemen to protect them from death by poisoning frequent in the Middle Ages. Unicorns, finally, were also the symbol of purity and of inaccessible love... Of course the best-known artistic representation of the fabled unicorn appears in the famous tapestry set, the *Lady with the Unicorn*, in the Musée de Cluny (see page 45). There it merely forms a part of the allegorical whole. But in the *Hunting the Unicorn* series shown here, the unicorn is the main theme of the hangings.

The Unicorn tries to escape   14 ft. × 12 ft. 0¾ in.

The Start of the Hunt   10 ft. 4 in. × 12 ft. 0¾ in.

The Unicorn at the Fountain   12 ft. 4¾ in. × 12 ft. 0¾ in.

The Unicorn at Bay   13 ft. 1¾ in. × 12 ft. 0¾ in.

The Capture of the Unicorn   4 ft. 3 in. × 6 ft. 6¾ in. (fragment)

The Unicorn is brought to the Castle   12 ft. 10¾ in. × 12 ft. 0¾ in.

The Captive Unicorn   8 ft. 2¾ in. × 12 ft. 0¾ in.

The six parts of this set are a fine example—which is both intact and in good condition—of what was called in the Middle Ages a "chamber of tapestry". They form a coherent whole because they represent the favourite pleasures and pastimes of lords and ladies at the time of Louis XII, around 1500. The background, typical of Gothic tapestry in the late Middle Ages, is in the "mille-fleurs" style—i.e. covered with tiny flowers, among which can be seen pansies and ragged robin, violets and primroses, buttercups and daisies, harebells and foxgloves, daffodils, bluebells, periwinkles and other wild flowers, not to mention assorted exotic birds with many-coloured plumage. But Renaissance influence can already be seen in the Italianate costumes and in various details of feminine fashion. For example, in *The Walk* (below), one of the ladies has her hair parted in the center and drawn back off the face, while her forehead is adorned with a narrow band after the manner of the Florentine ladies. A similar detail is seen in the celebrated portrait of *La Belle Ferronnière* in the Louvre. But it must be stressed that these Italian touches are only in the details and that the work as a whole was produced according to the spirit and traditional techniques of the 15th-century master-weavers. Overall, the tapestries show the attention to detail and realistic handling of familiar objects which are typical of mediaeval art. In the *Reading* scene, a small dog—obviously the lady's pet—is shown barking at the cat which is rolling over on its back and playing with a ball of wool. Another cheerful detail is seen in *The Bath*, where ducks are splashing busily around in the puddle formed by the bath's outlet. *The Departure for the Hunt* is only a fragment but an interesting point is that the figure on the right is almost identical to one shown in an engraving by Dürer and entitled "The Six Warriors" (1495). The set was woven on fairly thick warp threads and the colours are all of vegetable origin: madder for red; pastel—a perennial herb like madder—for blue; and weld—a variety of reseda—for yellow. Shading, or the transition from dark to light, is achieved by means of yellow and white hatching; this process in fact gives the impression of light falling from the top of the pannels and creates a great feeling of decorative unity.

The Walk   11 ft. 11 in. × 9 ft. 2 in.   Reading   7 ft. 10¼ in. × 9 ft. 5¾ in.

Embroidering 7 ft. 4 in. × 8 ft. 6¼ in.

The Bath 8 ft. 7 in. × 9 ft. 3 in.

The Departure for the Hunt 5 ft. 9½ in. × 8 ft. 4¼ in.

Scenes of Gallantry 12 ft. 2¾ in. × 8 ft. 6½ in.

COATS OF ARMS
MONOGRAMS (DETAIL)
BRUSSELS MILLE-FLEURS TAPESTRY

These illustrations are not from a set but are three examples of tapestries constructed around a number of repetitive motifs, especially popular in Gothic times. The first uses coats-of-arms to make a decorative frieze; the second mingles flowers with monograms and the third is an example of Flemish heraldic tapestry. The latter is in Berne's Historical Museum, but similar specimens can be found in many other collections—one of the most spectacular being the tapestries with a pink background in the Hospice of Beaune, in Burgundy.

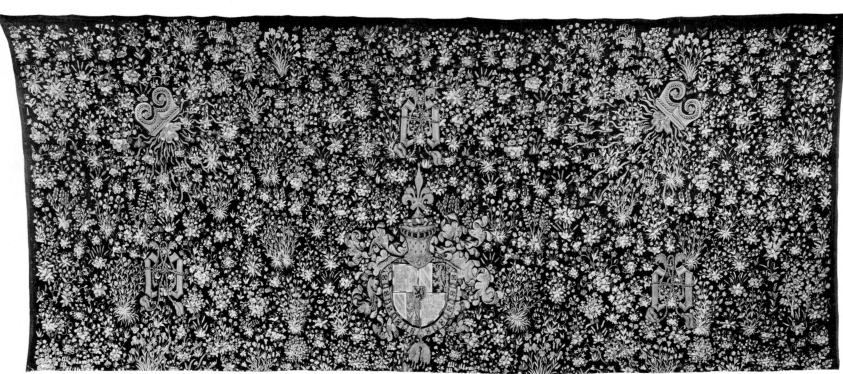

INVENTORY
OF GOTHIC TAPESTRIES

AUSTRIA

VIENNA: Kunsthistorisches Museum.
  The Triumphs of Petrarch, 6 pieces, 16th century.

BELGIUM

BRUSSELS: Musée du Cinquantenaire.
  The Presentation in the Temple, Arras, 14th century.
  Battle of Roncevaux, Tournai, 15th century.
  The Childhood of Hercules, Tournai (?), 15th century.

TOURNAI: Cathedral.
  The Story of Saint Piat and Saint Eleuthère, 20 pieces, Arras, 15th century.

FRANCE

AIX-EN-PROVENCE: Musée des Tapisseries.
  The Life of Christ, 16th century.

ANGERS: Musée des Tapisseries, Château d'Angers.
  The Apocalypse, 77 scenes, France, 14th century.
  The Lady at the Organ, 16th century.
  The Passion and the Resurrection, Arras (?), 15th-16th century.
  Angels Bearing the Instruments of the Passion, 16th century.

ANGERS: Cathedral.
  The Story of Saint Maurille, Paris, 15th century.

BEAUNE: Eglise Notre-Dame.
  The Life of the Virgin, 5 pieces, 15th century.

BEAUNE: Hôtel-Dieu.
  Tapestries with flowers and monograms, France, 15th century.

BEAUVAIS: Cathedral.
  The Story of Saint Peter, 6 pieces, Tournai, 15th century.
  The King of Gaul, 5 pieces, Beauvais, c. 1530.

LA CHAISE-DIEU (Haute-Loire): Church.
  The Life of Christ, Flanders, 15th century.

MONTPEZAT (Tarn-et-Garonne): Church.
  The Story of Saint Martin, 5 pieces, Loire, 16th century.

NANCY: Musée Lorrain.
  The Story of Esther, 2 pieces, 15th century.

PARIS: Musée de Cluny.
  The Story of Saint Stephen, 15th century.
  The Story of Saint Peter, 15th century.
  The Offering of the Heart, 15th century.
  Aristocratic Life, 6 pieces, 15th-16th century.
  Life of Saint Gervais and Saint Protais, 5 pieces, 15th century.
  Grape-pickers and Vine-growers, Loire, 15th century.
  The Lady with the Unicorn, 6 pieces, France, 15th century.

PARIS: Louvre.
  The Noble Pastoral, 16th century.

PARIS: Musée des Arts Décoratifs.

Two Figures under a Dais, Tournai, 15th century.
The Woodcutters, Tournai, 15th century.
Scenes from a Romance Novel, 5 pieces, France, 15th century.
Tapestries of courtly subjects, Arras, 15th century.

PARIS: Musée des Gobelins.

Shepherds and Shepherdesses, France, century.

PARIS: Musée Marmottan.

Susannah the Chaste, 5 pieces, 15th century.

REIMS: Musée des Beaux-Arts.

The Story of Clovis, 6 pieces, Arras (?), 15th century.
The Life of Saint Remy, 10 pieces, France or Flanders, 15th-16th century.
The Life of the Virgin, 17 pieces, France or Flanders, 15th-16th century.

ROUEN: Musée des Antiquités.

The Story of Diana, 15th century.
Winged Stags, France, 15th century.

SAUMUR: Church of Notre-Dame-de-Nantilly.

The Savages' Ball, Tournai, 15th century.
The Capture of Jerusalem, fragments, France, 15th century.
Cavaliers, fragment, France, 16th century.
The Life of the Virgin, 2 pieces, 16th century.

GREAT BRITAIN

LONDON: Victoria & Albert Museum.

The Chatsworth Hunts, 4 pieces, Arras, 15th century.
The War of Troy, 4 pieces, 15th century.

ITALY

ROME: Palazzo Doria.

The Story of Alexander, 2 pieces, Tournai, 15th century.

NORWAY

OSLO: Kunstindustri Museet.

The Twelve Months, fragments, Germany, 11th-13th century.

POLAND

CRACOW: Church of Saint Catherine.

The Swan Knight, Tournai, 15th century.

SPAIN

SARAGOSSA: Cathedral el Pilar y la Seo, Tapestry Museum.

Esther and Ahasuerus, France, 15th century.
The Story of the Passion, Arras (?), 15th century.
Exaltation of the Holy Cross, Flanders, 15th century.
The Story of Jephthah, France, 15th century.
The Story of the Virgin, France or Flanders, 15th century.
The Ships, France, 15th century.

PASTRAÑA: La Colegiala.

Portuguese Conquests, 4 pieces, Tournai, 15th century.

ZAMORA: Cathedral.

The War of Troy, Arras or Tournai, 15th century.

SWITZERLAND

BERN: Historical Museum.

The Adoration of the Magi, Tournai, 15th century.
The Story of Herkenbald, 15th century.
The Story of Julius Caesar, 4 pieces, Flanders, 15th century.

BASEL: Historical Museum.

Card Players.

U.S.A.

MINNEAPOLIS: The Minneapolis Institute of Arts.

The Tapestry of Esther, 15th century.

NEW YORK: The Metropolitan Museum of Art, The Cloisters Collection.

The Giving of the Roses, Arras or Tournai, 15th century.
The Hunt of the Unicorn, 7 pieces, 15th century.
The Nine Heroes, 15th century.
The Seven Sacraments, 3 pieces, 15th century.
The Departure of the Falcon Hunt, Tournai, 15th century.
The Triumphs of Petrarch, 15th century.

SAN FRANCISCO: California Palace of the Legion of Honour.

David and Melchisedech, Tournai, 15th century.

WASHINGTON: Corcoran Gallery.

Rustic Scenes.

CLASSICAL TAPESTRY

from the 16th to the Early 20th Century

MICHEL FLORISOONE

Director General of the Mobilier National and of the Gobelins and Beauvais Manufactories

Because tapestry was fundamentally bound up with the daily life of society's ruling classes, and because it reflected the customs and religious spirit of the times, the art became directly involved, around the turn of the 15th century, in that revolution in aesthetics known as the Renaissance, and in the evolution which the Renaissance worked upon civilization as a whole.

This revolution was largely the work of the monarchs and great men of the age—Charles V of the Holy Roman Empire, Philip II of Spain, Francis I and Henry II of France, the Infante Ferdinand of Portugal, Ferdinand of Aragon—all highly cultured men and confirmed humanists. It was only natural that they should buy many works of art, including tapestries. It was also natural that what they bought should encourage tapestry-makers towards new standards of taste.

These traditional purchases were soon increased, in Italy, France and the Flemish lands, by the demands of a growing middle-class clientèle, rich, opulent and pervasive, which developed alongside the old, privileged castes. Although they were no doubt satisfied with the commonplace commercial tapestries currently on sale, the demands of these new buyers nevertheless forced the Flemish workrooms to expand production and work swiftly, which won for them an undisputed supremacy in the trade lasting for more than a century.

The dawn of the 16th century in fact found the Arras workshops in ruins after the dispersal of the Parisian industries that had followed the 100 Years' War. Although Tournai was then in its richest period, its activity was soon cut back by the sieges of 1512 and 1521, and finally its tapestry workshops disappeared completely, victims of the bloody struggles between the kings of England and France and the Emperor Charles V. Many weavers became refugees of war. They had to split up into nomadic groups, travelling from castle to monastery, to abbey in search of customers. Some tried to re-establish their trade abroad, and this was how the small tapestry centers started in Holland (Harlem, Leyden, Delft), Denmark, Germany (Frankenthal, Wesel, Munich, Nuremberg), Hungary and Italy. The process was hard for the weavers. But the result was that good tapestry-making gradually became international and stopped being a sort of privilege confined to a single country and caste.

During the changes caused by the intrusion of the Renaissance spirit into art, a purely technical change was also at work which was to modify the entire conception of tapestry. The Italian Renaissance gave painting pride of place over the other plastic arts and this reversal of values ushered in the classical age. Tapestry-making in its turn bowed to this domination. From then on until 1940 its history was, in a certain sense, a story of the ever-increasing ascendancy of the painter over the weaver. From being a free and creative art, as in its great Gothic days, tapestry-making sank to the rank first of an interpretative, and then of an imitative, art. Before this change, complete freedom had been given to the weaver as an artist. His artistry was restricted—and yet at the same time heightened—only by the limitations imposed by technique and the loom itself. The weaver was tied to the model he worked from only insofar as his own taste and his material resources dictated. The models were merely used as rough ideas. Often they were simply sketches on cloth, touched up with a light scumble of colour. The tapestry-maker could change the composition as he wished, dropping or adding details and even figures. If the colour scheme was simply indicated by a vague "red" or "blue" with no specification of the value, he was free to transpose the colours in whatever way the dyeing process required. The final decision fell to him as an artist capable of creating a personal work on the basis of a graphic idea. He alone was responsible for the blending of colours, and for the tones and combinations which determine contrasts and accentuate planes. He was, in short, a complete architect in wool free to construct something capable of adorning and sustaining an architecture of stone. But from the time of the change, tapestry's aim became more and more simply to find means of copying more and more faithfully the accents and modulations of painting. The weaver was expected to try to compensate for lack of individual character by the flawlessness of his reproduction.

HOW THE FLEMISH LOOMS WERE SCATTERED

It was by way of Brussels that the spirit of the Italian Renaissance first reached tapestry-making. Flanders, of course, with weaving centers in Antwerp, Bruges, Enghien, Valenciennes, Lille, Ghent, Tournai, and Brussels, dominated the art. The first direct contact with Italy came in 1509, when the painter Jean Gossart of Maubeuge journeyed to Rome in company with Philip of Burgundy. Besides being the bastard son of Philip the Good and an admiral of the fleet, Philip of Burgundy had been named Emperor Maximilian's ambassador to Pope Julius II. "Gossart", relates Carel van Mander (1604), "was one of the first to bring back to Flanders the correct way of composing and executing detailed works peopled with nude figures and subjects taken from fables, which until then had never been the custom in our country." Despite this contact, tapestry-making might have remained faithful to mediaeval aesthetics much longer had it not been for Pope Leo X. The Pope placed an order with Pietr van Aelst of Brussels for tapestries representing the *Acts of the Apostles* to be woven from cartoons by Raphaël. These tapestries were intended for the Vatican's Sistine Chapel. The cartoons were completed in 1516, the hangings in 1519, and van Aelst, who had worked for Philip the Fair, eventually became "tapestry maker to the Pope." Leaving aside the actual merits of the weaving and the heavy rendering of the design, such an order had widespread effects. In the first place, of course, it came from an august personage. In the second, it confronted Flemish weavers with an entirely unprecedented situation: they were no longer required to *create* a tapestry from a model, but to *copy* as exactly as possible completed paintings which, moreover, were of a style and inspiration entirely foreign to them. Nevertheless the weavers of Flanders and elsewhere kept their own personality and independence for quite a considerable time. The Brussels weavers, for instance, did not hesitate to scatter flowerets over Christ's robe, which they considered much too empty.

The *Acts of the Apostles* was nonetheless the first blow against tapestry's autonomy. The work was carried out under the control of an Italianate Flemish painter, perhaps Bernard Van Orley, apparently helped by Tomaso Vincitore. The latter, who is thought to be of Flemish birth, helped Raphaël prepare the ten cartoons which made up the sequence. The greatest number of changes in decorative style can be seen in the borders, which repeat the Vatican loggias' greco-roman "grotesques". These motifs, so called because of their stylized "grotto-esque" or "grotesque" natural elements, were inspired by the craze prevalent among Italian princes for decorating certain rooms of their palaces to resemble grottoes. The idea was picked up from antiquity and an example can be found in the ruins of Pompeii. From the 16th century, they were to inspire all French and Flemish borders up until the 1800's.

When it was finished, this tapestry was exhibited in Rome where it aroused great admiration. Numerous copies were woven. Such a sensational success prompted a flood of orders for Brussels. Leo X commissioned a *Life of Christ* from drawings by various pupils of Raphaël. The Bishop of Mayence, the King of Portugal, the King of France and the Cardinal of Ferrara also became assiduous customers. A lively trade soon developed between Genoa and Antwerp, which became an important marketing center for the sale of tapestries—both false and authentic. In order to combat increasing counterfeits, an edict dated 1528 required weavers of Brussels tapestry to add, in the lower selvedge, two capital B's, woven in a lighter wool than the background and separated by a red escutcheon. Makers were also obliged to sign their work with a distinguishing mark. In 1544, Charles V extended these prescriptions to all the centers in the Low Countries. Bruges, Tournai, Lille and others created special symbols. Audenarde, for instance, chose as its device a yellow shield crossed by three red bars and resting, appropriately, on a broken pair of spectacles.

In Brussels the Italian paintings were accepted without too much reluctance as models. Such celebrated tapestries as the *Story of Psyche* and *Vulcan* were copied from the school of Raphaël. In the same spirit Geubels produced the *Triumphs of the Gods* copying Mantegna, and Jules Romain's superbly animated cartoons served as models both for the *Fructus Belli* and the successful 22-piece *Life of Scipio*, commissioned by Francis I. *Vertumnus and Pomona*, with its décor of caryatids and gardens, is another of the most beautiful tapestries of the period.

Bernard Van Orley was the Flemish painter who undoubtedly brought the greatest foreign contribution to his native looms. An avowed disciple of the

64

Italian school, he was skilled in the science of perspective and every painting technique. Nevertheless, through his fervour for the beauty of antiquity— demonstrated in works such as the *Last Supper*, the *Foundation of Rome* (1524) and certain panels of the Passion—he showed his continued Flemish temperament. It is this that was responsible for the characteristic mixture of idealism and realism, refinement and breadth of power especially noticeable in *Great Hunts of de Guyse or of Maximilian* woven by François Geubels at the request of the Governess of the Low Countries, Charles V's sister Mary of Hungary. It is, in fact, evident that in this work, whose subject is inspired by the *Book of King Modus and Queen Ratio* the painter was content to remain realistic and natural. He presents the houses and monuments of Brussels as a town dweller, but seems to offer the countryside through a countryman's eyes. He interprets forms and beings in a Nordic, or more precisely a Germanic, spirit.

In the 16th century, more and more princes adopted the habit of using tapestries to commemorate their military achievements. In 1531, Charles V had the States-General of Flanders present him with a woven version of the *Battle of Pavia* and the Brussels looms produced, for the same monarch, a *Conquest of the Kingdom of Thunes* to celebrate a naval expedition against the Barbary pirates. From 1549 to 1554 the *Conquest of Tunis*'s twelve panels were woven of gold, silver and silken threads by William de Pannemaker to re-create Jan Vermeyen's design. Vermeyen had been commanded by the Emperor to paint in the "best and brightest hues" the "large-scale drawings" he had made during the expedition itself. Not to be outdone, the Duke of Alba also commissioned de Pannemaker to immortalize his *Victories* and the Archduke Albert chose Martin Reymbouts to portray in seven parts his *Battles* including those of Calais and of Hulst. No personal initiative whatever on the part of the weaver was permitted to intrude into these detailed narratives, whose topographical and technical precision was rigorously controlled. Some tapestries of this period, in fact, are nothing more or less than geographical maps.

Swamped with orders, obliged to work rapidly, neglecting their borders, Flemish weavers began abandoning their technical discipline and could no longer renew their originality. Serious deterioration set in during the second half of the 16th century. The policy of religious proscription and confiscation adopted by the Duke of Alba against the Protestants precipitated events. Many weavers sought asylum in the States of the Prince of Orange, particularly in Delft which, in the late 16th century and early 17th, became one of the main centers of European tapestry-making. One by one all centers in the Spanish Low Countries died out. A native of Brussels, Josse Jean Lanckeert, set up business in Delft and in 1587 created a *Deliverance of Leyden* from Hans Liefrinck's cartoon. The famous master, François Spierinck, who supplied the States-General of the United Provinces with a large number of tapestries, also moved to Delft. Lord Howard, conqueror of the "invincible" Spanish Armada, later ordered Spierinck to make woven copies of cartoons by the Dutch painter Henri Cornelis de Vroom, which represented various phases of the battle.

A certain number of these banished weavers also found refuge in the Palatinate. There, thanks to the patronage of Frederick III, they were able to organize a high-warp industry at Frankenthal. With Pierre de Waeyere as chief and Everard Van Orley as the main painter, it was very busy for a time. At Lauingen, Bavaria, Prince Othon-Henri of Neubourg in 1540 received more Flemings to weave tapestries for his castle.

At Wesel, in the Duchy of Cleves, looms went into operation for a time under the direction of Jean Le Blas of Tournai. Weavers installed at Munich in 1603 were not so fortunate. They were placed under the inadequate management of Jean van der Biest, of Enghien, and of de Witt, from Bruges, who had been Vasari's pupil in Florence under the name of Candido. As a result the workshop soon began to wilt.

Flemish exiles also found sanctuary in England around 1567 where on the whole they had a great success. Tapestries, by Robert Hiks, already existed at Burcheston in 1540. According to the fashion of the day, most of them consisted in large-scale geographical maps of the counties of Worcester, Warwick, Oxford and Gloucester. In 17th-century England, however, there unexpectedly occurred what might be called an "English tapestry phenomenon". It started because King James I entrusted the Mortlake workshop to Sir Walter Crane. Sir Walter put Josse Ampe of Bruges in charge of its eighteen looms and fifty workmen. Naturally enough the latter were mainly Flemings from Audenarde.

From this workshop, which did its best work under Charles I, came tapestries whose beauty is still admired today. Best known is the *Acts of the Apostles*, for which Raphaël's cartoons had been purchased (with the intercession of Peter Paul Rubens). Among the others: the *Story of Vulcan*; the *Story of Diana and Calisto*; the *Four Seasons*; the *Twelve Months*; the *Five Senses*, etc. Up until 1658, the workroom's cartoon painter was François Cleyn or Klein from Rostock in Mecklembourg who is responsible for the tapestry *Hero and Leander*. Under Charles II, the industry underwent a fresh surge of prosperity thanks to the vigorous administration of Sir Sackville Crow who appointed Antonio Verrio of Lecce as cartoon painter. But after 1667 it began to wilt and finally died out completely around 1688 at the end of the Stuart era. As Guillaume Janneau correctly points out: "The tapestries produced at Mortlake possess an unfailing harmony, a tempered brilliance and a rare richness which are absolutely unique." The Flemings scattered as far as Spain where in 1624 François Tons of Brussels started weaving at Pastraña in New Castille. About the same time, Spain's Antonio Ciron set up four looms near Madrid at Santa Isabel, where Velasquez painted his *Spinning Women*.

The hard-working Flemings came down on Italy in colonies but stable workrooms and recognized centers were rare. Workshops sprang up and disappeared easily. Very often weavers, looms and models alike were all jumbled together in any sort of shelter. Often the entire personnel consisted of two or three artisans, and sometimes all of them were from the same family. As soon as their commission was completed and delivered, they packed up lock, stock and barrel and went off to seek their fortune elsewhere.

The Flemish "invasion" of Italy first began in the 15th century. Although the Italian princes, particularly the Gonzagas of Mantua, owned notable collections of French and Flemish tapestries, there were no native weavers. Eventually Flemings settled at Perugia, Corregio, Bologna, Modena and many other towns. But the very first colony was at Mantua. In 1419, two weavers who came to be known as Jean and Nicolas de France sought asylum at the Gonzagas' court. Other weavers from the North joined them and soon the art was being taught on the spot. Several years of great prosperity followed. In 1444 Luigi de Gonzaga, a great lover of Flemish tapestries, sent for Boteram of Brussels to whom the Italians gave the name Rinaldo di Gualteri. Boteram spoke of himself as a "master tapestry weaver after the fashion of Arras," and was best known for his woven interpretation of Mantegna and especially the latter's *Triumphs of Julius Caesar*, now preserved at Hampton Court. Unhappily the new Mantua tapestry center's development was cut short in 1478 by the death of Luigi de Gonzaga.

The record shows that, before going to Mantua, Boteram worked in various places. In 1438, for example, he founded a workshop at Siena where he had a two-year contract, later renewed. But in 1442 he was replaced by an Arras weaver, Jacquet by name, who is said to have produced over forty works including a *Story of Saint Peter* for Pope Nicholas V. Boteram wandered to Ferrara where another group of Flemings was already at work. Of these, Giacomo di Friandria had arrived in 1436 and Pietro de Andrea di Friandria in 1441. A native of Bruges, Liévin Gillisz, who had founded the first workshop in Florence, later found himself unwanted and, in 1457, he too moved on to Ferrara, where he was reckoned the best interpreter of Cosimo Tura's works.

Towards 1464, Marquis Borso d'Este brought Giovanni Mille and Rinaldo Grue, both high-warp weavers, from Tournai to Ferrara. Until 1471 the workshop's cartoons were supplied by Cosimo Tura, Battista Dosso, Giovanni Pordenone, Benvenuto Tisi, known as "il Garofalo" and Jules Romain. Then Hercules I succeeded the Marquis Borso and lured Sabadino, an Egyptian of great renown, to Ferrara.

The pinnacle of Ferrara's fame was eventually reached, however, between 1534 and 1559, when Hercules II brought together a team of weavers with Jean Roost (or Van der Rost), Hans and Nicolas Karcher and eight other Flemings. Ferrara's output is probably the best illustration of the new artistic and technical conceptions of tapestry. Hans Karcher, who was in charge until 1562, did not immediately abandon the traditional Flemish virtues as can be seen in his interpretation of *Ovid's Metamorphoses*, where tonal contrasts and a limited range of colours are used with great success (1535-1545). But the series on the *Life of Saint Maurelius* (1550-1552) and the *Story of the Virgin* (1562) show complete and utter submission to the finished Italian paintings which were used as cartoons.

"Weaving thereupon ceased to be a means to an end," says Guillaume Janneau, "and became an end in itself."

After the death of Hercules II the workshop quickly fell upon bad days. However Nicolas Karcher and Jean Roost had already taken root in Florence. Cosimo I de' Medici (1537-1574), wishing to free Florence and Italy from dependence on Flanders, gave great encouragement to the Florentine weavers, and production soared. However, it was never able to catch up with the rising demand and eventually the Flemish tapestry centers, instead of losing because of Italian competition, gained from the increased interest it created. The twenty-four Florentine looms turned out several very beautiful sequences: the 20-piece *Story of Joseph* (see page 92) from 1547 to 1550, now in the Palazzo Vecchio, *Parnassus* (1556), and *Marsyas* (1560)—all three after Bronzino; then the *Story of Saint Mark* with its gold, silver and silken threads, woven in 1550 by Roost following art-work by Jacopo Sansovino and now in Venice's Basilica; the *Twelve Months* (1552-1554), and a series of *Grotesques on a Yellow Ground* from pictures by Francesco d'Ubertino, known as "il Bachiaca"; the 10-piece *Human Life*; the *Story of Lorenzo the Magnificent*; a set of *Hunting Scenes*; *Lot fleeing Sodom*, now in the Gobelins Museum, and many others.

In the second half of the 16th century Bronzino, the accredited painter to the Florentine workshop, was succeeded by Alessandro Allori who had designed the classical Stories of *Latona, Paris, Phaethon, Niobe*, and *Bacchus*, and various Christian themes. Of Allori's cartoons Jules Guiffrey says rightly: "The tendency to substitute a picture for a decorative composition became more pronounced daily; the weaver was nothing but an interpreter, more or less skilful, more or less experienced, of the painter's invention."

Orders, however, continued to pour into the Medici workshop from as far away as Venice and Spain. After the death of de Roost in 1562, his son, Giovanni di Giovanni Roost, took charge. But the death in 1574 of Cosimo I brought to a temporary close the Florentine workshop's period of greatness. It was revived somewhat in 1630 by Parisian Pierre Lefèvre. But we can agree with Guillaume Janneau that in Florence "cartoon painters, influenced by the new creed of the superiority of painting over auxiliary crafts, had ceased to respect the rules of tapestry-making."

Under Pierre Lefèvre and his sons, the Florentine workshop operated briskly for half a century. Pierre Lefèvre worked with cartoons by Rubens, Cristofano Allori, Raphaël and Andrea del Sarto. He drew not only on historical and biblical subjects like the *Story of Alexander* and the *Story of Tobias*, but on contemporary themes—such as the *Story of Lorenzo the Magnificent*. Another important master-weaver, Bernardino van Hasselt, who had set up a rival workroom in the Palazzo Vecchio's outbuildings at the same period, was responsible for many more tapestries, including the *Story of Moses*, which is now preserved at the Mount of Piety, Rome.

Venice, like Antwerp, was a marketing center for tapestries. This fact is probably evidence that an industry existed there in the 16th century. Most likely it was an outgrowth of the one established in 1421 by Jean de Bruges and Valentin d'Arras, which created the *Life of Christ* series in the church of Santa Maria dei Angeli, and the *Story of Semele* now in the Hall of the Ten in the Doge's Palace. At Genoa in 1551, Vincentius della Valle and Pierre de Bruxelles attempted to establish a workroom but were replaced in 1553 by Denis de Bruxelles who from 1560 to 1564 used Lazare Calvi's cartoons as the basis of his work. And at Modena, Giovanni de Gesulis took over, in 1528, from Antonio de Gerardino who had founded the industry in 1488. Both were Flemish, despite their Italian names.

At Vigevano, however, the looms were actually manned by Italians—under the direction of Benedetto da Milano. But by a remarkable coincidence, as it has been pointed out, "this entirely Italian group produced a pure example of traditional technique, using the cartoon to serve tapestry's own ends but without trying to create the illusion of an exact reproduction of painting." This "pure example" is the *Twelve Months* set (see page 93), woven for the Trivulzio Palace from cartoons by Bartolomeo Suardi. The most dignified of the twelve parts is the October tapestry, devoted, naturally, to the harvest. There is nothing glamorous about the simple peasants realistically portrayed with their homely carrots, beets and other crops. Yet a monumental, almost architectural quality invests the figures, and especially those of the statuesque foreground women. For perhaps the first time ever in tapestry's history, the work is signed, and the Latin inscription *Ego Benedictus di Mediolani hoc opus feci cum sociis in Viglevani* (I, Benedetto da Milano, made this work in Vigevano with my associates), is the only symptom of the new individualistic spirit.

SUPREMACY OF FRENCH TAPESTRY IN THE 16TH AND 17TH CENTURIES	By the early 16th century French tapestry was installed at Blois following in the wake of King Louis XII who had come to the throne two years earlier. Forced by the troubled times to roam up and down France visiting castles, monasteries and abbeys, the weavers sometimes settled, for varying lengths of time and according to prevailing circumstances, at the seat of some provincial lord who was glad to have his walls hung with good warm wool and so improve his comfort. These nomadic workshops spread more swiftly along the Loire, customarily following in the footsteps of the king and his court. They were at Bourges during Charles VII's stay there. They were at Tours with Louis XI, at Angers with Charles VIII, and finally at

Blois under Louis XII. These industries are generally lumped together under the name "Loire workshops". There is, in fact, little appreciable difference between them. But from the point of view of style, they brought about a fundamental conflict, of great importance for the future of the art—a conflict between the values of mediaeval miniaturism and the new Italian influences of the Renaissance. The latter made an appearance in the *Life of Saint Gervase and Saint Protais*, created at Le Mans in 1509, and in certain details of the *Life of Saint Florent* produced at Saumur (1524). They blaze in sheer splendour through the *Life of Saint Saturnine* woven at Tours from models by one of Andrea del Sarto's pupils. Gothic tapestry's golden age, on the other hand, comes to an end with the *Life of the Virgin* and the *Story of Saint Remy* at Rheims (1532), as well as with such works as the *Triumphs of Petrarch* and the *Kings of Gaul* (1530).

The roaming life of French and Flemish weavers accounts to a large extent for the creation of workshops in the provinces of the Marche (now the Departments of La Creuse, Haute-Vienne, Indre, Vienne and Charente) and Auvergne. By 1456 Jacques Bennyn had set up a first workroom at Felletin, a busy town on the Lyons-Bordeaux trading route. The plant soon became prosperous, so much so that the inventory of Charlotte d'Albert, Duchess of the Valentinois country who died in 1514, mentions in all seventy-five Felletin tapestries.

Strangely enough, Aubusson, the name which was to have the longest and most glorious history in the growth of tapestry weaving, apparently came relatively late to the craft. Apart from the *Story of Saint Peter* and the *Story of Simon the Magician* which, in 1551, belonged to the Church of Saumur, it is not until 1560 that the town records of Ahun refer to weaving at Aubusson. But by 1648, in his "Geographical Survey of the Kingdom of France" Jean Boisseau writes that "the artisans of Aubusson are still more highly thought of than those of Felletin." Even then the work was distinctive. Aubusson weavers used especially thick warps and thick wefts. The result was a very noticeable simplification of the design and colour scheme. The effects of this technique can be seen even in the choice of subject, which most often was confined to woodlands, or verdure of the "cabbage-leaf" variety. Customarily, real or legendary animals frolic against a background of towns or castles. A good example is the set of ten tapestries by Anglars of Salers. Aubusson's family craftsmen, content to meet the demands of local gentry, bourgeois customers and the churches, worked fast and sold cheap. However, they managed to create important works too, notably the Stories of *Ahasuerus, Saint Martial* and *Saint Peter* as well as a series of *Heroes* which all reveal great care and skill. Although Flemish in origin and of low-warp, the Marche tapestries are very French in rhythm, feeling and technique. This is most clearly demonstrated in certain "verdures" and particularly in the *Saint Stephen* series at Toulouse.

During this period the Parisian workshops, despite their financial difficulties, had not completely abandoned their work. We know, for instance, that they supplied twenty tapestries for the wedding of Princess Renée of France and the Duke of Ferrara. There were other orders too, some of them from Francis I, although in general the latter preferred to purchase from Antwerp or to send cartoons to Brussels. But court tapestries were continually being put up or taken down, and moved from place to place to accompany the king on his travels. Small wonder then that they rapidly wore out, and the cost of replacing them put a heavy strain on the royal treasury. Like Cosimo de' Medici, Francis I wished to become independent of the Flemish weaving industry. But the Parisian weavers, who had not yet recovered from the devastation caused by the English occupation in the 100 Years' War and were still weighed down by their craft's cumbersome feudal organization, could not give the king the service he needed. Exasperated, Francis I decided to create a private weaving industry which would work exclusively for him and on which he could impose the new style. He therefore ordered the Superintendent of Royal Buildings, Philibert Babou de la Bourdaisière, to recruit foreign weavers, probably from Tournai, and establish them, with their looms, in the Palace of Fontainebleau, which was the springboard of the French artistic Renaissance. France's first royal workshop opened in 1539, probably under the direction of Pierre and Jean le Briès. It only operated for twelve years. But it produced a number of masterpieces, among them the sequence *The Wanderings of Ulysses*, copied from Francesco Primaticcio's frescoes in the Palace's Galerie des Réformés. It is believed that the workroom was kept going for a while by Henry II after the death of Francis and it may have produced the *Story of Diana* designed by Philibert de l'Orme, a series done in honour of Diane de Poitiers, the king's mistress, commissioned as a gift from the king and intended for the château he had given her at Anet.

But Henry no doubt wanted to revive the Paris weaving industry. To help do so he established and endowed with special privileges the Hôpital de la Trinité workshop in the rue St. Denis. Using 136 orphans recruited from the Trinité hospice, and probably aided by the Fontainebleau weavers, he set up a professional school there where tapestry-weaving was taught side by side with painting, wool carding and spinning. The king went even further, when, in direct contradiction to established guild laws of the time, he decreed that Trinité apprentices could rise to the rank of master craftsmen at no cost to themselves.

The decision shook Paris's hidebound mediaeval workrooms to their very foundations. Nevertheless nothing of great style came out of the Trinité workshop, although its 12-piece *Life of Christ* (1584-1594), destined for Saint Médéric's church, is notable for its free and powerful interpretation of the cartoons made by Henri Lerambert, the "painter for the king's tapestries." The same can be said for the *Legend of Saints Crispin and Crispinian*. More important, however, the workshop did produce two artists who made significant contributions to the future of tapestry in France—Maurice Dubout and Girard Laurent. These two weavers were in fact called in, some years later, by Henry IV to help in the realization of a special scheme he had worked out. While still only King of Navarre, he had thought of creating his own "domestic" workshop but he did not have the time then to carry out the project. Once having conquered Paris, and become King of all France, he picked up the threads of the idea and extended his scheme on a national scale. In the old Jesuits' House, Faubourg St. Antoine, in Paris, he set up a weaving plant in 1597 under the direction of Dubout and Laurent, with a view, like Henry II before him, to revitalizing France's weaving trade. When the Jesuits (who had several years previously been expelled from France) were given permission to return in 1606, so forcing Dubout and Laurent to quit the premises, Henry IV installed them in the newly-finished "galleries" of the Louvre itself. He had decided to create there a "seminary of the best and most competent workers," wishing, as contemporary texts record, "to promote an alliance between intellect and the fine arts, on the one hand, and members of the nobility and the military on the other." Here then, armed with patents dated January 4 and December 22, 1608, Dubout and Laurent "opened shop" and took up residence. With this recognition of their merit the Louvre workshop proceeded to reach a high standard of perfection.

Henry IV's idea, however, was not merely to create a "conservatory for higher technical education" as the Louvre workshop has been called. The aim of his economic and artistic policy was to industrialize France using silk manufacture and tapestry-making as a basis. Surveying the means at his disposal—the Trinité workshop struggling to survive after the departure of its best masters, the independent Parisian industries openly hostile to any form of change, the wandering provincial weavers and the Marche workrooms with their isolation and lack of scope—Henry was quick to see that none of them could possibly create a true, national tapestry industry, or hope to surpass the highly polished art of Brussels. The king therefore took a bold decision. Paris, it must be explained, was the stronghold of high-warp weaving, which, as the guild-masters rightly protested, was "far better and more valuable than that (low-warp weaving) practised in the Low Countries." Into this Paris, Henry introduced... Flemish low-warp weavers! He saw that, with their speed and dexterity, these were the only craftsmen capable of creating for France a tapestry industry and trade which might compete with those of Brussels and Antwerp.

In 1599 the Superintendent of Royal Buildings, Jean de Fourcy, began to approach Flemish tapestry-makers. A royal warrant dated January 12, 1601, announces the arrival of "foreign workers whom His Majesty has brought from the Low Countries to man the tapestry industry in the town of Paris." On the 29th of the same month, three Flemings from Audenarde—Marc de Comans, Jérôme de Comans, and their brother-in-law Frank van der Planken (soon to become known as François de la Planche)—went into partnership with a view to forming and exploiting a tapestry workshop. For Marc de Comans, Fourcy rented the Hôtel des Canaye, purchased from the Gobelin family only thirty years earlier by a draper named Michel Charpentier. This building stood just across the way from the Hôtel des Gobelins which Philibert Gobelin had sold two years before. François de la Planche, at first lodged in the Hôtel des Tournelles, soon found these quarters too cramped, and so joined Marc de Comans, taking over the premises obligingly made available to him by the Gobelins family to whom he was distantly related. The Gobelins were in fact descendants of the celebrated "dyer of scarlet", Jehan Guobelin of Rheims who had come to Paris in the 15th century to exploit a secret dyeing process which he had discovered in Venice. By April, the two workshops were installed on the banks of the Bièvre, a tributary of the Seine which today is in the 13th district of Paris. In September, an edict proclaimed that it was "from now on forbidden for anyone to bring into the kingdom from foreign countries any tapestry depicting figures, woodlands or foliage." Finally, in January 1607, Henry IV decided, over protests from Parisian master-craftsmen and from his own minister Sully—who favoured an exclusively agricultural policy—to seal the foundation of this new Faubourg St. Marcel industry by a fresh royal edict.

The letters patent, dated 1607, contain exceptional trading clauses on the basis of which Louis XIV was later to support the Gobelins. They confer nothing less than a monopoly. For a period of fifteen years—later prolonged—it was decreed that "no-one may imitate the products" of "my lords" François de la Planche and Marc de Comans. The ban on foreign tapestry imports was confirmed. The tapestry market in France was thus cornered by the two brothers-in-law. Furthermore, the king bore the cost of their lodging and that of some 200 workers who became, *ipso facto*, naturalized Frenchmen. In addition they were to be exempt from all taxes and tolls during fifteen years. Master-craftsmen and apprentices could, after three years and six years respectively, open up their own business without first having to produce the customarily required masterpiece.

The king went even further to encourage his new industry. The royal Treasury paid the upkeep of the apprentices, who at the end of three years numbered 65. All raw materials used, with the exception of gold and silk, were exempt from tax, and the king granted an annuity of 1500 pounds to each of the two masters, plus an allowance of 100,000 pounds to offset initial costs. As if this were not enough, Marc de Comans and François de la Planche were recognized as noblemen and "table-companions" of the king. In this way, tapestry-making and trading were raised to a rank not unworthy of the nobility. One last clause which carried great weight and which may, perhaps, have been decisive, was a grant to the two masters, enabling them to open a brewery and sell beer.

In return, Marc de Comans and François de la Planche undertook to maintain eighty looms in constant activity—sixty in Paris and twenty at Amiens. They also agreed not to sell their products at higher prices than those hitherto paid for Flemish tapestries. It is worth noting that de Comans and de la Planche remained responsible for the smooth running—commercial and financial—of their workshops. They could trade as they wished and were free to weave for private buyers. And although the king subsidized them, if he wished to make a purchase he just had to take his turn in the queue along with the other customers!

Even after the death of François de la Planche in July 1627 and the signing over of Marc de Comans' rights to his son Charles, the industry throve. Charles found himself in business with his cousin Raphaël de la Planche. The pair separated in 1633 and thus the Manufactory split in two—Charles staying at the Gobelins to become Head of the Faubourg St. Marcel factory, and Raphaël setting up near the Hôpital des Teigneux, Faubourg St. Germain. The rift in no way altered the royal privileges already bestowed, which continued to be enjoyed by the two workshops. Their output was both plentiful and of high quality and the eighty looms of Paris, Amiens and finally of Tours produced some celebrated series. Among them: the *Story of Coriolanus*, the *Story of Diana*, *Children's Games*, the *Story of Psyche*, and the *Story of Constantine* ordered from Rubens by Louis XIII. From the Faubourg St. Marcel factory came the *Story of Artemis* from cartoons by Henri Lerambert which were adapted from Antoine Caron's illustrations for a manuscript by Nicolas Houel (1562). These latter drawings had been produced in honour of Catherine de' Medici.

In 1627, painter Simon Vouet arrived in Paris from Italy, setting afoot a new and original movement—one might almost call it a school—which became noted for its great decorative richness and a brilliant use of colour. Vouet founded a whole work-room of cartoon painters ready to work from his drawings and paintings. His models, as interpreted by de la Planche and the two Comans, as well as by Maurice Dubout at the Louvre, resulted in the *Wanderings of Ulysses*, *Story of Reginald and Armida*, *Loves of the Gods*, *Scenes from the Old Testament* and *The Philistines' Banquet*.

Vouet entrusted his *Elijah taken up into Heaven* and the seven parts of the *Loves of the Gods* to the Amiens factory. His composition, the beauty of the colours and his understanding of the technicalities of tapestry-making all earned him the complete and intimate trust of his weavers. The latter, working with relative freedom and a certain boldness, yet also with deep respect, adapted and transformed Vouet's paintings into tapestries throbbing with life and vigour.

By 1650, however, the gradual evolution of technique can easily be discerned. As a result, old individual characteristics peculiar to tapestry were subdued or smoothed out, while greater and greater skill and virtuosity were sought as a kind of compensation. The classical age, with its emphasis away from the specific and realistic and towards universality and generalization, was fast approaching. For the weaver this meant simply effacing his own personality and producing a regular, unostentatious and carefully-woven fabric.

Some of these changes may be seen in works produced in the Louvre workshop in the middle of the century like the *Story of St. Gervase and St. Protais* from cartoons signed by Philippe de Champaigne, Sébastien Bourdon, Eustache Le Sueur and Goussé. Most of the parts comprising *The Life of the Virgin* (from pictures by Poerson, Jacques Stella and Philippe de Champaigne) are believed to have been woven in a small workshop set up by Pierre Damour in the cloisters of Notre-Dame. Damour was a pupil of Daniel Pepersak, a Fleming with a workshop at Charleville in 1601. Later called to Rheims, Pepersak wove a twenty-nine piece *Life of Christ* for Archbishop Henri de Lorraine, and in 1648 received, from the Chapter of Notre-Dame de Paris, a commission for this *Life of the Virgin,* which he passed on to Pierre Damour.

Another weaving plant, at Maincy, a kind of modernized "domestic" workshop, was begun in 1660. It was built up from scratch by Nicolas Fouquet, the powerful and luxury-loving Superintendent of Finances, in the park of his fabulous Château de Vaux-le-Vicomte, and was run by an outstandingly skilful and ambitious painter, Charles Le Brun, who helped decorate Versailles for Louis XIV. Le Brun was aided by a team of artists who turned out whole series of cartoons, some of them original, some replicas of works by Raphaël. The Maincy factory, manned by twenty-five Franco-Flemish weavers headed by a Parisian named Loÿs Blamars, came as close to modern "mass production" as was possible in its age. During its three years' existence its output was three times greater than that of all the other Parisian workshops. Some of its principal products, used to adorn the château at Vaux, were "door-pieces" devoted to *Famous Men*, and such works as the *Triumphal Chariot*, the eight-piece *Story of Constantine*, the *Muses*—also in eight parts—and the ten-piece *Meleager's Hunts*.

Unhappily Nicolas Fouquet was denounced by Colbert, the king's minister, and imprisoned for misappropriation of public funds. Along with his property, the Maincy workshop was confiscated by Colbert, who saw in this a chance to complete the plans laid by Henry IV in 1607. The financial situation of the Parisian workshops was lamentable, and the Faubourg St. Germain factory would have collapsed completely had the king not appointed its Director, Raphaël de la Planche, to the additional and well-paid post of Royal Treasurer. During the minority of Louis XIV, which was troubled by unrest among the nobility and an increasing struggle for influence on the part of the parliament, the difficulties became still graver. From geographical, administrative and artistic points of view alike, it was obviously of paramount importance to regroup the profession and centralize it. The workshops were so scattered that any attempt at reform was worthless. The competitive spirit, so systematically fostered by Francis I and Henry IV, had degenerated into sterile rivalry. There existed in Paris five privileged weaving plants: the Faubourg St. Marcel workshop, headed by the last of the Comans; the Maincy industry; the Louvre galleries workshop under the son of Girard Laurent; the Tuileries plant set up by Jean Lefèvre, son of the director of the Florentine industry; and the Faubourg St. Germain group.

Colbert decided to bring all these together under the roof of the Gobelins. On June 6, 1662, he bought the old Hôtel Canaye which had been let to one of Henry IV's stewards and which is referred to in the deed of sale as the "house of the Gobelins family." Next came a piece of land belonging to Le Brun, a house owned by Hippolyte de Comans—Marc de Comans' third son and successor—and several other lots of land, making a total of nine consecutive purchases.

First to move into this new complex were three high-warp workshops whose directors still enjoyed full responsibility. Chief of these was Jean Jans, also called Jean de Bruges, at the head of 67 workmen and numerous apprentices. The second workshop was directed by Jean Lefèvre and the third by Henri Laurent from the Louvre galleries. In the same manner, the low-warp industries were regrouped under Jean de la Croix.

At the height of its activity, the new complex employed approximately 250 workmen, not including apprentices. Later on two more low-warp groups were added. In 1667 the Gobelins Manufactory was organized on a permanent footing under letters patent which incorporated it in the Royal Furniture Manufactory. The artistic direction of the Gobelins was entrusted to the fortunate Charles Le Brun, from the Maincy plant at Vaux-le-Vicomte.

Although Le Brun was one of the leading figures in the artistic evolution of the time, his directorship was nevertheless characterized by respect for traditional tapestry-making techniques. In practice his principal task was to "produce designs for the tapestries and have them executed correctly." The trade term "design" or "idea" meant the artist's original work; a "design" differed from a "model" which was a painting made to the exact size of the tapestry and modified only by its author. It differed also from the "cartoon" or "pattern" used for the actual weaving. Usually, Le Brun executed a design, as in the case of the *Legate's Audience* or the *King visiting the Gobelins*. A sketch was then painted by one or more other artists, under his supervision, and the model was finally produced by yet more artists regularly employed by the factory. If the painting to be used was already in existence, the model was prepared immediately, as in the case of the *Battles of Alexander* sequence. It should be noted therefore that, although the weaver no longer worked directly from a sketch on cloth touched up with colour as in the Middle Ages, neither did he have to follow a finished picture in deference to the Renaissance idea of the supremacy of painting.

What he now used was a copy of an original specially prepared for weaving as a tapestry. In fact Le Brun, who was familiar with the requirements and limitations of the dyeing process, gave the weavers a completely free hand as far as colour went. His design and his relief were another matter and had to be copied faithfully. At no time did Le Brun attempt to subordinate tapestry-making to painting. On the other hand he did not hesitate to modify legs and arms drawn even by the great Raphaël himself. One of the first measures taken by Le Brun on arrival at the Gobelins was to send the apprentices to compulsory drawing classes by Louis Licherie.

Le Brun was not alone in following such a policy. Sébastien Bourdon, Eustache Le Sueur, Errard, Michel Corneille, Claude Vignon, Moillon and La Hyre also refrained from finishing off paintings intended for weaving, in order to leave the weaver a free choice of colours. Even the famous François Boucher remembered this precaution in the mid-18th century when tapestry was again completely dominated by painting.

The necessity of preparing these cartoons and models obliged Le Brun to enlist a whole team of painters. We know the names of about fifty of them. They included Baudrin Yvart, who had already worked with Le Brun at Maincy, Louis Licherie, Verdier, Louis Testelin, René-Antoine Houasse, Pierre de Sève, Baptiste Monnoyer, the Coypels, the Boullongues, Poerson, etc. Each had his own speciality, his own talent, and they were divided into groups each under its own chief. Some painted architectural subjects, others worked on ornaments, animals, scenery and so on. For example in the *Royal Houses* set Baudrin Yvart and François Bonnemer were responsible for the large foreground figures, van der Meulen for the scenery and groups of silhouettes, Guillaume Anguier for porches, Nicasius Bernaerts and Peter Boëls for all the animals, Monnoyer for foliage, François Desportes for the fruits in the foreground, and Jean Garnier for musical instruments. For the *Battles of Alexander* the models were painted by Louis Licherie, Baudrin Yvart, Verdier, Louis Testelin and René-Antoine Houasse.

Several copies were made of each set produced by the Gobelins up to 1683. Distributed, as royal gifts, all over Europe, they were intended purely as propaganda to emphasize the greatness of Louis XIV's reign and especially the personal glory of the sovereign himself.

There was nothing particularly new about this. Louis XIV—no doubt with more show and splendour—was merely enlarging upon the ideas of the Emperor Charles V, Henry III, Cosimo de' Medici, Lorenzo the Magnificent and others. The sets were finished off systematically, and for twenty years the entire resources of the Manufactory were exclusively engaged in carrying out the king's plan. But this plan was only revealed little by little, and with a certain amount of prudence. The first model given to the weavers by Le Brun was for the *Elements* (see page 96) series, particularly notable for its magnificent borders in which mottoes and inscriptions composed by the Little Academy sing the praises of Louis XIV. Next came the *Seasons*, again with the hidden flattery in the borders but also depicting four of the finest royal châteaux with the pastimes appropriate to each according to the season: *Spring and Versailles* with "the king on horseback in the ring," *Summer and Fontainebleau* with Minerva and Apollo holding a picture showing the Tuileries under construction, *Autumn and Saint-Germain* in which Bacchus and Diana are holding a picture representing the king hunting, and *Winter,* with a ballet theatre.

The Story of Alexander, a splendid five-part epic decorated with moral-bearing scrolls, recalls the highly idealized gallantry and magnanimity of the great conqueror and civilizer, and implies a worthy modern counterpart in the person of Louis XIV. The weaving of the *Story of the King* (page 94), begun in 1665, shows the king in fourteen different attitudes corresponding to the most princely acts in the life of Europe's greatest monarch. These episodes were drawn from his private life, his military career and his diplomatic activities. The *Months*, or *Royal Houses*, set completes this pompous survey by boasting the magnificence of the French court which, month by month, could change its paradise without changing its god. The old "months" theme is thereby brought up to date in the most realistic manner. This series of twelve tapestries was woven seven times in all, together with eight window-pieces. The whole group, with its porches, pilasters, terminals, columns and balustrades, speaks volumes for the merits of French architecture.

Le Brun was not merely an innovator. He was also the man who carried out amply, generously and beyond their wildest hopes the plans laid down years before by Francis I and Henry IV. From the technical angle, he perfected and disciplined the old family craft whose independence and prerogatives were thereby safeguarded throughout the length of his control.

However, Colbert had not forgotten the Marche workshops. Since the edict of 1601 they had been protected against all foreign competition and as a result business was booming. Colbert raised the status of the private Aubusson factories to that of royal weaving plants and this was ratified by letters patent dated July 1665. In 1689 the same privilege was accorded to Felletin. A stimulating influx of experienced Flemings brought the number of weavers up to 2,000 and Aubusson's output improved noticeably.

But these workshops were still badly in need of an artist who could produce original cartoons and advise their weavers. It was not until the mid-18th century, however, that the situation was remedied. Still, during the 17th century, the Aubusson works passed through a fine period under the direction of Evrard Jabach of Cologne, a celebrated collector and art-lover, and a friend of Antoine Van Dyck, Charles Le Brun, Adam-François van der Meulen, Nicolas de Largilierre, and Hyacinthe Rigaud noted today mainly for his Louvre portrait of Louis XIV. In 1668 Jabach bartered his paintings for the right to set up a personal workshop and to organize a factory for the processing of hemp, wool and silk. Then, around 1683 the Duke de la

Feuillade, who had just become Viscount of Aubusson, established at Aubusson what has since been called his own "Gobelins" workshop, with "his painter in ordinary", Pierre du Mesle, in charge.

This workshop, according to Cyprien Perathon, created hangings comparable to those produced in Flanders, and one of its masterpieces was a beautiful sequence on Joan of Arc. However, in 1685 the Edict of Nantes was revoked by Louis XIV; this Edict had protected the religious liberty of the Protestant minorities in France since 1598. The revocation and the persecution which then followed led to a mass exodus of Protestant workers, including the Flemish weavers.

Along with the Marche workrooms and apart from those already noted at Amiens, Tours, Charleville and Rheims, several other centers existed in France. They were either local industries or old nomadic workshops which had finally taken root. An ex-head of the first Gobelins manufactory, Claude de Lapierre, who had served his apprenticeship at the Trinité center, founded a workshop at the Hôpital de Bordeaux and another, in 1632, in the Duke of Epernon's castle at Cadillac. Here was woven the *Story of King Henry III* of which only the *Battle of Jarnac* remains. At Lille the industry was relaunched in 1625, thanks to the vigour of Vincent van Quickelberg from Audenarde and Guillaume Waerniers of Brussels. From 1701 to 1758 Waerniers was in charge of twenty-one looms which are reputed to have equalled the Gobelins for the beauty of their work. We know that from 1625 to 1650 a factory was in operation at Rouen, and the quality of its tapestries is proved by the fact that both Raphaël de la Planche and Chancellor Michel Le Tellier possessed some. Nancy, together with Saint-Mihiel, had been an important regional center since the 15th century, and in the early 17th century several Brussels weavers could still be found there. But around 1697 two bigger factories were founded, one of them under Nicolas and Pierre Durand, in the attics of the Boucherie, and the other, belonging to Charles Mité, in the château de Malgrange where two sequences were woven: *Victories of Charles V, Duke of Lorraine* and *Arabesque Months*. A little later, F. Josse Bacor, a one-time Gobelins apprentice, and Sigisbert Mangin set afoot at Lunéville a workroom which was transferred to Malgrange at a later date. The "door-pieces" bearing the *Arms of Lorraine and Orleans* were the most notable works to come from their looms. In 1734 Jean Bella from Aubusson established a high-warp and a low-warp industry in Nancy.

More important to the development of French tapestry weaving was the institution by Colbert, in 1664, of a factory at Beauvais which, though under the king's protection, remained a private enterprise. It was directed first by Louis Hinart who seems to have used designs by Jacques Fouquières. It is Hinart who deserves credit for the *Picardy Wedding* and *Children's Games* sets. The next director, from 1684, was Philippe Béhagle from Tournai and under both these men the factory enjoyed a period of great success. Many of their works were officially qualified as being "excellent"; for example a tapestry based on Raphaël's *Acts of the Apostles* for the cathedral of Beauvais, the *King's Conquests* and a series of *Sea Ports* after Kerchove and Campion (before 1693). Béhagle's most important contribution, however, was to sponsor a new standard of taste and the subsequent complete divorce of the craft from Le Brun's ideals and aesthetic values. With its set of *Grotesques on a Yellow Background*, or *Spanish Tobacco*, the young Beauvais factory opened the door to a renovation of style in the art of tapestry-making. The theme of these grotesques was taken from antiquity through the intermediary of Raphaël: slim architectural structures raised on colonnades, supporting porches and arbours intertwined with leaves, birds, bouquets, garlands, trophies, and incense-burners; and in the foreground a whole throng of delicate legendary figures, mingled with characters from the Commedia dell'Arte, dancing, moving, singing, and playing music.

Jean Berain whose drawing ability had earned him commissions from both the king and the Royal Academy of Music, played an important role in the new aesthetic movement. He helped in designing the borders of the *Conquests of the King of Sweden* (see pages 108-109) set, from cartoons by Jean-Baptiste Martin, and was entirely responsible for the models of *Marine Triumphs* woven in Béhagle's private Parisian workshop. The *Triumphs* might have been lifted straight out of the décor of one of Lulli's operas, with its wealth of colonnades, caryatids, shells, corals, and fountains. In the midst of all this appear Eurus, the god of tempests, Amphitrite, Venus and a young warrior of antiquity who turns out to be none other than the Count of Toulouse. The next following style was determined by Philippe Béhagle and Jean Berain, even before Le Brun's removal, for the grotesques were designed before 1689.

However, the Beauvais technique was still very patchy and the tapestries were criticized for their "unequal and knotty texture, ill-planned colour schemes, their shaggy wools and their fast-fading colours."

Known as the 1690 crisis, the events which turned the life of the Gobelins workshops upside down from 1683 to 1694 brought in their wake, in 1699, a complete renewal of the spirit and aesthetics of tapestry. The crisis had three causes, corresponding to three aspects of the craft: personalities, technique and aesthetics.

At the root of the trouble lay a rivalry between two artists, Charles Le Brun and Pierre Mignard, and a parallel rivalry between two ministers, Colbert and Louvois. On September 6, 1683, Colbert died, broken by the ingratitude of the king who had disgraced him after twenty years of loyal service. He was succeeded by his bitter enemy Louvois, whose first care was to remove Le Brun—Colbert's creature—from the Royal Furniture Manufactory. Although Le Brun remained nominally in charge, it was in fact the Controller of Buildings, Monsieur de la Chapelle-Bessé, who took over the actual direction of the workshop. And the old spirit of grandeur and opulence was immediately replaced by one of economy. Economy stopped the work on the *Story of the King* which required a great deal of gold thread. Deprived of new cartoons, "ideas" and models, the weavers took up once more some old Brussels favourites: *Maximilian's Hunts, Fructus Belli* and the *Lucas Months*. The king's cabinet yielded up sundry drawings and paintings, such as *Subjects from Fables* by Jules Romain and Raphaël, and the *Story of Moses* by Nicolas Poussin; Raphaël's *Triumphs of the Gods* and the *Arabesque Months* were rejuvenated by Noël Coypel. It was also decided to weave a series of eight large pictures painted by the Dutchman Albert Eckhout in Brazil during the expedition undertaken by Maurice de Nassau. The resulting set, called the *Old Indies*, was greeted with enthusiasm and is undeniably a masterpiece of its exotic kind.

Le Brun died in 1690 and Mignard, then aged 78, succeeded him. For the artistic world, the rise of Mignard consolidated official recognition of the new attitude and strengthened a sense of aesthetics based on the preponderance of sensitivity and colour and no longer on logic and design. This artistic revolution, so long clamoured for by the younger generation, brought painting "into line" with the ideas of the great writers of the time—Racine, Madame de La Fayette, Madame de Sévigné and Boileau—headed by the incomparable Molière (who had just written a poem "to the glory" of one of Mignard's works, the dome of the Val-de-Grâce convent). Molière had shifted the spotlight of writing from duty and heroism to frothier works in which the pill of truth is sugared with wit and sensitivity, and presented in the most charming possible manner. Thus Mignard, the master of the Gobelins, saw in his new post simply another instrument placed at his disposal in the service of painting. His programme was therefore restricted to the reproduction in wool of six of his decorations for the Gallery of the Château de Saint-Cloud, painted at the request of Philip of Orleans, the driving force behind the whole movement.

Mignard was not long in charge of the Gobelins because in 1694 the workshops, which had been marking time since the exhaustion of the Royal Treasury, had to close down. However, these four years sufficed to effect a radical change in the entire conception of tapestry, its basic aims and its use as a means of expression. Its role from then on was to relate fables and to be merely decorative and ornamental. Devoid of spirituality, tapestry was content to entertain and to amuse. It must be admitted however that it achieved these aims in the most pleasant manner.

It was inevitable that this new conception of tapestry should entail changes in weaving and dyeing techniques. The weaver was required to make an exact copy of a painted model, imitating its every shift of tone, its movement, its brightness, its delicacy. To do this he was forced to abandon the traditional method of sharp chromatic contrasts, the use of frank and durable colours, composition in broad and well-defined planes, and even colour hatching to produce intermediate shades, which were now replaced by a system of pigmentary mixtures. He was forced also to widen his range of colours and deliberately infringe Colbert's statutes of 1671. These had been based on the old dyers' regulations and those of the guilds, and divided colours into two groups: "fast" or strong and durable dyes, and "unstable" or transient ones. The 18th century saw the triumph of "unstable" dyes. The "fast" dyeing agents, such as weld for yellow, madder for red, woad and pastel for blue and cochineal for carmine, were now joined by a whole gamut of new dyes, authorized by new regulations drawn up in 1737 by a chemist named Dufay. Indigo and logwood, soot black and walnut stain, yellow-wood, turmeric, orchil, annatto, safflower, all were accepted. Fragile "turchino" blue was imported from Venice; Saxe blues appeared in 1740, and Prussian blues, prepared with ferrocyanide, in 1747; both were invented by another chemist, Barth. To obtain even greater variety of colour and graduations of tone, mordant agents such as alum, tin, copper, iron, zinc, bismuth and chrome were used. In fact, as far back as 1665, the head of the Gobelins dye-works, Jacques van Kerkhove, had brought from Holland the secret of "tin scarlet". Grey, because of its infinite variety, was now at the very base of the weaver's palette, but was to be the principal cause of the deterioration of tapestries dating from this period. Colours, as it has been seen, proliferated. In the Middle Ages, some forty different colours had been sufficient; in the Angers *Apocalypse* there are only twenty-four. Le Brun had helped popularize three new colours—black, white and dark brown—though these were not unknown before his time. For the *Legate's Audience*, woven by Jean Lefèvre in 1680 after Le Brun, 79 tones were used, without counting silk, silver and gold threads. *The Bloodhound*, one of the *Louis XV's Hunts* set (see page 97) woven from a picture by Oudry in 1740, required 364. In 1780, 587 tones were used in *The Two Bulls* from the *New Indies* sequence, a vast quantity compared with only 75 in 1687 for *The King borne Aloft* from Albert Eckhout's *Old Indies* set. And in 1852, 672 different colours were required for the figures in a replica of the *Story of Psyche* from Raphaël.

The increase in the number of colours was really a neglect of traditional discipline because these new dyes were less durable than the tried and trusted fast colours. The chief culprits for this change were Mignard, Jean-Baptiste Oudry and, to a lesser degree, François Boucher who succeeded Oudry at Beauvais and the Gobelins.

Oudry, an animal painter, replaced Jacques Duplessis as draughtsman to the Beauvais plant and director of the drawing school, on July 22, 1726. In 1734 he became Nicolas Besnier's co-director of the plant. Reigning over his "kingdom", to use Voltaire's term, Oudry regarded the weavers as his subjects and demanded an exact transcription of his paintings. Because of his speciality, his choice of subject fell naturally on hunting scenes—*New Hunts*; peasant life—*Rural Pleasures* (1730); and realistic themes—*Fine Ver-*

dures (1736). Oudry excelled in every kind of animal subject, and he portrayed pheasants, ducks, bitterns, bustards and dogs with equal ease and freedom. His inspiration was not, however, limited to the animal world and thus he also exploited the vast resources offered by literature, both ancient and modern, from the *Metamorphoses* and *La Fontaine's Fables* to the *Story of Don Quixote* illustrated by Charles Natoire. This tapestry, although it did not reach the standard of perfection set at the Gobelins by Charles-Antoine Coypel, is nevertheless admirable. Boucher, who had been called in by Oudry, gave a remarkable display of virtuosity with cartoons for several sequences: *Italian Festivals* (1736), the *Story of Psyche* (1741), the *Chinese Hangings* (1742) following the then current trend in exotic subjects introduced by way of the new trade by the India Company, and the *Noble Pastoral*. With their cleverly constructed décors, their ruined temples and lovers' fountains, their rocks, clouds, Italian pines, and general bric-a-brac of arabesques and draperies; with lovely curved figures complacently displayed to arouse admiration, these tapestries adapted themselves more successfully to the norms of tapestry-making than the landscapes of Oudry.

Beauvais was content to produce its celebrated tapestry chair-seats and pictures designed to fit into the panelling of softly-lit drawing-rooms, and this suited its rich bourgeois customers perfectly. But the Gobelins refused to submit to the wishes of Oudry, who in 1733 was appointed superintendent of work there. The conflict lasted for thirty years, despite the efforts of Le Normand de Tournehem, Superintendent of Buildings, to resolve it. "It cannot be denied," argued the weavers, "that it is the master (i.e. the director of the workshop) who should be responsible for his own works. No-one is better equipped than he to decide on the best way to bring them to perfection; and should it be that he is in need of advice, he can easily obtain that of history's most skilful painters." The weavers were in fact saying that it was for them, and them alone, to decide on the best way of transposing their models into tapestries. This was an essential prerogative of their craft and they had no intention of surrendering it to the superintendent. In token of protest, the workshop directors stayed away from the Gobelins on Oudry's visiting days. According to an old text, they even went so far as to dismiss, for alleged administrative reasons, "all our most skilled weavers." The revolt was only quelled by the death in 1755 of Oudry and the accession of Boucher as superintendent.

Throughout the century, Beauvais and the Gobelins poured forth the kind of tapestry most calculated to please the elegant, sensitive and refined society of the day, tapestries which were in complete harmony with the prevailing concept of life and the feminine taste which impregnated its setting. The new style, inspired by the creations of Berain at Beauvais, spread to the Gobelins (reopened in 1699) where its influence can be seen in *The Gods* door-pieces and the *Grotesque Months in Bands* (1709) (see page 95), both the work of Claude Audran III. Most characteristic, yet with greater originality, is the *Story of Don Quixote*. Between 1714 and 1794 this series was put on the looms nine times, with variations in the colours and in the richly imaginative "surrounds" (borders) dreamed up by Blain de Fontenay, Claude Audran III and Louis Tessier. The subject itself was inserted as if it were a painting, in a setting of flowers, trophies, putti, animals, architectural motifs and scrolls, the whole laid out with an exquisite feeling for balance and charm, on backgrounds of imitated fabric, and finished with a painted wooden frame. Similar "surrounds", equally beautifully designed, can be found in the *Scenes from Opera, Tragedy and Comedy*, and in the *Gods' Sequence* from François Boucher (1758). With its dazzling illusory effects, its acrobatically-woven imitations and fascinating make-believe, this set incontestably represents "the high-water mark of 18th-century Gobelins output." Painting at the time was beginning to draw its aesthetic inspiration from opera. In a similar way the *Story of Esther* (1737-1740) (see pages 106-107) and the *Story of Jason* (1743-1746) are precisely reproductions of theatrical scenes. In the same spirit Charles Parrocel composed his *Entry of the Turkish Ambassador to Paris* through the Tuileries Gate, which looks like a sort of equestrian ballet on a background of minor characters and cardboard architectural scenery. Yet, side by side with this flood of artifice and invention, it would have been surprising if the Gobelins, under the direction of Oudry, had not produced works whose main theme was nature. *Louis XV's Hunts* (1734-1745) (see page 97) based on art-work by Oudry himself, is a good example, as is the "europeanization" by François Desportes of Eckhout's *Indies* (1735-1741), with its curious mixing of animal and vegetable life from the old world and the new.

If the 18th-century output of the three main French tapestry centers—the Gobelins, Beauvais and Aubusson—is compared, they are seen to have at least one thing in common. This is their choice of subject and steady adherence to the artistic fashion of the day, however it switched, from rustic to exotic, to relatively realistic, or to purely decorative.

Echoing the craze for Chinese and Turkish scenes (Amédée van Loo's *Turkish Costume* was to be woven at the Gobelins in 1772-1775), Jean-Baptiste Le Prince at Beauvais, just back from Muscovy, launched a Russian trend in 1769 with his *Russian Games* (see page 100) which, to tell the truth, despite its promising title, showed little more than a variety of bucolic gatherings.

Country Pastimes (see pages 98-99), a set of eight paintings by François Casanova, was woven at Beauvais in 1772, as well as *Gypsies* in 1777 composed of six paintings by the same artist. Jean-Baptiste Huet supplied the ten models for *Pastorals with Blue Draperies and Arabesques*. All the innovations of Paris and Beauvais were mirrored by Aubusson which produced its own copies of Oudry's *Rural Pleasures*, *Metamorphoses* and *Louis XV's Hunts*, and also freely-adapted versions of Boucher's *Chinese Scenes* including the *Return from Fishing, Tea, Gardening* and *Rice Milling*.

Several Chinese landscapes were taken from Jean Pillement's works: Aubusson borrowed right and left and made use of every available motif. At long last, too, Aubusson had been supplied with an official "painter to the king"—first Jean-Joseph Dumons in 1731 and then Nicolas Jacques Juillard. It was thanks to these two that the Marche workshops were kept supplied with cartoons by artists of every calibre. Also, a collective supervision of raw materials and dyestuffs seems to have been instituted around 1750. Some notably successful workshops were those directed by Grellet, Picon, Furgaud and Vergne.

By virtue of its similarity of inspiration, mention must be made of Spanish tapestry from the Santa Barbara plant, and especially of those pieces woven from Goya's cartoons. This establishment was created by Philip V, who in 1720 placed it in the charge of Jacques van der Goten from Antwerp. High-warp weaving was introduced there by Antoine Lenger of France. In 1746 the Santa Barbara and Santa Isabel factories merged and between them brought out sequences on *Telemachus, Don Quixote* and the *Conquest of Tunis*. *Rustic Celebrations* and *Village Scenes* were also woven either from works of David Teniers or in his style, as well as *Hawking* and scenes from everyday life. In the forty-five tapestries based on Goya's cartoons the life of the people is portrayed with a more than ordinary warmth of feeling and nimbleness of execution.

FRENCH TAPESTRY FROM
THE 19TH CENTURY ON

For tapestry, the modern era begins in 1785 with the weaving of Lavallée-Poussin's *Conquest of the Indies*, the last reference to the exotic style and the first act of submission to academic standards. Tapestry, more and more tightly bound to painting, followed step by step its treatment of chosen themes, which were now taken from the pages of French history. Among the various topics used were the *Story of Henry IV* from designs by François-André Vincent (1782-1787), *Scenes from the History of France, Continence of Bayard* and even one entitled: *The Fronde Partisans arresting President Molé*. During the Revolution, the work continued along the same historical lines—though it had to be brought up to date from time to time because events moved so rapidly, and the situation was constantly changing. The Government set up a competition which required participating artists to "draw their inspiration above all from great moments of the French Revolution and to recall all those acts of virtue which have honoured humanity." Tapestry's mission was to commemorate "those who have earned the gratitude of mankind through their example of liberty, patriotism, courage, benevolence, wisdom, kindly morality and in general of all the virtues." In 1805, the Empire in its turn instructed the Director of the Gobelins weaving plants to choose subjects "from the History of France and particularly from the Revolution. As His Majesty's reign will be one of the most glorious eras in French history," continued the official text, "I have no doubt but that you (the director of the plants) will use as models those paintings which retrace his victories or his beneficent deeds." No more than this suggestion was needed. The Gobelins promptly and dutifully reproduced *Napoleon visiting the Victims of the Plague at Jaffa* and *Bonaparte distributing Swords of Honour after the Battle of Marengo* by Gros, J.B. Regnault's *Death of General Desaix*, and David's *First Consul on Horseback*. A set of tapestries on the Emperor was begun in imitation of Le Brun's *Story of the King*, and some "door-pieces" were woven for the Tuileries.

The Empire, indeed, might have given the Gobelins the chance to restore the magnificence it had known under Louis XIV. It only needed a repudiation of the 18th century's technical mistakes—principally in the search for new dyestuffs. But unhappily the discovery of new mordant chemicals led increasingly to more subtle colours being placed at the weaver's disposal. After tartar and salts of ammoniac, the properties of alum, salts of tin, copper, iron, chrome and bismuth were employed to create colour variants. Charles-Axel Guillaumot, who was then director of the Gobelins, saw fit to use this abundance of chemical agents in order to bring the weaver's colour range even closer to the painter's, little knowing that in so doing he was building into his tapestries a far greater susceptibility to the ravages of time and light. The almost perfect matching of dyes to paints achieved by chemical progress was seen by Guillaumot as a great and undreamed-of step forward. It led him to declare triumphantly: "Today, the preparation by the dyer of the subtlest shades of colour, and the use by the weavers of silks and wools so treated, have reached a pitch of perfection which has to be seen to be believed. Today a Gobelins tapestry is no longer a tapestry; it is a replica in wool and silk of a painted picture." And Anicet-Charles-Gabriel Lemonnier, director of the Gobelins under the Restoration, in sending the king a *Story of Henry IV* for the new hangings of the Throne Room, together with a bust of Louis XVIII, expressed the hope that His Majesty might thus "appreciate the standard reached by his weaving plant in the art of imitation of every kind."

Around this time Michel-Eugène Chevreul, the colour physicist who direct-ed the Gobelins dyestuffs laboratory from 1824 to 1889, composed a palette of 14,400 tones, based on his theory of the chromatic circle. So equipped, Gobelins weavers were able, throughout the 19th century and into the first forty years of the 20th, to produce copies of every kind of painting, old and contemporary alike, by Horace Vernet, Ingres and Paul Baudry, or by Raphaël, Philippe de Champaigne, Le Brun, Mignard, Boucher, and Rubens, including the vast *Life of Marie de' Medici* whose original paintings take up one whole room in the Louvre. A set known as the "Grand Décor," in the Tuileries' Louis XIV Salon, seems to have had quite a grandiose effect, and a series of portraits representing the builders of the Louvre was woven for the Galerie d'Apollon.

A few more clear-sighted persons, however, were concerned over the fate which had befallen tapestry-making. Chevreul himself, startled by the way

86

in which his discoveries were being applied, sounded a firm warning: "Tapestry should not waste its time by competing with painting and trying to reproduce effects and details for which it is not intended. The ribbed and fibrous aspect of its colours is bound to resist such efforts." Another very good reason for having fewer colours was to use only those which would not fade. From 1859 on, these dangers came to the notice of official committees which demanded a return to the old, simple technique. In 1919 the director of the regional Decorative Arts School, Marius Martin, suggested that the weaver's colour range should be reduced to simple and, above all, durable tones.

However, in 1911 the Gobelins decided to abandon the use of natural colours (which had become more and more ephemeral through the unrestricted use of "unstable" dyes) and to adopt colours based on anthracene which are much brighter. Thanks to these, Gustave Geffroy, the then Gobelins Director, was able to re-create the finest details and shades of Impressionist paintings. Perfect copies were made of Claude Monet's famous *Nymphéas* (Water-Lilies), and of Chéret's and Bracquemond's decorations, of Odilon Redon's chairs. Alas! all that remain of these bright and subtly-blended colours today are dull greys and wine-tints.

Geffroy's idea had been to interest the most advanced painters of his time in tapestry with a view to obtaining models from them. His idea was followed up by Jean Ajalbert, director of the Beauvais factory, who enlisted the collaboration of Louis Anquetin, Jean Veber, Emile Gaudissard, Leonetto Cappiello, Paul Vera and Raoul Dufy. Then, from 1919 to 1938 Marie Cuttoli supplied the Aubusson workshop with paintings by Rouault, Braque, Picasso, Miro, Matisse, Léger, Le Corbusier (see pages 144-145). But the art of tapestry-making had not yet broken out of the period of imitation, and the painters themselves, when asked to prepare special cartoons for weaving, followed in Mignard's footsteps with a finished painting. Happily, today a new movement to correct many of the earlier errors in technique has been born. It will be assisted by progress in the chemistry of synthetics which has already solved almost all the problems involved in making available the widest possible range of colours and at the same time ensuring that the colours, once fixed, will not fade.

ADAM AND EVE DRIVEN FROM THE GARDEN OF EDEN   21 FT. × 15 FT. 3 IN. – BRUSSELS, 16TH CENTURY   Accademia, Florence

This is a notable example of the many tapestries on all sorts of biblical subjects which the Brussels workshops wove throughout the 16th century. Among the Flemish master-weavers' greatest and most noble clients were members of the Austrian imperial house of Hapsburg— whose collection of tapestries is now displayed in the Kunsthistorisches Museum, Vienna. Another client, King Sigismond-August of Poland, also had a magnificent collection of religious scenes (see pages 104-105) which still hangs on the walls of Wawel Castle in Cracow, Poland.

STORY OF JOSEPH: JOSEPH REUNITED WITH HIS FATHER, BY A. BRONZINO
14 FT. 5½ IN. × 18 FT. 2½ IN.   FLORENCE, 16TH CENTURY

Palazzo Vecchio, Florence

FRVMENTA TERRÆ REDDERE/
STABVLIS/ APIBVS/ ET VINEIS
CAVERE/ POMISQVE/ INSERI
OCTOBER ARBOREM ET MONET

THE TRIVULZIO MONTHS: THE MONTH OF OCTOBER, BY IL BRAMANTINO – 19 FT. 6¼ IN. × 17 FT. 5½ IN. Castello Sforzesco, Milan
VIGEVANO, 1503-1509

October is the month of harvest, of heaped-up fruits and vegetables ready to be sold or stored
away for the winter months. It is an old theme brought up to date and implanted in a setting
which lets the painter display his skill in perspective, so dear to Renaissance artists. The twelve
Months were woven for Marquis Gian Giacomo Trivulzio and remained in his family until 1935.

STORY OF THE KING: THE CROWNING OF LOUIS XIV, BY LE BRUN — 18 FT. 10½ IN. × 12 FT. 7½ IN.   GOBELINS, 1665-1680   Les Gobelins, Paris

This tapestry, entitled *The Crowning of Louis XIV*, represents the coronation in Rheims Cathedral on June 17, 1654. On the right is Cardinal Mazarin and in a gallery behind him, Anne of Austria, Louis XIV's mother. The tapestry belongs to a set called *The Story of the King*, comprising fourteen subjects by Le Brun and six more by other painters. This set, which was intended to impress the neighbour-states with the prestige of France's king, was woven eighty-three times in all, and distributed all over Europe. The last weaving was between 1736 and 1741, when the series was reduced in size to only six tapestries. Today, only fifty-five sets remain.

94

THE TWELVE "GROTESQUE" MONTHS: APRIL TO SEPTEMBER, BY CLAUDE AUDRAN
16 FT. 5 IN. × 12 FT. 5 ½ IN. – FRANCE, 1709

The Twelve "Grotesque" Months were designed by Claude Audran and his pupil Antoine Watteau. So called because of their "grotesque" or "grotto-esque" motifs of highly stylized natural elements (above), they are sophisticated mixture of animals, birds, flowers and signs of the zodiac, surrounding ornate porches with Venus, Apollo, Mercury, Jupiter, Ceres and Vulcan symbolizing the months of April to September. January, February and March still exist too but the three remaining *Months* mysteriously disappeared around 1830.

95

THE ELEMENTS: WATER, BY LE BRUN 11 FT. 5¾ IN. × 20 FT. 10 IN.   Les Gobelins, Paris
GOBELINS, SECOND HALF OF THE 17TH CENTURY

LOUIS XV'S HUNTS: THE PACK, BY J.-B. OUDRY — 14 FT. 1¼ IN. × 25 FT. 11 IN. GOBELINS, 1743   Uffizi Gallery, Florence

COUNTRY PASTIMES: THE DRINKING TROUGH, BY FRANÇOIS CASANOVA – 19 FT. 6¼ IN. × 12 FT. 4¾ IN. BEAUVAIS, 1772   Mobilier National, Paris

The Drinking Trough (above), one of the eight-piece *Country Pastimes* by François Casanova, was produced between 1772 and 1779, in the Beauvais Manufactory. After 1760, Beauvais tapestries became increasingly naturalistic and picturesque ... Charming bucolic gatherings were particularly popular as themes for tapestries "made entirely to please the eye of the indoor beholder." Such new fashions, typified by the Trianon village and the simplistic romanticism of Rousseau, are especially noticeable in Casanova's tapestries, and the choice of subject indicates a desire to break away from the courtly frills and furbelows inherited from François Boucher.

THE BIRD CATCHERS, BY LE PRINCE — 11 FT. 9¾ IN. × 12 FT. 1 IN. — BEAUVAIS, 1769-1793

Musée des Tapisseries,
Aix-en-Provence

In doing his Russian log-hut, Jean-Baptiste Le Prince endeavoured to follow the current trend towards depicting foreign and/or exotic subjects. But the rest of the scene, with beribboned peasant women and their admirers, smacks of a more refined—almost decadent—style. The *Russian Sports* sequence, to which the *Bird Catchers* belongs, is far more French than Russian.

CATALOG
OF CLASSICAL TAPESTRIES

During the 16th century, princes and noblemen abandoned their feudal castles in favour of more comfortable and luxurious residences, and secular tapestries were then used as status symbols to show off the magnificence of their owners. They served to decorate state rooms, galleries and drawing rooms in the various royal establishments, and were sometimes sent abroad as gifts (or on loan) in order to impress other crowned heads and courts with the grandeur of the donor. In this way, Louis XIV sent all over Europe, with the maximum of publicity and ostentation, tapestries which trumpeted the greatness of his reign and his personal glory. From the 16th to the 20th century, tapestries on religious topics—and particularly those inspired by the Bible—increasingly lost the sense of their sacred mission and their role of edification, and followed in the worldly and secular footsteps of painting. This two-fold evolution is illustrated by the hangings reproduced in the following pages. These hangings come from varying workshops—Brussels, the Gobelins or Beauvais—but all have belonged, or still belong, to celebrated collectors; in the past, to the Kings of France and Poland; and nowadays to the Pope and to the King of Sweden. So closely linked to the lives of the great in bygone days, these tapestries are for us mirrors of forgotten splendours and mute witnesses of historic moments.

17 ft. 5 in. × 11 ft. 5 ¾ in.

17 ft. 3 ½ in. × 10 ft. 6 ¾ in.

Practically nothing is known of the origin of these four magnificent "Indian" tapestries, which are now the property of the Abel de Lacerda Foundation in Caramulo Museum, Portugal, except that they were woven at Tournai in the early 16th century. In these works the familiar allegorical motifs of the Middle Ages are replaced by exotic and highly imaginative designs inspired by contemporary Portuguese conquests in the East Indies (as India was then called). Unicorns were supplanted by camels and hunts gave way to processions loaded with bizarre wonders like tropical birds more fantastic than anything ever dreamed of by a feudal lord. All four tapestries seem to give off the breezes of distant oceans and the spirit of *conquistadores* bent on adventure and the conquest of foreign lands. The archives of Tournai mention several tapestry sets "in the fashion of Portugal and the Indies" (1504), "of wild beasts and peoples after the manner of Calcutta" (1520) and the "travels of Caluce" (1513).

16 ft. o¾ in. × 11 ft. 5 in.

28 ft. o½ in. × 11 ft. 11 in.

THE STORY OF NOAH
Wawel Museum, Cracow, Poland

From the chronological point of view, this sequence devoted to the *Story of Noah* comes after the *Paradise* set (6 tapestries) and before the *Tower of Babel* set (4 tapestries); all are produced in the same style. In the upper borders can be found texts from Chapter VII of the Book of Genesis which is illustrated by the tapestries. Around the middle of the 16th century, this set was bought by King Sigismond-August of Poland to decorate the royal Castle of Wawel, at Cracow. (A panegyric written on the tapestries in 1553 is the earliest reference attesting to their presence.) They were woven of wool, silk and gold thread in the Brussels workshops, and the cartoons were painted by Michel Coxien. Altogether, the museum of Wawel owns eleven sets (136 tapestries) which were purchased by Sigismond-August. The most sumptuous order given to the Brussels weavers was for a sequence of *Verdure with Animals* comprising different-sized pieces calculated to fit the varying shapes and dimensions of the rooms of Wawel Castle; there are forty-eight tapestries in the set. Now one of the greatest tapestry museums in the world, the Castle of Wawel contains forty other tapestries from various places. About thirty more are housed nearby in Wawel Cathedral.

God speaks to Noah   21 ft. 10½ in. × 15 ft. 5 in.

The Building of the Ark   25 ft. 11¾ in. × 15 ft. 4¾ in.

The Animals enter the Ark   25 ft. 11 in. × 15 ft. 3 ¼ in.

The Deluge   27 ft. 5 ¼ in. × 15 ft. 7 ¼ in.

The Animals leave the Ark   29 ft. × 15 ft. 3 in.

Noah's Sacrifice   23 ft. 1 ½ in. × 15 ft. 2 ¾ in.

God blesses Noah   19 ft. 10 ½ in. × 15 ft.

The Drunkenness of Noah   16 ft. 8 ¾ in. × 15 ft. 5 in.

THE STORY OF ESTHER   Uffizi Gallery, Florence

Esther's Banquet   17 ft. 4 in. × 14 ft. 0¼ in.

Esther faints   17 ft. 5¾ in. × 13 ft. 9½ in.

Esther's Coronation   17 ft. 8½ in. × 14 ft. 4 in.   Esther's Toilet   13 ft. 5 in. × 14 ft. 0½ in.

Mordecai's Disdain   17 ft. 3¾ in. × 14 ft. 2 in.

The Condemnation of Aman   16 ft. × 14 ft. 1 in.

These tapestries represent the *Story of Esther*, the beautiful Jewess who protected her people by marrying Ahasuerus. Woven at Tournai during the 15th century, they are now divided between Minneapolis Museum (USA) and the Musée Lorrain, Nancy. Jean-François de Troy (1679-1752), the renowned Parisian painter responsible for the cartoons, picked up and modernized a topic which had been a favourite in Gothic times, and gave these tapestries all the magnificence and splendour usually associated with the Venetian masters.

Esther's banquet, for instance, puts us in mind of Veronese's rich "Wedding at Cana" in the Louvre—or perhaps of some gorgeous operatic setting. Up until 1772, seven more sets on this same theme were woven, and in all one hundred tapestries belonging to the suite came off the Gobelins looms. Examples of these can still be seen in France at the Mobilier National, the Gobelins, the Château of Fontainebleau and the Château of La Roche-Guyon; others are in the Uffizi Gallery, Florence, and Windsor Castle, England.

Mordecai's Triumph   24 ft. 7¾ in. × 14 ft. 0¼ in.

The Battle of Lund, First Day   16 ft. 9 in. × 13 ft. 2½ in.

The Battle of Lund, Second Day   17 ft. 2½ in. × 13 ft. 2½ in.

The *Conquests of the King of Sweden* series comprises four tapestries now in the royal palace at Stockholm. Other pieces were planned but some were left unfinished and the remainder were never started. The cartoons were made by Jean-Baptiste Martin from paintings by the patriotic-minded Swedish artist Johan Philippe Lemke (1631-1711), and the borders by Berain were apparently inspired by those invented by Le Brun in 1668 for the *Months* set. Berain, in fact, employs the same idea of using the border to create a kind of balcony overlooking the entire composition. Berain's sketches were finished off by Louis-Guy de Vernansal. The *Battle of Landskrona* was woven at Beauvais in 1699. *Lund* was finished by a Gobelins weaver, Dominique de Lacroix, who signed it, while the two other pieces were woven in Béhagle's Parisian workshop. Even the tapestries shown here might never have been completed because the Beauvais factory was almost bankrupt whilst they were being woven.

THE KING OF SWEDEN
Royal Palace, Stockholm

The Battle of Malmö   16 ft. 8 ¾ in. × 13 ft. 5 ½ in.

These four tapestries, *The Conquests of the King of Sweden*, recall an heroic chapter in Sweden's history. Charles XI, born in 1655, became king in 1660. The early years of his reign were troubled by war and in 1675 the Swedish troops were defeated by the Grand Elector of Brandenburg. The young king, who until then had remained indifferent to the situation, pulled himself together, appointed new ministers, and beat the Danish army at the battles of Halmstad (April 1676), Lund (November 1676) and Landskrona (July 1677). He was also the victor at Malmö. An ally of the King of France, he naturally turned to this country's craftsmen to immortalize the glorious events of his reign. Perhaps the Swedish ambassador was influenced by the 14-piece *Story of the King*, woven from 1665 to 1680, and decided to have Charles' commemorative tapestries produced in the same style. Charles XI, a great king who did not lose the common touch, turned Sweden into the principal Baltic power.

The Battle of Landskrona   17 ft. 6 in. × 13 ft. 2 ½ in.

TAPESTRY BY MAILLOL

This small tapestry was woven in the early part of this century from designs by the sculptor Aristide Maillol. Its goddesses are graceful but it lacks the dimensions required to make it a great piece of mural decoration.

RINALDO
IN THE GARDENS OF ARMIDA

Later, from November 1930 to September 1932, the Gobelins produced this *Rinaldo in the Gardens of Armida* from cartoons by a Symbolist painter, Maurice Denis. It was inspired by the *Jerusalem Delivered* written by 16th-century Italian poet Torquato Tasso. But despite the quality of the painter and the weaver's efforts, the piece remains nothing more than a stylistic exercise.

Gobelins, Paris   2 ft. 11 ½ in. × 2 ft. 11 ½ in.

Mobilier National, Paris   11 ft. 8 in. × 9 ft. 0 ¼ in.

SELECTION
OF CLASSICAL TAPESTRIES

AUSTRIA

VIENNA: Kunsthistorisches Museum.

1. *Tapestries of the 16th century*

Scenes from the Life of Moses, 9 pieces, from Raphael, Holland.

The Story of Abraham, 10 pieces, from B. van Orley, Brussels.

Scenes from the Life of Saint Paul, 4 pieces by P. Coecke van Aelst, Holland.

Scenes from the Book of Tobias, 8 pieces, from B. van Orley, Brussels.

Scenes of the Romulus and Remus Legend, 8 pieces, Holland.

The Twelve Months, 12 pieces, Brussels.

The Seven Virtues, 8 pieces, from P. Coecke van Aelst, Brussels.

Pomona and Vertumnus, from Ovid's Metamorphoses, 9 pieces, Brussels.

The Life and Great Deeds of João de Castro, Viceroy of the Portuguese Indies, 10 pieces, Brussels.

The Life of Christ, 3 pieces, Holland.

The Sufferings of Christ, 6 pieces, Holland.

The Seven Deadly Sins, 7 pieces, from P. Coecke van Aelst, Brussels.

The Lucas Months, 9 pieces, Bruges.

Biblical Scenes from Genesis, Joshua and Judges, 8 pieces, Brussels.

Scenes of the Life of David, 7 pieces, Audenarde.

Scenes from the Life of Alexander the Great, 8 pieces.

Biblical Scenes from Exodus and the First Book of Kings, 5 pieces.

Biblical Scenes from the First Book of Kings, 10 pieces.

Six Ages of the Earth, 6 pieces, Brussels.

David and Bathshebah, 10 pieces.

The Triumphs of Petrarch, 6 pieces, Tours (?).

Scenes of the Story of the Apostles, 9 pieces from Raphael, Brussels.

2. *Tapestries of the 17th century*

Scenes of the Life of Alexander the Great, 11 pieces, from Ch. Le Brun, Gobelins, Paris.

The Great Deeds of Publius Cornelius Scipio Africanus, 5 pieces, from Willem van Leefdael, by Everaert Leyniers and Heinrich Reydams, Brussels.

Scenes from the Life of Constantine the Great, 6 pieces, from Rubens, Gobelins, Paris.

Hunting Scenes, 7 pieces, from Rubens, Brussels.

The Riding Lesson of Louis XIII, 8 pieces, from Jordaens, by Everaert Leyniers and H. Reydams, Brussels.

Scenes from the Life of Moses, 6 pieces and 7 pieces.

Scenes from the Life of Jacob, 8 pieces, from B. van Orley, Brussels.

The Twelve Months, 6 pieces, from Jan van den Hoecke, Brussels.

Scenes from the Life of Abraham, 10 pieces, Brussels.

The Fruits of War, 16 pieces, from Giulio Romano, Brussels.

Scenes from the Life of Consul Decius Mus, 5 pieces, from Rubens, Brussels.

Scenes from the Life of Alexander the Great, 9 pieces, Brussels.

Scenes from the Life of Roman Emperor Augustus, 8 pieces.
The myth of Diana, 5 pieces.
The myth of Diana, 8 pieces, by Toussaint Dubreuil, Paris.
Scenes of the Life of Samson, 8 pieces.
The Representation of the 7 Planets and Time, 7 pieces, Brussels.
Allegorical scenes of the Powers that reign on the Earth, 8 pieces, from Ludwig van Schoor, Brussels and 8 other pieces, Brussels.
Zenobia, Queen of Palmyra, and Aurelian, 7 pieces, Brussels.
Scenes from Greek-Roman history, 8 pieces.
Scenes from the Legend of Aeneas and Dido, 8 pieces from Giovanni Francisco, Netherlands.
Scenes of Rural Life, 8 pieces from Jordaens, Brussels.
Antony and Cleopatra, 8 pieces, School of Rubens, Brussels.
The Old and the New Testament, 3 pieces, from Rubens, Brussels.

3. *Tapestries of the 18th century*

Mythological scenes, 8 pieces from Coypel, Gobelins, Paris.
Heroic Deeds of Charles V, Duke of Lorraine, 5 pieces, Nancy.
Victories of Charles V of Lorraine, 23 pieces, from Ch. Herbel, La Malgrange.
The Emperor Charles V at Tunis, 10 pieces, from Jan Vermayen, Brussels.
Tapestries from the frescoes of Raphael in the Vatican, 4 pieces, Gobelins, Paris.
Tapestries of Calcutta, 8 pieces, from Desportes, Gobelins, Paris.
Pastoral scenes, 6 pieces, Brussels.
The Arms of Duke Leopold of Lorraine and of E. Charlotte of Orleans, 13 pieces, La Malgrange.
Grotesques with the Arms of Lorraine and Orléans, 2 pieces.
Fénelon's Adventures of Telemachus, 5 pieces, from a French (?) painter.
Scenes of peasant life, 6 pieces, from D. Teniers, Brussels.
Scenes of Cervantes' Life of Don Quixote, 6 pieces, from Ch. Ant. Coypel, Netherlands.
Scenes of rural life, 13 pieces, Brussels.
Scenes of military life, 4 pieces, from Hyacinthe de la Peigne, Brussels.
Scenes from Roman history, 9 pieces, Brussels.
Allegory of the Powers that Rule the World, 8 pieces, from Ludwig van Schoor, Brussels.
Apollo, Minerva and the Muses, 8 pieces, Brussels.
The Myth of Perseus and Andromeda, 6 pieces, Brussels.
Mythological scenes, 8 pieces, from Ludwig van Schoor, Brussels.
The Four Seasons, 2 pieces, from Le Brun, Gobelins, Paris.
The Four Elements, 1 piece, from Le Brun, Gobelins, Paris.
The Twelve Months of the Year, 10 pieces, La Malgrange.

FRANCE

AIX-EN-PROVENCE: Musée des Tapisseries.
Tapestry of Don Quixote, from Natoire, Beauvais, 18th century.
Wall-hanging of the Russian Sports, from Le Prince, Beauvais, 18th century.

ANET (Eure-et-Loire): Château.
The Story of Diana, 4 pieces, Fontainebleau, 16th century.

CHANTILLY: Château.
Wall-hanging of the Arms of the Count of Toulouse, 10 pieces, Gobelins, Paris, 17th century.

COMPIÈGNE: Château.
The Muses, 10 pieces, from Le Brun, Gobelins, 17th century.
The Story of Esther, 17 pieces, from de Troy, Gobelins, 18th century.

FONTAINEBLEAU: Château.
The Story of Artemis, 1 piece from Lerambert, Gobelins I, 17th century.
The Seasons, 3 pieces, from Le Brun, Gobelins, 17th century.
The Story of the King, 3 pieces, Gobelins, 17th century.
The Story of Alexander, 2 pieces from Le Brun, Gobelins, 17th century.
The Triumphs of the Gods, from J. Romain and N. Coypel, Gobelins, 17th century.
Maximilian's Hunts, 4 pieces from Van Orley, Gobelins, 17th century.
Louis XV's Hunts, 1 piece, from J.B. Oudry, Gobelins, 18th century.
The Story of Esther, 6 pieces, from de Troy, Gobelins, 18th century.

LYON: Musée des Tissus.
La Fontaine's Fables, 5 pieces, Beauvais, 18th century.

PARIS: Louvre.
Maximilian's Hunts, or de Guise's Hunts, 12 pieces from van Orley, Brussels, 16th century.
The Story of Artemis, 1 piece, from Lerambert, Gobelins I, 17th century.
The Old Testament, 1 piece, from Simon Vouët, Louvre, 17th century.
The Story of Henry III, 1 piece, Château de Cadillac, 17th century.
The *portière* of Mars, 2 pieces, from Charles Le Brun, Gobelins, 17th century.
The Arabesque Months, 5 pieces, from the Grotesques of de Guise, Gobelins, 17th century.
The Lucas Months, 2 pieces, Gobelins, 17th century.
The Story of Scipio, 2 pieces, from J. Romain, Gobelins, 17th century.
The Chambers of the Vatican, 1 piece, from Raphaël, Gobelins, 17th century.

The Story of Moses, 5 pieces, from Poussin, Gobelins, 17th century.

Subjects from the Fables, 6 pieces, from J. Romain and N. Coypel, Gobelins, 17th century.

Triumphs of the Gods, 1 piece, from J. Romain and N. Coypel, Gobelins, 17th century.

Loves of the Gods, 4 pieces, from Boucher, van Loo, Pierre de Vieu and Lagrenée, Gobelins, 18th century.

PARIS: Musée des Arts Décoratifs.

The Story of Tancred and Clorinda, 4 pieces, Gobelins, 17th century.

The Battle of Granique, 1 piece, by Le Brun, Aubusson, 17th century.

The market, seaport, 1 piece, from Teniers, Brussels, 17th century.

The Offering to the God Pan, Beauvais, 18th century.

PARIS: Musée des Gobelins.

Arabesques, 1 piece, Fontainebleau, 16th century.

The Acts of the Apostles, 4 pieces, from Raphaël, Paris (Louvre), 17th century.

The Story of Saint Crispin, Paris (Trinité), 17th century.

The Story of Gombaut and Macé, from L. Guyot, Tours and Aubusson, 17th century.

The Story of Constantine, 3 pieces, from Le Brun, Gobelins, 17th century.

Maximilian's Hunts, 3 pieces, from van Orley, Gobelins, 17th century.

Louis XV's Hunts, from J. B. Oudry, Gobelins, 18th century.

The Story of Esther, from de Troy, Gobelins, 18th century.

New *portière* of Diana, from Perrot and Cazes, Gobelins, 18th century.

The Story of the King, 2 pieces, from Le Brun, Gobelins, 17th century.

PARIS: Mobilier National.

The Story of Diana, 8 pieces, from T. Dubreuil, Gobelins I, 17th century.

The Story of Artemis, 6 and 8 pieces, from Lerambert, Gobelins I, 17th century.

The Story of Psyche, 7 pieces, from Coxcie, Gobelins I, 17th century.

The Story of Constantine, 2 and 5 pieces, from Rubens, Gobelins I, 17th century.

The Acts of the Apostles, 2 × 10 pieces, from Raphaël, Mortlake, 17th century.

The Story of Coriolanus, 17 pieces from Lerambert, Gobelins I, 17th century.

The *portière* of Mars, 12 pieces, from Le Brun, Gobelins, 17th century.

The *portière* of the Triumphal Chariot, from Le Brun, Gobelins, 17th century.

The Elements, 12 pieces, from Le Brun, Gobelins, 17th century.

The Seasons, 3 pieces, from Le Brun, Gobelins, 17th century.

Story of the King, 3 pieces, from Le Brun, Gobelins, 17th century.

The Story of Alexander, 31 pieces, from Le Brun, Gobelins, 17th century.

Royal Houses, 15 pieces, from Le Brun, Gobelins, 17th century.

Window-pieces of the Thermal Baths, 14 pieces, from Le Brun, Gobelins, 17th century.

The Arabesque Months, 6 pieces, from the Grotesques of de Guise, Gobelins, 17th century.

The Lucas Months, 8 pieces, Gobelins, 17th century.

The Gallery of St-Cloud, 12 pieces, from Mignoud, Gobelins, 17th century.

The Chambers of the Vatican, 39 pieces, from Raphaël, Gobelins, 17th century.

The Story of Moses, 13 pieces, from Poussin, Gobelins, 17th century.

Subjects from the Fables, 8 pieces, from J. Romain and N. Coypel, Gobelins, 17th century.

Portières of the Gods, 14 pieces from Watteau and Audran, Gobelins, 18th century.

Don Quixote, 27 pieces, from Ch. Coypel, Gobelins, 18th century.

The New Indies, 4 pieces, from F. Desportes, Gobelins, 18th century.

The New Testament, 13 pieces, from Jouvenet and Restout, Gobelins, 18th century.

New *portière* with the Arms of France, 12 pieces, from Perrot, Gobelins, 18th century.

The Story of Jason, 8 pieces, from de Troy, Gobelins, 18th century.

The Story of Esther, 7 pieces, from de Troy, Gobelins, 18th century.

Country Pastimes, by François Casanova, Beauvais, 18th century.

PARIS: Petit Palais.

The Hunter's Rest, Aubusson, mid-18th century.

PAU: Musée des Beaux-Arts.

The Lucas Months, 10 pieces, Gobelins, 17th century.

The Arabesque Months, 6 pieces, Gobelins, 17th century.

Wall-hanging with the Arms of the Duke d'Antin, 9 pieces, Gobelins, 17th century.

Royal Houses, 15 pieces, from Le Brun, Gobelins, 17th century.

SAINT-LÔ: Musée.

The Story of Gombaut and Macé, 8 pieces, from Laurent Guyot, Tours and Aubusson, 17th century.

STRASBOURG: Cathédrale.

The Life of the Virgin, 14 pieces, from Ph. de Champaigne, Brussels, 17th century.

GREAT BRITAIN

LONDON: Buckingham Palace.

Loves of the Gods, 3 pieces, from Boucher, van Loo, Pierre de Vieu and Lagrenée, Gobelins, 17th century.

LONDON: Victoria and Albert Museum.

The Acts of the Apostles, 2 × 10 pieces, from Raphaël, Mortlake, 17th century.

WINDSOR: Castle.

The Story of Esther, 7 pieces, from de Troy, Gobelins, 18th century.

Portières of the Gods, 6 pieces, from Watteau and Audran, Gobelins, 17th century.

ITALY

FLORENCE: Galleria degli Uffizi.

The Story of Jacob, Florence, 16th century.
Wall-hanging of the Festivities for Henry and Catherine de' Medici, Brussels, 16th century.
Louis XV's Hunts, 9 pieces, from Oudry, Gobelins, 17th century.

FLORENCE: Palazzo Pitti.

The Elements, Gobelins, 17th century.
The Infant Gardeners, Gobelins, 17th century.

FLORENCE: Palazzo Vecchio.

The Story of Joseph, Florence, 16th century.
The Hunts of Poggio a Cajano, 3 pieces, 16th century.

MILAN: Castello Sforzesco.

The Trivulzio Months, 9 pieces, Milan, 16th century.

ROME, City of the Vatican: Vatican Picture-Gallery.

The Acts of the Apostles, from Raphaël, Brussels, 16th century.

POLAND

CRACOW: Wawel Museum.

Wall-hanging of Paradise, 6 pieces, from Michel Coxien, Brussels, 16th century.
The Story of Noah, 8 pieces, from Michel Coxien, Brussels, 16th century.
Wall-hanging of the Tower of Babel, 4 pieces, from Michel Coxien, Brussels, 16th century.
Verdure with animals against a landscape, 44 pieces, from Guillaume Tons (?), Brussels, 17th century.
Grotesque Suite, 13 pieces, from C. Bos, Brussels, 16th century.

CRACOW: Wawel Cathedral.

Wall-hanging of the Trojan War, 8 pieces, Flanders, 16th century.
The Story of Jacob, 8 pieces, Brussels, 16th century.

PORTUGAL

CARAMULO: Abel de Lacerda Museum.

Tapestries on Indian Themes, 4 pieces, Tournai, 16th century.

LISBON: National Museum of Art.

The Story of Marcus Aurelius, Antwerp, 16th century.
The Story of Mark Antony, Flanders, 17th century.
The Story of Alexander, Flanders, 18th century.
The Story of Achilles, Brussels, 18th century.

LISBON: Palacio Nacional da Ajuda.

The Story of Alexander, Gobelins, 17th century.
The Story of Alexander, Aubusson, 18th century.
Scenes of Life in Madrid, from Goya, Santa Barbara, 18th century.

SPAIN

MADRID: El Escorial.

The adventures of Telemachus, from Arnault, Beauvais, 17th century.
The Story of Decius Mus, from Rubens, Brussels, 17th century.
Goya's Tapestries, 46 pieces, Santa Barbara, 18th century.

SANTIAGO DE COMPOSTELA: Cathedral.

Scipio and Hannibal, Brussels, 16th century.
Wall-hanging of Achilles, said "Tesnières", Lille, 17th century.
Wall-hanging of Lovers, Flanders, 17th century.
Goya's Tapestries, 12 pieces, 18th century.

SWEDEN

STOCKHOLM: Royal Palace.

The Conquests of the King of Sweden, 4 pieces, from J. B. Martin and Lemke, Gobelins, 17th century.
The Story of Jason, 2 pieces, from de Troy, Gobelins, 17th century.

UNITED STATES

BALTIMORE: The Baltimore Museum of Art.

The Story of Aeneas, 2 pieces, Paris, 17th century.

BOSTON: The Isabella Stewart Gardner Museum.

Castles and Gardens, 4 pieces, Paris, 17th century.

HARTFORD (Connecticut): Wadsworth Atheneum.

The Story of Cupid and Psyche, from Raphaël, Gobelins, 17th century.

MINNEAPOLIS: Minneapolis Institute of Arts.

The Prodigal Child, Flanders, 16th century.

NEW YORK: The Metropolitan Museum of Art.

The Story of Diana, 2 pieces, Fontainebleau, 16th century.

SAN FRANCISCO: California Palace of the Legion of Honour.

The Story of Moses and Aaron, 6 pieces, Flanders, 16th century.
Life of Joan of Arc, 4 pieces, by J. P. Laurens, Gobelins, 18th century.
Portières of the Gods, 4 pieces, from Claude III Audran, Gobelins, 18th century.

CONTEMPORARY TAPESTRY

ADOLF HOFFMEISTER

Director of the History of Art, Prague

"Tapestry: a piece of tissue or handiwork used for decorating a bedroom or any other room of a house. This furnishing can be made of all kinds of material: brocatelle, Bruges satin, calamanco, caddis, etc. ..." This 18th-century definition of tapestry, printed in the Encyclopaedia of arts, crafts and sciences published by Diderot and d'Alembert, shows in part the state of decadence into which a once noble art had fallen. From the heroic and heraldic richness of Gothic days, from its status as a unique and precious work of art, tapestry had now sunk to a position ranking no higher than curtains, sets of chairs, china, or other items of household decoration. It remained in this depressed state for nearly two centuries and from these depths it is now at last re-emerging. The rebirth of tapestry in the 20th century is, therefore, little short of prodigious. In this age of plastics and television, electronics and automation, nuclear energy and mass indoctrination, it is comforting to find more and more people who are interested in tapestry, real tapestry in the old sense of the word—that creation of artists and craftsmen, that wealth of innumerable threads cunningly interlaced, packed down and welded to the warp with skilful knots, in which history and gallantry and religious faith, all, at one time or another, found themselves enmeshed.

We are today rediscovering the true worth and meaning of tapestry. Wool, the very flesh and blood of tapestry, not only provides warmth and covering for the bareness of the wall, but it also deadens noise and imparts its own special feeling of comfort and restfulness. Its chief mission, however, is to illuminate man's everyday life with remarkable beauty and a kind of textured poetry. Far from being space-consuming, tapestry, like painting, can actually increase our living area by opening on uplands of the imagination: Tapestry is a full counterpoint to the often grey monotony of daily existence. Opaque sunshine-flooded windows, gardens in which the eye can wander and please itself with sensual memories:

> "No, my Isabella, it is not just a kerchief;
> It is a great moonlit garden.
> Acacias I see and sinuous pathways,
> So strange that passers-by must stop and wonder."
>
> K. and J. Capek, "The Fatal Game of Love"

In every tapestry a viewer's first glance tends to follow and then take in the overall structure—horizontal lines, circular movements, and repetitive symmetry. A second glance probes further and discovers patterns full of subjects. Tapestry should not be expected to conform to orthodox rules, for here artistic licence is all-important; tapestry is a decorative two-dimensional art working with flat surfaces, little concerned with depth and perspective, a shadowless painting in which the interplay of pure colours and the pleasure they give the onlooker are the main precepts. This is one of the principal differences between modern and classical tapestry. Today, tapestry is no longer a *copy* of a finished *picture* by a master, such as a hunt in the forest of Compiègne (see page 97). Even the figurative compositions of present-day cartoon-painters are treated without recourse to tricks of perspective. This is true of tapestries by Marcel Gromaire, Jean Lurçat and Jean Picart Le Doux and of the non-figurative compositions of younger cartoon-painters.

But the crux of the matter is this; that every tapestry, whether it is figurative or otherwise, has a special role to fill on the architectural scale. Jean Lurçat, the painter, stresses its mural function: "Tapestry is an essentially mural object, going hand in hand with architecture", and Le Corbusier, the architect, explains its role in 20th-century living: "The destiny of modern tapestry is clear—it is the 'mural' of our times. We are 'nomads' living in communally-serviced apartment blocks and we change apartments as our family requirements change... We cannot have a mural painted on the walls of our apartment. However, a woollen wall of tapestry can at any time be taken down, carried away and put in place elsewhere. This is why I have called my tapestries 'muralnomads'."

And in apartments, it is the architecture itself, not the furniture, which is the determining factor. Modern tapestry at its best, like much of Gothic tapestry, is not intended to fill the little gap between the divan and the cupboard, but to follow the line of the whole wall, to fit up against the ceiling, the floor or the corner. Wedded to the wall, tapestry shares its functions of mitigating atmospheric conditions and deadening noise; at the same time it satisfies the need for intimacy.

The role of tapestry is better understood if we compare the walls of a 19th-century European apartment with those of a modern structure. The carved wooden panellings and gold-flecked stuccoes of the last century left only a small—and secondary—place for tapestry. Today, on the contrary, walls are stripped bare and, like the walls of the Middle Ages, they require a covering which corresponds to their size. It can, therefore, be said that the evolution of architecture has encouraged the growth of modern tapestry. But Lurçat and Le Corbusier, and with them the majority of modern cartoon-painters, think chiefly in terms of large wall surfaces—the bigger the better—in public or official buildings. As in the age of the *Unicorns* and the *Apocalypse*, tapestry retains its solemn and public character; as it was once part of the liturgy and inseparable from the pomp of kings, so today it naturally finds its place in presidential palaces, parliaments, embassies, concert halls, factory board-rooms ... and, once more, churches. In the Centre Aéronautique in Paris, for example, are two large tapestries by Mario Prassinos on the *Denizens of the Sky*, while the church of the Plateau d'Assy, in Haute-Savoie (France) is decorated with an *Apocalypse* by Jean Lurçat. Its ceremonial tradition had bestowed on mediaeval tapestry an emotive and monumental character; we of the 20th century are now witnessing a resurgence of

117

this character. Gone are the finicky and wishy-washy copies damned by the Encyclopaedia's faint praise. By what miracle did this return to the original source of tapestry come about? How, after centuries of affectation, did warmth and feeling once more revive? The Answer is due to a collection of personalities and circumstances which must be retraced one by one.

The first real effort at renovation came around 1920. And, perhaps inevitably, it came from a great historic name in tapestry-weaving—Aubusson. Marius Martin, the director of the town's School of Decorative Arts, had grasped the essential requirements for a revival of the craft and understood that the time was ripe for a change. He advocated a limitation of the range of colours, the use of colour hatching and a return to a decorative style. It was a perfectly realistic programme but it failed because painters—like Paul Deltombe—who were asked to supply cartoons indicated every detail, even down to the form of hatching to be used, thus depriving the weaver of all inventiveness and the tapestry of any savour. The weavers themselves, too-accomplished copyists, had long since forgotten the role of "flames," "tongues", hatching, and other technical means of obtaining subtleties of colour shading.

Hardly anybody in the trade had yet heard of Jean Lurçat who had been experimenting continuously since 1916. "In the absence of any likely commission for my cartoons," Lurçat explains it now, "I had no alternative but to bear the cost of executing them myself. This is an extremely serious decision to take at the age of twenty! Being unable to obtain a high- or low-warp loom or to pay a professional weaver, I was obliged to fall back on cross-stitch embroidery which does not require a highly trained specialist. My first cartoon was, in fact, a water-colour twelve inches by twenty; and my mother spent several months embroidering it with tiny stitches. The finished product was, on analysis, simply a copy and, like all copies, however faithful, its design and colours were only approximate. A large number of different shades were used. Had I been obliged to pay my needlewoman, my experiments would have stopped short there and then. I soon understood that I must readjust my sights and above all cut expenditure. Any work of art, whatever it may be and whatever may be thought of it, starts from a budget. Especially at the age of twenty! There was nothing for it but to reduce wool purchases—in other words to choose a narrower colour range—and to use a larger stitch. This I resolved to do and my second cartoon, measuring two square yards, was embroidered in the same time as the first. But, even more important, it had a decidedly more mural aspect: I was on the right track ... Sent home by a timely war wound a year later, I turned out two more panels, approximately four square yards and five square yards respectively, and requiring only about fifty colour shades ... Around 1919, wanting to launch forth into large-scale hangings, I tried to double the size of the stitch used in my second experiment. The attempt failed and taught me a sharp lesson. The too-broad handling of the subject had resulted in a slipshod effect. Such treatment was tolerated by foliage, water and sky, but the human face collapsed completely. Its design was primitive and askew, and it lacked solidity. The best intentions in the world do not excuse defective technique! The only thing to do was to start again from square one, 1916. Having made a long study of 15th-century textures, I realized that the craftsmen of that period had discovered the secret of balance as far as density of weave was concerned. I needed no second bidding!" Jean Lurçat continued his experiments, and by 1930 several hundred square yards of his work had been woven.

Similarly, hundreds of miles away from Aubusson, Marie Teinitzerova-Hoppeova, in her workshop at Jindrichuv Hradec, Czechoslovakia, was instinctively returning to a great soberness of colour and weaving in tapestries intended for the Czech pavilion at the 1925 Exhibition of Decorative Arts, Paris.

Several years later, in 1933, Marie Cuttoli launched a new venture in ordering cartoons from the principal artists of the time—Dufy, Derain, Léger, Braque, Picasso, Rouault, Lurçat and Miró. The first canvas—a Picasso 4 ft. 9½ in. × 3 ft. 8¾ in.—was copied in Delarbre's workshop at Aubusson. As far as finance went, if Marie Cuttoli did not actually buy the artist's painting or cartoon she repaid him with a woven copy of his work. At other times, however, she was able to sell the tapestry at a higher price than that paid for the model. Most of these artists, with the exception of Lurçat and Miró, knowing nothing of the rules of the craft, sent or lent oil paintings instead of cartoons. The result was both admirable and disappointing; admirable for the precision and fidelity of even the subtlest harmonies, disappointing because from a distance it was impossible to distinguish the painting from the woven replica, which amounted to the very negation of tapestry. The operation had led to a dead end ... but at least it was seen that another path must be sought. And Marie Cuttoli was far from having wasted her time. The ball had been set rolling and artists and weavers alike were beginning to think about tapestry and to ask questions.

A fresh stimulus was given by the meeting in 1933 of Jean Lurçat, the artist, and François Tabard, the master-weaver. Neither was a novice in the art of tapestry-making; Lurçat had by then been experimenting for nearly twenty years, and Tabard came from a family with a two-centuries-old tradition of weaving. Lurçat—and others after him—visited Aubusson. But his true revelation was awaiting him at Angers. "I can hardly describe the shock that I felt, in 1938, when I first saw the *Apocalypse* ... in that month of July heavy with menace and omen ... I returned from my visit more than ever convinced that the methods I had planned and attempted until then were the right ones, persuaded that painting's way out of its present troubles lay in close collaboration with architecture and architects ... The Angers *Apocalypse*, besides being a prophetic guide for the painter, constitutes, for all who can read its meaning, the cross-roads of all our terrors."

What did this prophetic guide advise? Chiefly a return to source, a search for virility and the adoption of a more solid weave. The pretty-pretty frivolities of such painters as Mignard and Fragonard must be replaced by broader and more substantial themes and feelings which are common to all mankind: respect for life, anguish in the face of death or war, man's adventure on the road to progress, in the cosmos, and so on.

In September 1939, the Ministry of National Education requested artists Dubreuil, Gromaire and Lurçat to settle at Aubusson in order to plan, create and if necessary supervise the execution of a series of large new tapestries. "We arrived one by one," recalls Lurçat, "with the air raid sirens of Paris still wailing in our ears. The town of Aubusson was bursting at the seams with refugees. We settled in as best we could, and soon got to know the weavers' homes, their workshops, their drinking places. Circumstances brought us into daily contact with our craftsmen and facilitated our team work with them. Together we tried out the different skeins of wool available: from Australia and from the various regions of France. Why were these wools so different from each other, both to the touch and in use? Some were brilliant, some were dull; some shimmering with light, some tired and flat as though crushed under their load of colour ... But for us, and for those who joined us later, the most advantageous aspect of our stay was the experience gained during the hours spent at the looms with the weavers, those humble, hard-working and earnest craftsmen—Dumontet, Lonjanie, Fougerolles, Couturier and others too numerous to mention here. These men were the descendants of such masters as Colard de Burbure, Pasquier Grenier, Montaigne, Jehan du Molin, Jouaneau and Jeanne La Franque who in olden days had filled every corner of Europe with the poetry and refinement of their *Nativities, Savages' Ball, Lady with the Unicorn, Scenes from Aristocratic Life* and so on.

"After a certain amount of groping, we decided that the first essential was to sample the various wools. Thus, we picked out from the skeins which were already dyed a relatively limited number of tones (20 to 40). These served a dual purpose: first as samples for the dyer, and second as boundaries for our palettes. In this way we were able to compose on the basis of a known and tried range of colours, and not according to those chance colour mixtures, improvizations and strokes of good or bad luck inherent in palette work. This restriction of colours is the best guard against a wandering back to the intricacies of oil painting. It forces the artist to think clearly and directly, and it means that the workshops have to stock only a minimum of dyed wools, which in turn lowers their costs. Simplicity of design, severity of colour scheme, and clearly explained cartoons all combined to bring about a return to the speed of execution typical of the 11th, 12th and 13th centuries—i.e. approximately two square yards per worker per month."

In the workshops of Tabard, Demontet, Goubely and Lauer, the cartoon-painters learned their craft. Then, until 1944, came the darkness of war, almost driving tapestry underground until, with the joy of peace, ensued the resurrection of French tapestry. In 1945, Saint-Saëns, Picart Le Doux and Lurçat founded the Association of Tapestry Cartoon-Painters. In 1946, the exhibition on "French Tapestry from the Middle Ages to the Present Day" at the Musée d'Art Moderne, Paris, met with a resounding success. The list of exhibitors was headed by those hard-working pioneers Gromaire, Dubreuil and Lurçat; then came Coutaud, Dom Robert, Guignebert, Lagrange, Picart Le Doux, Saint-Saëns, Hélène Détroyat and three new recruits from painting—Dufy, Brianchon and Savin.

This memorable exhibition toured the capitals of Europe and America. Its consequences were beneficial for the cartoon-painters who won a reputation and a place in the sun, and the result of what then was only a beginning is now apparent everywhere in the art world. Naturally enough, there were arguments, hurt feelings and struggles for control of the market, but the opposite would have been worse—a sign of indifference. This emotional side of the history of contemporary French tapestry is already fading out of memory and the concrete facts remain: there are now painters creating cartoons, weavers to weave them and an ever-increasing public to admire—and buy—them.

The recent but nevertheless already notable near-past has given rise to a fertile and boisterous present. The pioneers of modern tapestry are still at work, of course, helping with their example the rising generation of young masters. One of the giants was clearly Lurçat himself (born on July 1, 1892 at Bruyères, France). An advocate of tapestry's new look, an attorney denouncing the abuses and obstacles of the bureaucratic muddle; he was above all a proselytizer delighted, as he put it, "at having spread the tapestry bug all over the world". His output was colossal. About a thousand of his cartoons have been woven and "that vast cosmogony of wool is governed by a central idea, the Apollinarian myth, which sets up the sun as the source of all life" (Germain Bazin). And it is true, Jean Lurçat thought big, saw himself planted in the midst of things—animals and humans alike—sharing with all his heart their now interdependent fate. "I can think of nothing more comforting," he once said, "than those big stretches of wall covered with grasses, friendly dogs, girls washing linen or guarding sheep, with cornflowers and sage, violets and thyme, prophets, ploughmen, horses." Thus the artist expressed his feelings through suns, stars, cocks, and a whole menagerie of friendly beasts. His persistent themes were the daily round, the pleasures of intellect and feeling, the conquests of science. But neither his means of expression nor his subjects quite sum up Lurçat's tapestry or the man himself. With Lurçat there is always a hidden something in reserve, like a continuously unfolding mystery; always something of that mediaeval magic which, merely by combining a sign of the zodiac with a leaf motif, could conjure up a vision of the universe in all its organic range, from dying star to living vegetable matter.

Jean Lurçat has had a tremendous influence on the renaissance of tapestry both in France and in the rest of the world. The rules which he has formulated on the basis of his experience may be summed up as follows: 1. Tapestry should not be a copy of a picture but a creation in its own right. 2. Tapestry is intended for a wall, and should be composed according to the purpose of the room in which it is to be hung. It should aim at monumental qualities, and is in fact seen to its best advantage in public buildings. 3. The cartoon should be created by the artist to the actual size of the future tapestry. 4. The texture of the weaving should be fairly coarse, like that used, for instance, in the 14th century for the Angers *Apocalypse* (see pages 37-39).

Marcel Gromaire (born on July 24, 1892 at Noyelles-sur-Sambre) spent four and a half years at Aubusson. The most austere of the pioneers with his solid architectural compositions and his sober palette—he sometimes uses as few as 18 shades—Gromaire was unfaltering in the cause of tapestry's renaissance. His *Woodcutters of Mormal* (see page 138) illustrates the heavy rustic texture of his weave (ten threads to the inch) and the monumental character of his work.

Our aim here is not to write a history of contemporary tapestry—that would need greater detachment and a better time perspective than is yet possible—but merely an introduction. Still, it is essential at least to mention two recruits of great merit who were among the first to join the early nucleus: Marc Saint-Saëns and Jean Picart Le Doux. Saint-Saëns (born on May 1, 1903, at Toulouse) met Jean Lurçat in 1941 and his first cartoon, *The Foolish Virgin* (see page 139), dates from 1942. Since then he has produced a considerable number of tapestries, impassioned, vibrant and grandiose. He has the imagination and sensitivity of a Latin, yet his technique is frugal of means. When creating his cartoon, Saint-Saëns considers not only the dimensions of the tapestry but also the volume of the room in which it will be hung and the use to which this room is put, as well as its furnishings, lighting and decoration. In this way, the tapestry plays a well-defined role as part of the overall decorative scheme.

Jean Picart Le Doux was born on January 31, 1902, in Paris. Actively encouraged by Jean Lurçat, he began to design cartoons around 1943, and these now number almost a hundred. Picart Le Doux also works according to those artistic rules which governed tapestry's golden age, and his inspiration reminds us of those verdures, pastorals and animal scenes beloved of mediaeval weavers. His tapestries are serene, tidy, logical; as in a French garden, imagination is deliberately kept in check, rhythm and colour are thoughtfully placed, and the apparently effortless effect is monumental.

During succeeding years other artists, who had not shared the trials of the early days, began to take an interest in cartoon-painting. Perhaps more important for the rebirth of interest in tapestry-making, some of them had already won renown. Léger and Le Corbusier are the best examples.

Already a world-famous architect, Le Corbusier (born on October 6, 1887, at La Chaux-de-Fonds, Switzerland) became interested in tapestry about 1949. He considers that his activities as a cartoon-painter complement his architectural work. His cartoons show an architectural influence but do not depend entirely on the craft's usual formulae. Le Corbusier, always ready with a fresh new approach, neglects hatching, colour shading and relief effects in favour of pure tones, mixed threads and vigorous line drawing. His tapestries are created in accordance with his general theories on architecture and the art of living. For Le Corbusier, tapestry must take its place as part of an integral whole, never private or individual, must take into consideration the viewers for whom it is intended, must always bear in mind its social role. The following is an example of the artist's inventive spirit: any photograph reproduced by the process of photogravure (for example in a newspaper) will be seen upon examination to consist of thousands of tiny black dots, which are spaced close together for the darkest parts of the picture and far apart for the lighter areas. Le Corbusier, working in collaboration with Victor Vasarely, had the idea of choosing interesting-looking sections of photographs so treated, enlarging them many times and using the result as an absolutely original and modern cartoon.

Fernand Léger (born at Argentan, 1881-1955) had a different artistic background from either Lurçat or Le Corbusier, but shared their view that tapestry must be integrated with architecture. Although he created a few cartoons, he was not a cartoon-painter in the proper sense of the term. However, certain of his works have been chosen for weaving and the enlarged version keeps all the vigour of the originals. In these tapestries with their simplified forms, their clear and radiant colours, a certain trick of light gives the impression that the central subject stands out from the background and remains hanging in mid-air (see page 145). The first requirement of anything produced by Léger—in ceramics, stained-glass windows or tapestries—is a markedly individual character. Similarly, his rare tapestries have earned a special place in the history of tapestry and modern painting alike, because of their combination of grave simplicity and originality.

Le Corbusier and Léger are both famous men. Their experiments, however, are far from being the only ones in this field and are not necessarily at the source of all the abstract cartoons now being given to the master-weavers of Aubusson or the Gobelins. There is of course a wide gap separating Lurçat, Gromaire, Saint-Saëns and Picart Le Doux from the abstract cartoon-painters. It would be wrong to compare or to contrast these two trends, since there is no reason to lay down *a priori* that cartoons should be produced according to the rules of figurative art in preference to any other. The only criterion is the result. And the last twenty years have given us many excellent tapestries of both kinds. What is essential is that the inspiration should be in harmony with the material, the colours and the destination of the tapestry. This brings us back to the basic differences between easel-paintings, and tapestries—differences in purpose, in matter and in technique—and the consequent independence of each in the family of plastic arts. To apply the same criteria to both painting and tapestry is a grave mistake, and to avoid falling into this error of judgment we have only to look as far as France, where each discipline has in its different way been practised with great success.

In 1946, the majority of cartoon-painters were producing figurative tapestries. As well as the artists already mentioned, we should refer to one or two more. Dom Robert, son of the Count of Chaunac-Lanzac (born on December 15, 1907, at Nieul-l'Espoir) and now a Benedictine monk, painted his first cartoons for tapestries in 1941. Encouraged by Lurçat, this cultured, self-taught artist passed from illuminations and water-colours to tapestry-designing without abandoning his love of luxuriant plants and animals which he depicts in a way that recalls poetic, fairy-tale Persian miniatures. His works, brimming over with leaves and fountains, birds and flowers, seem to awaken an inborn memory of a wonderful and long-lost earthly paradise.

We have on several occasions mentioned the direct influence of Jean Lurçat on many budding cartoon-painters. But some came to tapestry-designing through other channels, for instance Lucien Coutaud (born on December 13, 1904, at Meynes), who was influenced around 1933 by Marie Cuttoli and later by Jacques Adnet. The latter, as head of the French Arts Company, was keenly interested in a renaissance of tapestry, and formed and directed a small group which included Oudot, Desnoyers, Brianchon and Coutaud. Coutaud is an original designer, his cartoons are daring and he sometimes takes liberties with reality. He may, for example, deliberately deform the proportions of a leg or of an arm, or alter the curve of a particular object, if he feels that by so doing he is achieving a better decorative effect. The narrative charm of his works reminds the viewer that Coutaud has also been an engraver and theatrical designer.

As for Jacques Lagrange (born on July 28, 1917, in Paris), his path was a solitary one. In 1939, when he was only twenty-two, he was stationed at Angers doing his military service. There he in turn discovered the *Apocalypse*, and, like so many men over the centuries, marvelled at its revelation. From that moment on, he determined to devote himself to the neglected art of tapestry, unaware that others were doing the same. Since 1946, Lagrange has used the excitement of life in Paris as his inspiration and his works reflect all the vigour and reality of everyday living.

Maurice André (born in Paris in 1914) is another painter who was at no time influenced by Lurçat. Trees, flowers and foliage are never found in André's tapestries, but in their place figures, machines, objects, sometimes animals. These are treated according to the cubist technique of breaking down forms into volumes, and usually with a very limited colour range. By deforming his motifs, Maurice André creates symbols rather than pictures and has moved towards a non-figurative art which is perfectly adapted to wall decoration and large dimensions.

Robert Wogensky (born on November 16, 1919, in Paris) opens yet another aspect of our panorama. He is first and foremost a painter but also designs cartoons—some fifty of which so far have been woven into tapestries. For him, painting and tapestry are two distinct arts and he does not attempt to transpose his conception of painting to the domain of tapestry. Many other artists have also designed cartoons and one might be tempted to divide cartoon-painters into two categories—those who are principally, if not exclusively, concerned with tapestries, and those who occasionally set aside their paint-brush (or their sculptor's chisel) to design tapestries. The work of Wogensky, an "occasional" cartoonist, has produced some excellent tapestries—better indeed than many tapestries designed by full-time cartoon-painters. The same can be said for Matisse, though not for many other painters who have at one time or another tried to express themselves in a medium which they have not mastered. Wogensky is interesting for another reason. Around 1945, his works were mostly figurative, with birds, cock-fights and so on. But in 1960 he switched to abstract subjects in that way bringing a taste of dreamland to prosaic daily life. Both styles result in true tapestries, fulfilling their role in every way. Wogensky thus avoids being drawn into the quarrel between figurative and abstract art, at the same time illustrating its futility and artificiality.

This is an appropriate moment to introduce further cartoon-painters whose theories and inspiration are in more immediate agreement with recent artistic trends. Significantly, perhaps, all these artists were born in the 20th century. The oldest, Victor Vasarely (born on April 9, 1908, at Pecs, Hungary), is a theoretician. From Lurçat he accepted the rediscovered technical laws of tapestry-making, but his artistic concepts are entirely his own. Since 1949, Vasarely has been responsible for the "experimental tapestries" produced at Aubusson by Tabard. For him, the terms "painter", "sculptor" or "cartoon-painter" are anachronisms. An artist, he believes, creates a two-, a three-, or a multi-dimensional work. It is no longer a question of different manifestations of creative feeling, but rather of the releasing of plastic feeling within different spatial confines. In practice, Vasarely shuns subjects or themes which involve a narrative of any kind, in favour of what he calls a "colour-form." His colours are not gaudy, his shading is achieved without subtle tone mixtures and his richness is neither offensive nor achieved by overcrowding. The less "colour-forms" there are in a plane surface, the greater the beauty, colour and "correctness" of that surface. The consequences are quickly drawn: Vasarely's colours are reduced to a minimum—two to five generally, as against the twenty or so used by Lurçat. He does not use broken lines or colour graduations but clear-cut contours, pure tones, and abstract, geometrical or imaginary forms (see page 169). It is in the context of these efforts and aesthetics that we should re-view and judge the works of Le Corbusier and Léger mentioned above, as also the tapestries of Jean Arp, Herbin and Mortensen, or those gouaches by Kandinsky and Sophie Taeuber-Arp which have been enlarged and woven.

The too strictly constructivist theories of Vasarely and his friends have not, however, convinced or satisfied all those modern cartoon-painters who felt (and feel) the need to find new means of expression. This is particularly true of such modern artists as Michel Tourlière, Mathieu Matégot, Mario Prassinos and Henri-Georges Adam.

Michel Tourlière (born at Beaune in 1925) is both sensitive and searching. He draws his inspiration from natural subjects and rhythms which are then transposed into a composition free of any narrative flavour. His tapestries (see page 140) are pleasing not only for the brilliant warmth and depth of their colours but also for the beauty of their weave. Because he is in close contact with the looms, (by virtue of his duties first as teacher and then director of Aubusson's national tapestry-teaching workshop), he expects from the weaver more than just a slavish copy of his cartoon. Thus he adds to the latter a freely-painted mock-up which gives details lacking in the cartoon and so helps the weaver determine the most suitable technical procedure to best interpret the artist's idea.

Mathieu Matégot (born on April 4, 1910, at Tapio-Sully, Hungary) gave his first cartoon to the weavers in 1946. Since then, solitary but enthusiastic, he has forged his way to success. Although he earns his living by designing and manufacturing cane and metal furniture, his great love is tapestry, for this is the medium which amply satisfies his creativeness and imagination. Although Mathieu Matégot accepts and respects the principles laid down by Jean Lurçat who was his mentor, his zealous path leads him in another direction. Like Tourlière, he attaches the greatest importance to the relationship between cartoon-painters and weavers; "I am like a composer whose work is at the mercy of the orchestra conductor", he says. Matégot provides a painting which he considers suitable for reproduction in wool and the weaver does the rest. His works are abstract, but not dried-up or intellectual like many other abstracts. On the contrary, his lines of force and the daring balances achieved, his unexpected colour effects and the interplay of light and shade, all give a dramatic intensity to those woven mirages which are his tapestries.

Mario Prassinos (born on July 30, 1916, at Constantinople) is a lyrical artist who cares less about abstract questions concerning tapestry's independence of (or dependence on) painting than about using tapestry as a means of expressing his own experience of nature and life. His aim is to create an image of his feelings—without reproducing the objects which have aroused these feelings. To achieve this purpose he uses plenty of reds, a few luminous highlights of yellow, dramatically opposed blacks and whites (see page 141) and a many-dimensional array of signs and powerful rhythms. His tapestries, like music, thus express sentiments which language is powerless to convey.

Henri-Georges Adam (born in Paris in 1904) occupies a place all his own among cartoon-painters. He is an engraver and his work shows qualities of engraving enlarged to mural proportions. Turning his back on coloured wools, he uses exclusively twelve different shades of white, grey and black and he demands a thread-by-thread weaving technique which results in starkly simple "engraving" made of wool.

Any description, however brief, of the various modern painters who have turned to tapestry, would be only half complete if we ignored the implications of the tapestry renaissance for the craftsmen and the luxury trade of France. For, unlike painting, tapestry is the idea of a creator realized by a team of craftsmen—and top-flight craftsmen at that. This aspect of the current renaissance can be illustrated by the following details.

Around the middle of the 18th century, tapestry weavers used some 30,000 colours. These in turn were divided up into nearly a thousand variations on each of 36 tones, shading from light to dark. In a classical tapestry, of dense weave and minute detail, eight inches of warp took up approximately 220 threads, and a weaver's output was about 6 to 8 square inches per month. Today, many tapestries comprise only 25 different shades of wool. A series of tapestries by Lurçat, for example, totalling around 270 square yards in area, required less than 50 colours (six yellows, five greys, two blacks, five ochres, two whites, five reds, five greens, five salmon-pinks, five blues and two background tones). With around 100 warp threads to eight inches an individual weaver can now produce approximately 1½ square yards per month—or roughly seven times the output of two hundred years ago. The first conclusion is obvious: nowadays tapestries cost less to weave and even very large works are, therefore, within the reach of a much broader market. In 1939, under the combined effects of economic crisis and slow artistic decadence, the craft was at its lowest ebb. The hundred or so remaining weavers—usually working alone—were kept busy only part-time. Now in 1965, many workshops and about 350 workmen are fully employed at Aubusson and, though the case of the Gobelins and of Beauvais is different since these are national factories whose workers are steadily employed by the State, the two centers are regularly busy. Thus, the second conclusion is no less clear: tapestry with its new technique and new inspiration, adapted to our contemporary life, is a living industry of considerable economic importance. The revival which has taken place in France over the last five years can be held up as an example to other countries, whether or not they have a "tapestry tradition." But although France's example is an encouraging guide, it should not lead anyone to try to impose the same weaving techniques and the same aesthetic approach upon other tapestry-weaving industries in other countries. The artistic climate of France is favourable to tapestry now as it was in the Middle Ages and the following centuries; but the fact that the French have usually excelled in the craft does not of course make it an exclusively French artistic province. For this reason a rapid and not necessarily comprehensive outline of what is being produced in other countries is now in order.

In this outline, however, the same words may not have quite the same meaning: for, according to the whim of geography or history, tapestry changes its inspiration, its weaving technique, even its raw materials. Some critics are inclined to think that many of the principal tapestries being made outside France are unorthodox. But however much one admires contemporary French tapestry, it is necessary to keep an unbiased attitude toward tapestries woven in other parts of the world. There is no one path to excellence, even in the art of tapestry-making. The diversity of tapestry techniques and aesthetic theories is one of the most fascinating things about the renaissance of this art. But many centers around the world work in relative isolation and too little is known elsewhere about what they do.

Incontestably Flanders is one of the countries which has given the greatest number of tapestries to Europe. This artistic activity died out when the last Brussels workshop (that of Jacques Van der Borght) shut down in 1794. A gulf of two centuries separates the ancient craft of Flanders from its modern Belgian counterpart. The first attempt at revival was similar to Marie Cuttoli's, and it failed for the same reasons. In 1945, a fresh and successful start was made thanks to the painters Louis Deltour, Edmond Dubrunfaut and Roger Somville working under the group name of "Forces Murales" (Mural Forces). In 1947, much new and constructive thinking was stimulated by the exhibition of French tapestry on tour from Paris, and the revival began in Tournai under the impulse of the "Forces Murales." Tones were limited and warp threads were thick; in the early days the system of numbered cartoons (in which the cartoons are drawn in black and white and the colours simply indicated by numbers—see pages 207-208) was used, but this was later abandoned. An uncompromising realism became the most characteristic mark of Belgian tapestry, confirmed in the First International Biennial Tapestry Exhibition at Lausanne. To the artists already mentioned were added Van Vlasselaer, Jan Van Noten, Mary Dambiermont, Liliane Badin and Jan Vaerten. Some painters, however, particularly Boel and René Guiette, eliminated not only those subjects traditionally used in religious or historical Flemish tapestries, but also figurative themes in general, and went on to specialize in abstract compositions. Every year brings forth new tapestries and it is hard to predict whether these forceful works will one day form a "Belgian school."

At different moments in history, weavers from southern Flanders have emigrated to the Netherlands and it is to them that Holland owes the temporary existence of weaving centers at Delft, Gouda and Leyden. It was also a Fleming, J. F. Semey, who attempted to bring about a revival of the craft during the period from 1918 to 1940. But for a long time the workshops did not pay and it was many years before the State came to their support by giving sizable orders. The post-1945 French example has stimulated greater official interest. Today there are more cartoon-painters working and there is a much greater popular interest. Outstanding among the cartoon-painters working today are Hans Bayens, Jan Bons, Dick Elffers, Lex Horn, Hans Van Norden, Herman Scholten and Marie Van Œrle Van Gorp. The Dutch artists have not followed the same path as their Belgian colleagues. They are more interested in creating a satisfactory decorative effect than in portraying the realities of daily life.

Surprisingly, although the Nordic countries possess many traditional crafts, tapestry-weaving is not one of them. Nevertheless, some mural tapestries are now being woven in Norway, Sweden and Denmark. In Norway, the origin of modern tapestry goes back to the end of the 19th century and was due to the influence of Gerhard Munthe (1849-1929) and Frida Hansen (about 1855-1930). Taking as his inspiration the example of the centuries-old tapestry preserved in the church of Baldishol, Munthe favoured a return to a rugged weave, colour hatching and cartoons aiming at a decorative two-dimensional effect as opposed to naturalistic attempts to render depth and volume. He also recommended the exclusive use of vegetable dyestuffs. Unfortunately, even during the short gap between the date of creation and today, the colours in his tapestries have not retained their original freshness.

Other artists (Ingeborg Arbo, Ulrikke Greve, and Emily Mohr) followed up the work begun by G. Munthe and Frida Hansen. The Second World War slowed down the work of artists and looms, but after further experiments had been carried out, one of Kåre Jonsborg's three monumental tapestries which was, intended for Oslo Town Hall, was put on the looms. Other contemporary artists who have turned their attention towards tapestry include Synnöve Aurdal, Ludvig Eikaas, Arne Ekeland, Else Paulson, Aksal Revold, Bjarne Rise, Alf Rolfsen and Else Marie Jakopsen. Special mention should be made of Hannah Ryggen, a self-taught weaver who works without the aid of a cartoon, guided only by her imagination and her visual memory. Her tapestries reflect the freshness of a sensitive and intelligent mind and express an inner vision in terms untainted by artistic dogmatism. Following a series of analyses and tests, Norwegian weavers now use thread made of the tough and lustrous top wool of the "spelsau" native breed of sheep. Great integrity of craftsmanship, the use of a wiry and shining wool and recourse to vegetable dyes characterize the Norwegian school.

Although in the past some tapestries were produced in Sweden, these were chiefly woven (or at least inspired) by foreigners, usually Flemings. Early in this century, Anders Zorn and Carl Larsson gave certain of their paintings to the weavers to serve as models. The results were far from satisfactory. Since then, however, younger artists have better understood the requirements of mural art and numerous works have been woven in recent years. Swedish artists are very close to nature, drawing inspiration from its elemental forces (Alf Wallander, G. G: son Wenneberg, Maja Sjöström, Gustaf Fjaestad), from Scandinavian mythology (Märta Måås-Fjetterström, Gunnar Hallström, Ossian Elgström, Olle Hjortzberg, Nils Von Dardel) and from Scandinavian tradition (Anna and Ferdinand Boberg, Sven Erixson, Hilding Linnqvist). Non-figurative tapestries can also be found as well as works based on folklore (Barbro Sprinchorn). In Sweden, tapestry now keeps four large weaving factories busy full-time. Though Swedish tapestries are little known abroad, at home they are often used to decorate public buildings such as town halls, theatres, libraries, banks. In spite of a few undeniable successes, the inspiration of Swedish tapestries seems in general to stem rather from folklore than from the broader trends of contemporary art. Similarly it is used rather as a furnishing than as an architectural element. Certain artists, like Lars Gynning, however, feel closer to their French colleagues and, like Egon Mathiesen of Denmark, have their cartoons woven at Aubusson.

Germany's contribution to the present-day rebirth of tapestry can best be described as sober and conscientious. Germany has a tapestry tradition which—setting aside one or two interruptions in the 17th and 19th centuries—goes back to the early Middle Ages, and the contemporary revival dates from the beginning of this century. The creation of the Scherrebek workshop (1896-1903) filled the long-standing gap between pure and applied art. Artists like Otto Eckmann, Hans Christiansen, Alfred Mohrbutter and Otto Ubbelohde collaborated in special designs to make tapestries which carefully took into account the special qualities and requirements of the materials to be used. They chose their subject "not for what it represented but rather for what it brought to the space it occupied" (Howaldt). The German expressionists (Franz Marc, August Macke, Ernst Ludwig Kirchner) became interested in tapestry because "the liberation of artistic methods, the development and the conscious use of decorative potential offered these painters a means of expression more real and more tangible than that of painting" (Urban). For the moment it is difficult to sum up German efforts over the last thirty years since these have been largely devoted to research. Many cartoon-painters, especially women, weave their own cartoons, though the cartoons of Irma Goecke and Fritz Winter are woven by German factories.

Up to 1920, no tapestry had ever been woven in Austria. However, the magnificent collections (over 800 tapestries) assembled by the Hapsburgs were often brought out to add the desired amount of brilliance and splendour to State occasions. After the fall of the monarchy, the imperial repairs workroom became a private factory and its director called in several great artists of whom the best known was Oskar Kokoschka. Following the last war, R. H. Eisenmenger composed a series of tapestries inspired by

Mozart's "Magic Flute", which now hang in Vienna's Opera House. The contemporary French example aroused great interest in Austria and the craft's promising future is in the safe hands of a number of artists. However, the group composed of Veronica Schmid, Josef Schulz, Fritz Riedl and their friends prefer to work without cartoons, letting their imagination play directly on the loom. For these artists, who are at the same time weavers, the act of weaving is all-important for the arrangement of the design, and the basic sketch is no more than a general idea. Fritz Riedl, the promoter of this new approach, found his vocation purely by chance on visiting the exhibition of French tapestries at Vienna in 1948 (the same tapestries which were displayed two years earlier in Paris). Subsequently, he served an apprenticeship at Aubusson under Jean Lurçat's aegis.

In Switzerland, "weavers of secular tapestries" used to produce works similar in style, technique and material to those of Alsace, Franconia and the central Rhine district. Usually practised in home or convent, the craft fell off during the 17th century. Now as then, no true tapestry factory exists in the Swiss Confederation. The very few active workshops owe their existence to the energy of a handful of enthusiasts. Cartoon-painters like Denise Voïta, Claude Loewer, Hans Stocker and others have their tapestries woven abroad, usually at Aubusson-Felletin. Others like Elisabeth Giauque on the other hand, prefer to do their weaving themselves.

In 1518, an Italian traveller who had attended the wedding in Cracow of King Sigismond I of Poland, approvingly noted the great range and beauty of the tapestries decorating Wawel Castle. One might easily assume that, besides Flemish tapestries, some of Polish origin were also on view. However, the oldest known Polish tapestries are of relatively recent origin, dating only from the mid-18th century. The craft's subsequent growth was hindered by the many upheavals which characterized the country's history, and the 19th century, as elsewhere in Europe, ushered in a period of decline. The first efforts at revival were made at the beginning of the 20th century, through the Polish Society of Applied Arts in Cracow, but the movement was stopped short by the outbreak of the First World War. In 1917, the "Lad" artists' co-operative was founded in Warsaw and out of it came tapestries by Josef Czajkowsky, Janina Konarska and Wanda Szczepanowska. The Second World War then intervened. After 1945, the art came to life again, particularly in Cracow, and the workshops began to get State support. Some artists use traditional motifs such as work and festivities in the countryside, great moments of national history, or the deeds of heroes and patriots; but many more combine striking simplicity of weave with great poetic originality of subject.

Three main varieties characterize Polish tapestry: first, the domestic kind, full of folklore and rich in venerable tradition, greatly appreciated by the home market; next the "Gobelins" type, which is working its way through the various concepts of contemporary art; finally the so-called "Polish kilims," which utterly intrigued visitors to the First International Biennial Tapestry Exhibition. The weaver—who usually doubles as cartoon-painter—uses thick and irregular woollen threads simultaneously with silk, string, and strands of all sorts of different substances in varying widths. With this rustic material the most astonishing plastic effects result. In addition, open-work weaving and variations of weave are introduced according to the artist's fancy. It might be thought that such homely materials and free handling would result in works suited only to museums of folk craft, but nothing could be further from the truth. Polish artists and weavers have created true and very beautiful tapestries (see page 147). This experiment, surprising no doubt for people used to the works of Gobelins and Aubusson, deserves great attention elsewhere in the world and should be pursued energetically in Poland itself.

In Czechoslovakia, a workshop was founded in the late 19th century by the painter R. Schlattauer at Valasské Mezirici. Subsequently, in 1910, a second factory was set up at Jindrichuv Hradec, thanks to the efforts of Marie Teinitzerova, the wife of a Buddhist philosopher and a pupil of William Morris and John Ruskin. Nowadays the majority of tapestries in Czechoslovakia come either from the Jindrichuv Hradec factory, or from the Antonin Kybal-Aloïs Fisarek workshop at the Prague Higher School of Arts and Crafts. The first monumental Czech tapestry dates from 1925 and owes its origin to Frantisek Kysela. This artist had a profound influence on the craft, which is now represented by two principal groupings: the first made up of painters, and the second comprising designers who have come over from the textile industry. In the former case, a painting is selected for its decorative qualities—sometimes even without the painter's knowledge—and an enlarged version, either a drawing or a photograph, is then often made to serve as a cartoon. The results so achieved are variable in the extreme...

In the case of the second group, the artist attempts to express himself through the medium of a cartoon designed specially for weaving. Interesting and widely differing works have been produced in this way; some of them influenced by French or Flemish tradition, others resolutely modern—such as Antonin Kybal's *Historical Monuments of Czechoslovakia*. Among the most successful of contemporary designers can be mentioned Josef Müller, Bohdan Mrazek, Jiri Fusek, Vera Drnkova—all pupils of Antonin Kybal. Others, such as J. Hladik were trained by Aloïs Fisarek. Despite a few successes, the renown of Czechoslovakia's artists and weavers has for many years past been confined to the country itself.

It is remarkable that the desire to revive the craft seemed to well up in many countries simultaneously (France, Scandinavia, Czechoslovakia, Hungary) around the beginning of the century. However, these praiseworthy efforts, usually championed by isolated artists, rarely came to anything.

We might pause for a moment to ask two questions—why were these attempts made, and why did they fail?—and to hazard a guess at the answers. The decadence of pictorial art toward the end of the 19th century had brought with it the decadence of tapestry, and some artists tried to correct this situation. They were usually closer to tapestry than to painting and this is why their efforts often had a somewhat homespun appearance. At the same time the trend towards large-scale works was taking root— perhaps under the influence of the Symbolists, with their pass-word "Walls to decorate ... Down with perspective!" But why then did these efforts fail? First, because of the absence of suitable models (the lesson had not yet been drawn from mediaeval tapestries) and secondly because of the lack of public interest and therefore of a market.

The same phenomenon occurred in Hungary where a few painters, grouped at Gödöllö near Budapest, tried to restore tapestry to its rightful place; in spite of a promising start, the enterprise failed and was soon forgotten. Experiments made some years later by Noemi Ferenczy, although not conclusive, at least kept Hungary's fragile native industry alive, and in the thirties, Ferenczy's pioneering work was continued—although along different lines—by Endre Domanovszky, using a very limited range of colours and a coarse weave. After 1945, Istvan Pekary in turn took up tapestry-designing and his works were as different from Ferenczy's as they were from Domanowszky's. Some were inspired by Hungary's past history, others by peasant life. Istvan Ban, with his *Parade of the Buso* (see page 148), followed in the footsteps of Pekary.

Like Czechoslovakia, Poland and other Danubian lands, Jugoslavia has inherited a magnificent rural tradition in embroidery, domestic weaving and wool dyeing. Her domestic workshops on the one hand, coupled with the rich resources of folklore on the other, have provided the impetus for the rise of Jugoslavia's new tapestry industry. A great many present-day artists are endeavouring to express the genius of their country in somewhat more modern terms. Their works are usually of medium size, since weaving techniques and the size of the looms apparently exclude the possibility of creating works anywhere near the size of the largest French tapestries. Designs by Milica Zoric and Mateja Rodici are still often based on the rich local tradition of popular myths. But other artists, like Nadja Volcko and Bosko Petrovic use rhythm and colour to fill a strictly decorative role. Once these weavers and artists have acquired a mastery of the craft comparable to that found in other countries, they will be capable of giving the world many pleasant surprises. But, like tapestry-makers elsewhere, their works need to be introduced to foreign markets.

Both Italy and Spain, in the past, possessed flourishing tapestry industries. Today, however, relatively little is being done. In Italy, in spite of a remarkable artistic and economic revival since the war, there are very few weaving centers and no painters devoted exclusively to tapestry design. If we set aside the tapestries produced by Felice Casorati, Corrado Cagli and Antonio Corpora for the liner *Leonardo da Vinci*, and those of Aroldi and

Enzo Brunori, tapestry looks very much like the pre-ball Cinderella of the peninsula's arts—especially in comparison to its importance in countries like France and Poland.

The situation is no better in Spain, although Catalonia has a certain amount of experience in the weaving of carpets. Only a few isolated artists, like Josep Grau Garriga and Jaume Muxart have proved that the mural craft is not altogether dead in Spain.

Paradoxically, Portugal is entirely different. Although her early conquests and far-flying geographical discoveries once provided inspiration for the Flemish weavers, Portugal never had a tapestry tradition of her own—apart from a brief spell of activity on the part of the Tavira factories. Fifteen years ago, however, an industrialist from Portalegre, named Manuel do Carmo Peixeiro, invented a new weaving process which was easier than the traditional French or Flemish techniques. In 1947, after several fruitless attempts, a painter who had spent some time in France created a set of cartoons which were woven into tapestry but which remained unknown both to the public at large and to prospective buyers. The creation of a market proved extremely difficult, particularly since neither the State nor the public showed any interest in these first courageous efforts. The exhibition of French tapestries held in 1952 at the Lisbon Art Museum (it was actually the same 1946 Paris exhibition still on tour) finally brought the art of tapestry before a large public and—almost as an afterthought—called attention to the existence of contemporary Portuguese tapestry. A rich harvest was reaped from this exhibition. Portuguese artists and weavers began to receive orders from the State. In 1958 the movement was boosted by a visit from the dynamic Jean Lurçat—so much so, in fact, that Portugal's weavers are now busily working on cartoons by Portuguese, French and Swedish artists for buyers all over Europe and America. The cartoon-painters' works are largely contained within the limits of conventional and stylized, well-accentuated forms. This is the case for Guilherme Camarinha, in particular, the doyen of the art, and Carlos Betelho (see page 157). Special mention, however, should be made of Rogerio Ribeiro whose volatile temperament is reflected in non-figurative cartoons reminiscent of the trends apparent in the decorative art of the pre-Second World War period.

It is hard for North and South Americans to make capital out of fabrics woven by Indians in bygone days, since for many years the only real admirers of these works were ethnologists! Efforts have been made to revive the ancient craft using native labour working with genuine or reinvented native designs and colours but, so far, these attempts have been too short-lived to be successful. Tapestry in America is a more or less faithful imitation of European tapestry, although it has none the less some characteristics peculiar to itself. This is primarily because American artists feel less bound than Europeans to traditional themes and forms. Experiments— usually isolated—conducted by artists and weavers are very different from those done in Europe, and sometimes seem bizarre to European eyes. North Americans, when they manage to free themselves from the small dimensions of domestic tapestry, show a decorative sense which can be both graphic—as in the case of Mark Adams (page 158), and forceful—as in the case of Sylvia Carewe and Lenore Tawney in particular. Other American artists like Allan Porter and Dana Romalo have made uncompromising efforts to adapt their ideas to the requirements of the weaver's material. There are no factories in the United States comparable to Aubusson. As a result, cartoons are woven either in Europe, or in very small workshops, or by the artists themselves.

In Canada, it is chiefly the French Canadians who are interested in tapestry-making. Folklore, naïve or unpolished, has a marked influence on the works of many of them, for example in the case of Thérèse Lafrance. The works of others like Krystyna Sadowska whose tapestries (page 146) resemble those done in Poland, still bear the stamp of their country of origin. Finally, we should refer to Paul Lacroix and especially to Mariette Rousseau-Vermette who, simply by using vertical colour movements, manages to obtain remarkably warm decorative effects.

In Brazil, two very different experiments are taking place. Genaro de Carvalho at Bahia utilizes tropical, often highly-coloured, themes, while Jacques Douchez and Norberto Nicola now working at São Paulo, create tapestries much nearer to international artistic feeling because they are so close to the world-renowned artistic activities of their town. All are experienced in French techniques because all have worked, for varying lengths of time, either with Lurçat or at Aubusson.

It is doubtful whether tapestry could maintain its precarious foothold on the rest of the South American continent but for a few dedicated artists such as Olga Amaral in Colombia and Armin Wexler working in Chile. Working alone, often isolated from current artistic trends and generally without a market, these courageous artists are nevertheless continuing their struggle to make tapestry known and appreciated.

The opposite applies to the United States where many European tapestries are sold and where home-woven works may one day find a better market... provided, however, that this luxury trade can successfully establish itself in an increasingly technically-minded society.

Tapestry has been woven in Japan since the 7th and 8th centuries—almost as long as in Europe. One of the most outstanding among these ancient tapestries is a *Buddhistic Paradise*, said to have been woven by Princess Choujô-himé, which has approximately 50 threads to the inch and measures a little over four square yards in area. Weaving techniques are to some extent similar to those practised in Europe. However, Japan's women weavers pack down the silk or woollen threads not with a comb but with their fingernails, specially shaped to a saw-tooth edge. For this reason, certain Japanese tapestries are known as *Tsouzouré-Nishiki*, which means

135

"tapestries woven with the fingernails." In modern Japan, large-scale decorative fabrics are in greater demand than tapestry; however, in 1960, Hirozo Murata had a hunting scene woven (page 149). This was produced by the *Tsouzouré-Nishiki* technique and embellished with gold thread.

As we think this survey shows, tapestry is a living art which is still growing all over the world. Cartoon-painters, more and more, are going beyond out-worn traditions (most notably the long infatuation with folklore) to create new styles and deal with new subjects. In designing their cartoons they are also disregarding the norms purely of painting in order to suit their work to the rhythms and functions of modern architecture. The isolated, frequently hit-or-miss experiments of individual weavers are being replaced by the work of factories busily creating tapestries according to improved or rediscovered techniques. Over the last thirty years, through the taste and interest of an ever-growing public and the active support of the great 20th-century patrons—public bodies, banks, industrialists—a flourishing market has been created. All in all a climate now exists which may lead to the blossoming of new masterpieces to enchant the mind and the eye: tapestries, in fact, to brighten our concrete walls with the joys, the fears and the achievements of 20th-century man.

COCKS' GARDEN, BY JEAN LURÇAT — 9 FT. 6¼ IN. × 8 FT. 2½ IN. — TABARD, 1939   Musée d'Art Moderne, Paris

Lurçat, with his strutting cocks and variegated foliage, praises the endless prodigality of Nature—rediscovered. His tapestry *Cocks' Garden* is directly descended from such works as the *Apocalypse* and the *Unicorn* series. For the concrete houses built by today's architects, their ally Lurçat provides those wonderful works which remind man of his real capital—the wealth of the mind.

WOODCUTTERS OF MORMAL, BY MARCEL GROMAIRE — 9 FT. 6 IN. × 8 FT. 6 IN. — GOUBELY, 1941   Lynedjian, Lausanne

The monumental character of the *Woodcutters of Mormal* is due to masterful drawing and to the balance achieved between different tones. The paintings of its author, Marcel Gromaire (born at Noyelles-sur-Sambre, France, July 24, 1892), can be seen in large museums in both Europe and America, but Gromaire's contribution to the contemporary revival of French tapestry is little known. His first tapestry was woven in 1939, at Aubusson, where he worked as a cartoon painter for nearly five years. It is now many, many years since he last supplied a cartoon. The understandable result is an increase in price of those works which already exist.

THE FOOLISH VIRGINS, BY MARC SAINT-SAËNS —
6 FT. 2¾ IN. × 8 FT. 0½ IN. TABARD, 1942

Collection of François Tabard

RUBY WINE, BY MICHEL TOURLIÈRE — 7 FT. 3 IN. × 5 FT. 0¾ IN. — PICAUD, 1952   Galerie La Demeure, Paris

Michel Tourlière produced this *Ruby Wine* in honour of the famous Burgundy vintages. He found its gleaming blues, reds and purples simply and pleasurably by looking into his wine-glass. His interest in the grape is only natural since his home-town is Beaune, in the very heart of Burgundy. He was born on February 15, 1925, and studied art and mural decoration in Paris. He later worked with Lurçat and in 1946 settled at Aubusson. In 1947, he was appointed instructor at the Ecole-Atelier Nationale de Tapisserie (a national teaching workshop) and he became its Director in 1960. All of Michel Tourlière's tapestries were woven at Aubusson.

PERSEPHONE, BY MARIO PRASSINOS – 6 FT. 4½ IN. × 4 FT. 6¼ IN. – GOUBELY, 1959   Galerie La Demeure, Paris

Persephone—honoured in this tapestry by Mario Prassinos—was the daughter of Zeus and the goddess of spring in Greek mythology. She was carried off by the god of the Underworld to be his queen and it was there that she spent the winter months. The artist, born at Constantinople on July 30, 1916, endeavours to use rhythm, texture and material as means to relate an intelligible human experience, and to describe the outer world in relation to the inner world. He usually constructs his works on the basis of the numbered cartoon (see page 208), without making a previous model. Exhibitions of his tapestries have been held in Europe and America.

THE SONG OF THE WORLD: THE GREAT MENACE, BY JEAN LURÇAT — 29 FT. 6¼ IN. × 14 FT. 5¼ IN. — TABARD, 1957   Property of the Artist

"The earth is round and wooded," says Jean Lurçat, rather feverishly, of this tapestry, "it is liquid and solid; above all, the earth is made up of human beings of every calibre, every type, every colour.   And the whole—germs, living beings, vegetables, minerals, winds that are like the earth's breath—all these are interdependent.   Whether the bomb is dropped by the Eagle or by the Beast, it will reduce the whole of creation to a poisonous quagmire . . .   On the right floats the bark of creation, with man at the helm.   It is he who steers because he is now the master of the universe.   Yes, the master indeed, since he has the power to destroy the universe or to pollute it; but above him is the brutish urus, whose ejaculation contaminates all of creation. This is why every animal and every plant in the vessel is already affected, diseased, even leprous . . .   The first explosions are tainting the sky—yet all is not lost!   Over man's head sits Pallas Athene's owl, the symbol of wisdom, perched near the rudder and keeping its vigil in spite of all.   And it is this which should ultimately save man—who was called Homo Sapiens— from the alternative fates of being burnt to ashes or lunacy; or in any event from a third fate, that of gross delusion by his leaders, his astrologers and his alchemists."   *The Song of the World.*

143

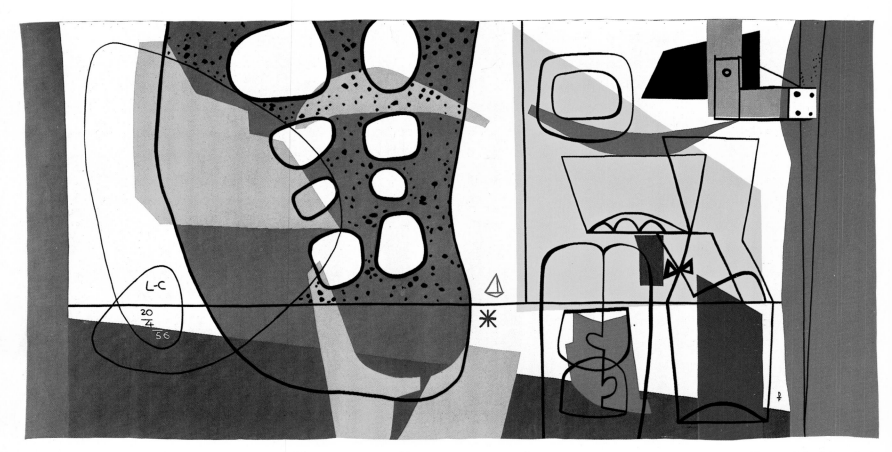

UNESCO, BY CH. E. LE CORBUSIER — 22 FT. 3¾ IN. × 11 FT. 3¾ IN. — PINTON, 1962

Unesco, Salle Suisse, Paris

Le Corbusier, the world-famous architect who created the Indian town of Chandigarh and built the extraordinary church of Ronchamp, also designs tapestries. Most are abstracts like this one. With clarity and sharpness he describes his concepts of tapestry perhaps better than any other modern artist: "We cannot have a mural painted on the walls of our apartment. However, a woollen wall of tapestry can at any time be rolled up, carried away and put in place elsewhere. This is why I have called my tapestries 'muralnomads'. Tapestry in one's home answers a legitimate poetic desire. With its texture, its matter, its tangibility, it adds a special warmth of its own to an interior. In a living-room, tapestry should be displayed at eye level. Its own height is therefore all-important: 7 ft. 2½ in., 9 ft. 6½ in., 11 ft. 9¾ in. which are the dimensions of the 'modulor' (or ideal proportions) minus 2 in. – 2¼ in. (7 ft. 4¾ in., 9 ft. 8¾ in., 12 ft., etc.). Tapestry thus becomes a useful element of construction and not merely a form of decoration. Furthermore, since wool absorbs sound, a wall covered with this substance can, in certain cases, fill a vital need from the acoustic point of view ... It was through the plastic arts—phenomena of pure creation—that I found the stimulus for my architectural and town-planning work ... My research is based on the uninterrupted practice of the plastic arts, and these are the source of my freedom of thought and my potential. Tapestries, drawings, paintings, sculptures, books and houses are, as far as I am concerned, simply one and the same manifestation of a stimulating harmony existing within a new, mechanically-minded society."

ABSTRACT COMPOSITION 1962, BY FERNAND LÉGER – 13 FT. 1½ IN. × 6 FT. 6¾ IN. – TABARD, 1962   Musée Léger, Biot

Fernand Léger, who died in 1955 at the age of 74, was one of the greatest of contemporary French painters. In addition to oil paintings, gouaches, monumental ceramics and stained-glass windows, he created numerous tapestries which are largely adventures in form and colour. Interviewed by Diane Vallier, he summed up his art in the following terms: "To attain complete freedom within the truth; that is the drama of the inventor, the artist and the poet. I use pure colours but of local tones; this means I never juxtapose complementary colours. In other words, I avoid placing a red beside a green, an orange next to a blue or a mauve by a yellow; because each of these colours loses its own local strength when seen side by side with another. The reason is the well-known phenomenon of vibration which is set up between complementary colours. This was thoroughly explored by the Impressionists and their relief effects were obtained through vibration. Whereas I, on the other hand, relate colours which give a constructive effect. If I have an orange, for example, I can put beside it a red, a yellow, or a green—anything but a blue. These are colours which stay put when juxtaposed. The result is less charming but incomparably stronger ... I range between two absolutes—black and white; the rest fall into harmony by themselves. Black is of tremendous importance to me. Early on, I used it for lines, to point the contrast between curves and straight lines. Later, as can be seen in my paintings, the black stroke became bolder and bolder, finally providing sufficient intensity of tone; and by stressing this I was able to make my colours stand out better ..."

THE MUSICIANS, BY KRYSTYNA SADOWSKA — 13 FT. 1½ IN. × 9 FT. 10 IN. — KRYSTYNA SADOWSKA WORKSHOP, 1960   Private Collection

With this tapestry, called *The Musicians*, Krystyna Sadowska evokes the fluid atmosphere of eternal poetry which invests those who need no words to express joy and sorrow. Full of youth and dynamism, *The Musicians* is similar in some ways to other contemporary Polish work, but its author has happily managed to avoid the pitfall of being over-influenced by folklore. Born in Poland on June 2, 1912, Krystyna Sadowska studied successively in Warsaw, London and Paris, finally emigrating to Canada some years ago, where she has now taken out formal citizenship. She paints and weaves her cartoons in her own workshop. Her tapestries have won many prizes in international exhibitions, notably a Gold Medal from the French Government in 1937.

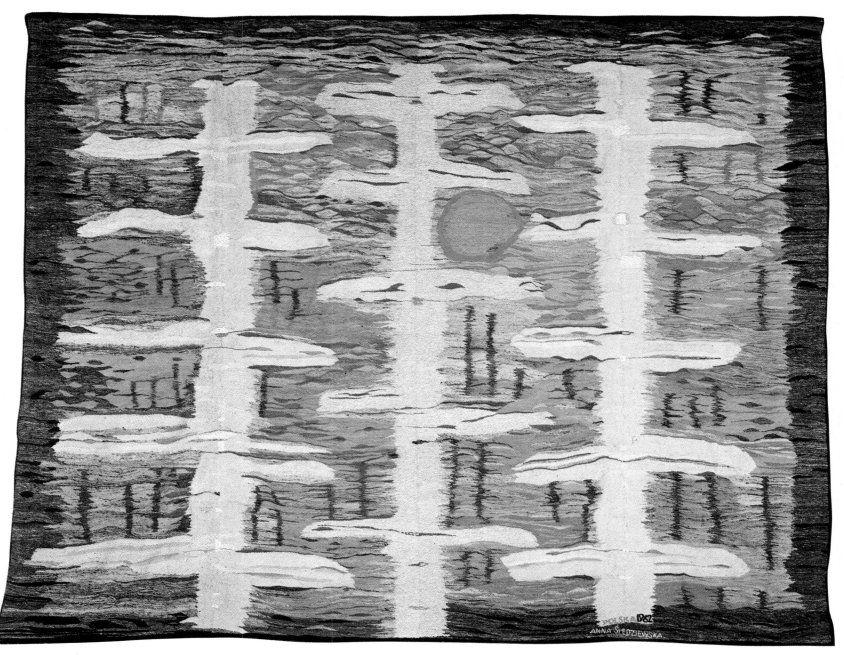

THE TREES, BY ANNA SLEDZIEWSKA – 13 FT. × 9 FT. 10 IN. – POLISH ARTISTS' WORKSHOP 1962   Private Collection

The Trees, by Anna Sledziewska, immediately calls to mind those great moss-grown trees of the vast northern European plains where the watery sunlight barely filters through low-hanging grey cloud ... A native of Poland, born on August 16, 1900, Anna Sledziewska studied at the Warsaw School of Fine Arts, where she is now an instructor in charge of the tapestry teaching workshop. She has produced a great number of decorative fabrics and "jacquards" (figured fabrics) and has written a book on modern Polish tapestry. Since 1950, she has taken an active part in Poland's artistic life through her teaching and through exhibitions at Lodz, Sopot and Warsaw. In recent years she has also exhibited in Paris, Moscow, Venice and Milan.

147

THE PARADE OF THE BUSO, BY ISTVAN BAN — 15 FT. 9¾ IN. × 10 FT. 10 IN. — H.G.R.M. WORKSHOP, 1957

Town Hall, Mohacs

The Parade of the Buso, made for his native town by Istvan Ban, illustrates an episode of mediaeval history, a battle between the Hungarians and an invading enemy, won by the inhabitants of Mohacs. The artist was born on March 31, 1922, at Mohacs (Hungary). He concentrates exclusively on tapestries and wall carpets produced according to a personal technique.

148

THE HUNT, BY HIROZO MURATA – 13 FT. 1½ IN. × 9 FT. 10 IN. – KAWASHIMA TEXTILE MILLS, 1962   Private Collection

The Hunt, by Hirozo Murata, was woven in a style which the Japanese call "Tsouzouré-Nishiki": in place of the comb normally used to pack down the thread (see page 218), the women weavers use their fingernails which are cut to a saw-tooth edge, a technique dating from the 6th century A.D. Hirozo Murata, born in Kyoto in 1920, is a painter and textile designer.

149

BOHDAN MRAZEK
PRESS CONFERENCE WITH
NEIL ARMSTRONG, 1970.
360 × 180 × 21
Woven by the artist

Bohdan Mrazek took part in the 3rd and the 6th Biennal. He was born in 1931, studied at the Higher School of Textile Industry in Brno, at the Higher School of Decorative Arts in Prague, as well as in Prague University. Beginning in 1958, he became involved in the tapestry revival in his country, and in 1961, began teaching at the Higher School of Textile Industry in Brno. Bohdan Mrazek is his own weaver: he has shown his tapestries in a great number of exhibits all over the world.

DEBRA E. RAPOPORT
TEXTURED, LAYERED GRID, 1975
305 × 244 × 61
Woven by the artist

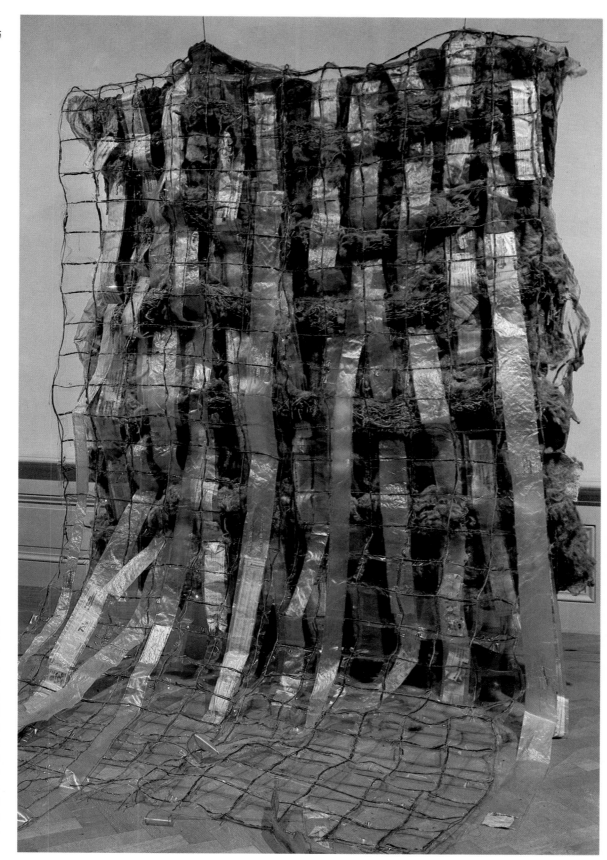

Debra E. Rapoport was born in 1945 in New York and attended Carnegie Institute of Technology and Berkeley University. She now teaches at Davis University in California. Besides taking part in the 5th, 6th and 7th Biennals, she has shown in many group exhibits in the United States—such as Austin (Texas) and Fort Wayne (Indiana). The tapestry at the 7th Biennal was executed in her own workshop in Berkeley from a mixed technique done with various materials.

SHIGEO KUBOTA — ECHO OF THE OCEAN, 1974, 260 × 300 — Woven by the artist

Born in Kyoto in 1947, Shigeo Kubota is a graduate of the Higher School of Art of Kyoto University. He took part in the 6th and 8th Biennal. Now a professor at the same school he once attended, he has participated in many individual and group shows, sponsored by the newspapers, Mainichi and Asahi. Like many contemporary artists, Kubota weaves his own designs.

CATALOG
OF CONTEMPORARY TAPESTRIES

A CATALOG OF CONTEMPORARY TAPESTRIES FROM ALL OVER THE WORLD

The next pages give an overall view of the world's present tapestry production from workshops in Europe, Asia and the Americas. Because of the size of this volume, there had to be a choice: this casts no reflection on the work of some artists that may unfortunately have been overlooked, nor on the work of others that cannot be shown here for lack of space. It had been planned to indicate prices of tapestries still or recently on the market. This proved impossible: too many factors had to be taken into consideration. What is shown follows the sequence of the Biennials, in order to acquaint the reader with the evolution of art of tapestry from the 1st Biennial in 1962 to the 8th in 1977.

Right now, what is tapestry? The range of the works now shown under this heading would make insistance on rigid technical characteristics most arbitrary. On the other hand, tapestry can no longer be limited by its previous uses. It does not fulfill its early specific functions: visual entertainment, warmth or acoustics. TV, central heating, and newer construction materials have replaced tapestry in this sense. Form rather than function determine new criteria.

No one can really set forth a definition that must eventually evolve from the works themselves. A proof of this are changes that have been brought to the rules of the Biennial, in order to give the jury greater latitude.

It seems useful to give a short definition of the different techniques that have been presented since the 3rd Biénnal.

Tissuterie: Art of lace, ribbon and trimming makers.

Passementerie: This category groups a number of edging and trimming materials, of cotton, wool, silk, steel, beads, etc., of numberless uses. *Passementerie* has existed since the remotest times. Several artists have brought its techniques up-to-date with astonishing results. *Passementerie* has little to do with weaving, since it requires no loom or a most rudimentary one. However, several artists use both weaving and *passementerie* in their creations.

Tortillé: A twist used to produce pleating or helicoidal ridges. The torsion of a rope.

Croisure: Crossover: an interweaving of crossed fabrics.

Braid: Flat trim made from intertwined materials.

Macramé: Textile object made from knotted twine or thread without the use of a loom.

Knots: An interlacement of one or more flexible bodies whose ends have been variously pulled or folded. Many of the new tapestries include lumps or knobs. More than sixty kinds of knots have been inventoried.

Knitting: A fabric formed by interlacing a single yarn or thread in loops, by the means of straight needles with one or both bluntly pointed ends. Flat fabric is knitted with 2 knitting needles, tubular shapes with 5.

Stitch: A single turn or loop of thread or yarn used in knitting, crochet or netting.

Appliqué: Material applied or laid in relief on another to form a design. *Appliqué* lace: one where flowers are made separately then sewn onto the background.

Collage-Piquage: This new technique appeared in the 3rd and 4th Biennals and was created by Alain Dupuis. He first glued bits of wool onto a background material, using paper and later cloth. By then machine-stitching the glued-on wool, he greatly reinforced the material. Hand gluing not only affords great freedom of composition to the artist, but it also offers the advantage of creating "decorative tapestries" at relatively low cost. Stitching can be in black, white or colour and a whole palette of stitches can be used. The technique is interesting as long as it does not slavishly imitate the effects of painting.

Net: Fabric woven or knotted into meshes. The thickness and the size of each mesh are extremely variable. Every stitch is knotted into place.

Embroidery: Stitched needle designs in relief on cloth or leather. Embroidery falls into three types. White embroidery is done on white cloth in cotton, yarn or silk of the same colour. Colour embroidery is designed on any material with either coloured, gold or silver thread. Needlepoint is slant-stitched in wools or silks on a canvas background. This enduring material is usually destined for hangings, cushions or seatcovers. The overall covering of needlepoint gives it a close resemblance to tapestry.

Crochet: The hook or *crochet* is used both for knitwork or lacemaking. The wool or cotton yarn is held in the left hand, between the first finger and the thumb. The work is held in the left hand, while the right hand draws the yarn in and out of the formed loops. There are five basic crochet stitches.

Fringe: An ornamental edging formed by groups of hanging threads, handknotted into another material.

To conclude, the Biennals serve to bring together artists, museum directors, art critics and historians. They give them an unique chance to meet ideas through spontaneous and group discussions that have proved highly stimulating. The Biennials have done much to promote the creation of tapestry workshops in many countries, as well as art galleries that specialize in tapestry; they have triggered other exhibits and shows, encouraged many collectors and stirred up a certain spirit of competitiveness among the exhibitors.

JEAN PICART LE DOUX — MIGRATIONS, 1962, 325 × 435 — Manufacture des Gobelins

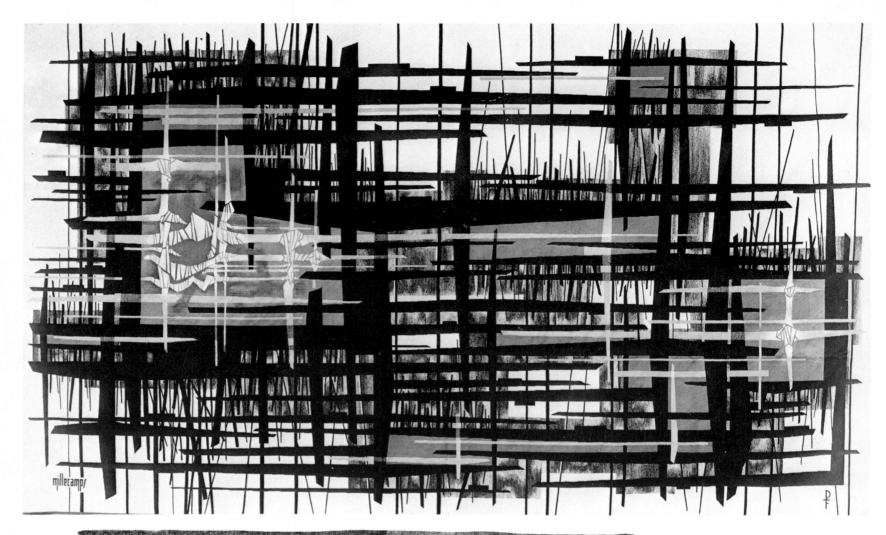

YVES MILLECAMPS
COUNTERPOINT, 1962, 270 × 450
Atelier Pinton, Felletin

H. GEORGES ADAM
GALAXY, 1960, 390 × 390
Atelier Goubely-Gatien, Aubusson

CARLOS BOTELHO — LISBOA, 1955, 378 × 450 — Manufactura de tapeçarias de Portalegre

MARK ADAMS
GREAT WING, 1962
Tissage Paul Avignon, Aubusson

YAN YOORS
PRIMEVAL NIGHT, 1957
Woven by the artist, New York

FRITZ AREND-MUTWILLIGES TRYPTYCH (DETAIL), 1961-61, 200 × 500 – Woven by the artist

ELISABETH KADOW
DORTMUND II, 1964, 273 × 375
Nürnberger Gobelin-Manufaktur

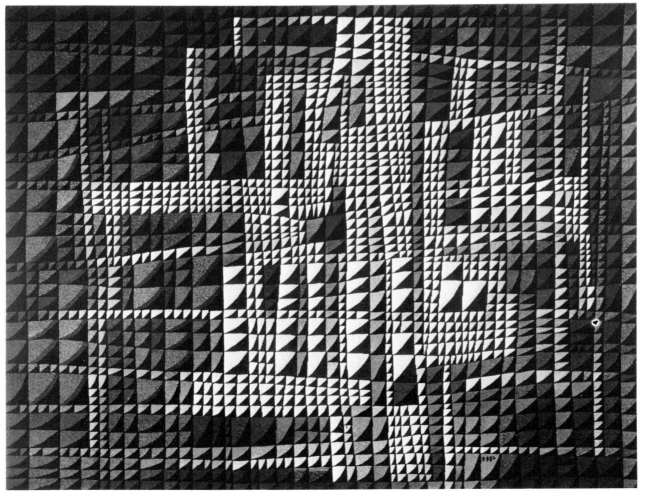

MARIA PLACHKY
DIAGONAL TRANSFORMATION
1965, 260 × 320
Woven by the artist

MARIO PRASSINOS
KING LEAR, 1963, 295 × 592
Manufacture Nationale des Gobelins,
Paris

AURELIA MUÑOZ
CONSTRUCTIVE ABSTRACTION
1965, 260 × 313
Woven by the artist

161

FRITZ RIEDL
THREE FIGURES, 1963, 275 × 420
Woven by the artist

MICHEL TOURLIERE
REDS OF THE VINEYARD, 1964,
220 × 380
Tissage Goubely-Gatien, Aubusson

BIENNIAL III

Barely a few months after Jean Lurçat's death, the 3rd Biennal was held. Yet the founder of Citam and the Biennals was fully present in his tapestry "Ornamentos Sagrados," the tenth piece of his masterwork, "Le Chant du Monde." At his death at the age of 74, Jean Lurçat left not only his many works, but the memory of a generous and passionate man. As the years pass, they reveal him not only as an artist and a reviver—along with François Tabard and Denise Majorel—of an art where French weavers had excelled for many centuries, but also as the initiator of a world-wide movement for the re-birth of tapestry. Under his impetus, artists prepared cartoons, workshops opened... and tapestries blossomed. However, in the very spring of the new tapestry movement, the influence of Jean Lurçat has lessened. Though each Biennial still remains a privileged moment that "tells men of all colours and walks of life of the concepts, both lyrical and architectural, of the artist faced with the Wall" (Jean Lurçat), it is far from certain that Jean Lurçat would enjoy all that fiber artists from all the world now offer to our admiring eyes. Could one expect that tapestry alone would escape the storms and uncertainties of our age?

JEAN LURÇAT — ORNAMENTOS SAGRADOS, 1966, 440 × 1050 — Manufacture Tabard, Aubusson

MAGDALENA ABAKANOWICZ
BLACK ASSEMBLAGE II, 1967
300 × 270
Woven by the artist

LOUISE PIERUCCI
GEOMETRICS 3, 1967, 167 × 320
Woven by the artist

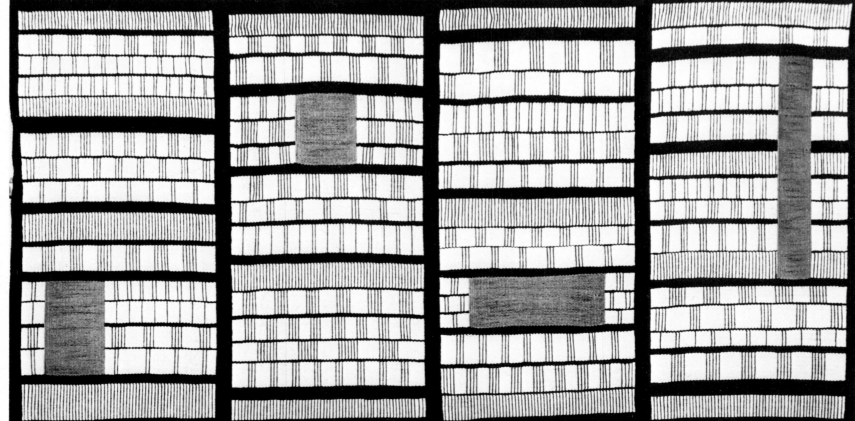

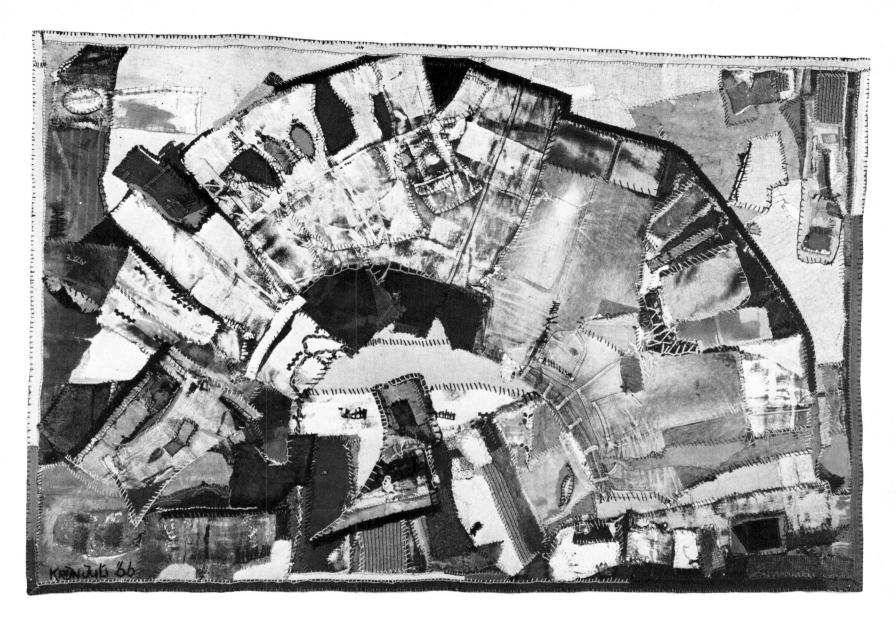

KRYN GIEZEN
KLEED, 1966, 190 × 300
Woven by the artist

LILLY KELLER
No. 44, 1966, 245 × 295
Woven by the artist

WOJCIECH SADLEY
SLEEPLESS NIGHT, 1968,
300 × 200
Wanda Cooperative, Cracow

166

ISIDOR VRSAJKOV
EPIQUON BALKAN, 1966,
290 × 210
Atelier 61, Novi Sad, Yugoslavia

ODETTE BLANC-FALAIZE
EB EL SAKI, 1965-67, 220 × 300
Atelier Caron, Ainab, Lebanon

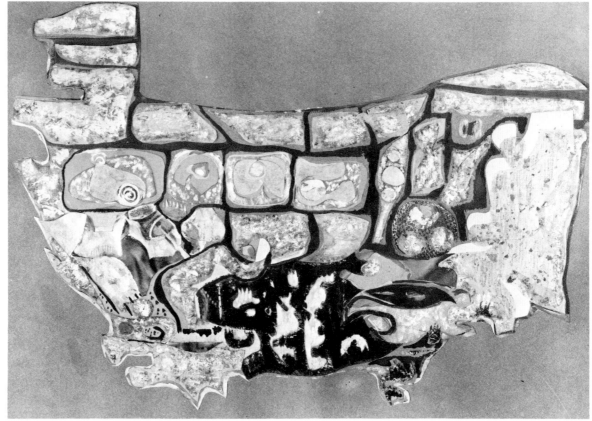

FRANÇOIS STAHLY
THE FOREST, 1967, 280 × 300
Woven by the artist

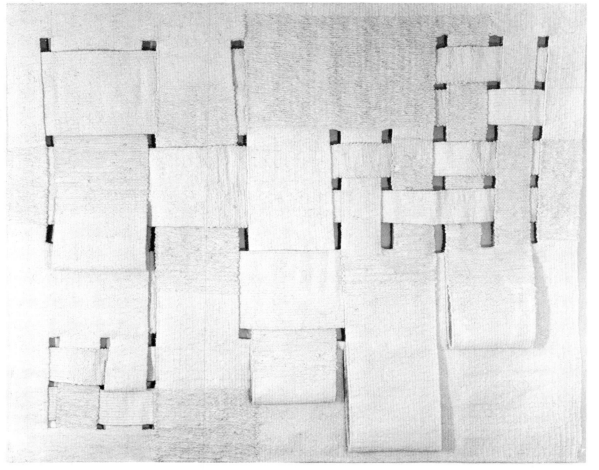

HERMAN SCHOLTEN
THE MIRROR, 1966, 215 × 255
Woven by the artist

VICTOR VASARELY – ORION GOLD, 1968, 260 × 246 – Manufacture Tabard, Aubusson

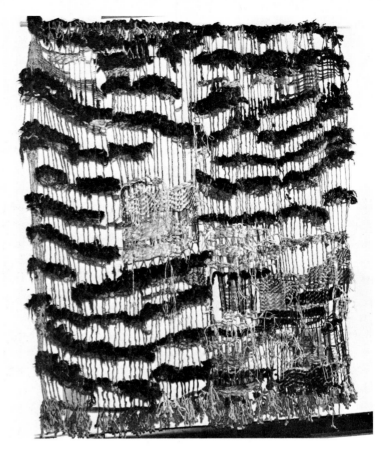

JEAN RIVIER
PASIGRAPHIE, 1969, 282 × 189
Manufacture Tabard, Aubusson

GUERITE FERA STEINBACHER
EASTER EGG, 1967, 276 × 184
Woven by the artist

ZORAVIA BETTIOL
CARNAVAL BANNER No. 1, 1968, 360 × 256
Woven by the artist

TADEK BEUTLICH – DREAM REVEALED (DETAIL), 1968, 230 × 225
Woven by the artist

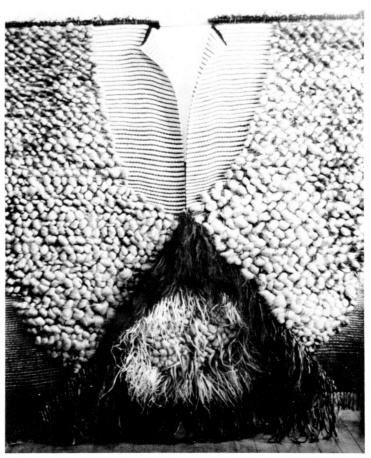

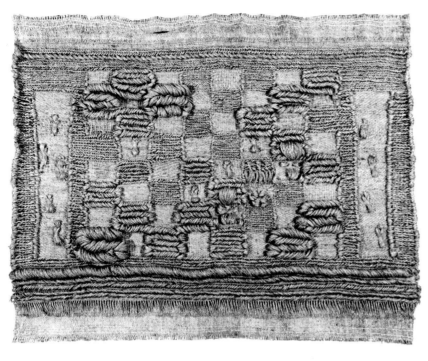

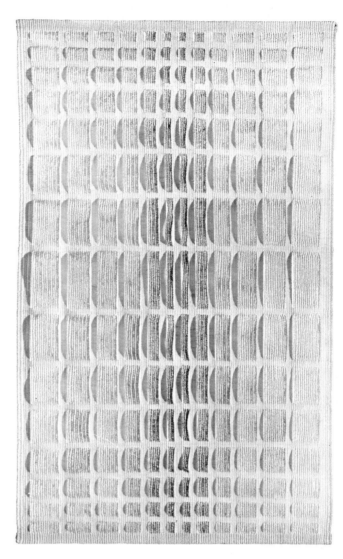

MARIA CHOJNACKA-GONTARSKA
THE KING'S MAST, 1968,
200 × 250
Woven by the artist

MOIK SCHIELE
TEXTILE RAUMSTRUKTUR, 1969
300 × 200
Woven by the artist

ALBERTO MAGNELLI
SATELLIC NATURE, 1969
425 × 525
Manufacture Nationale des Gobelins

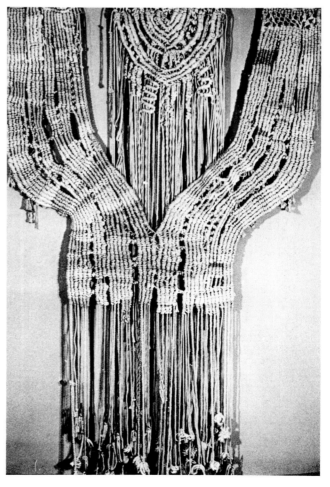

AURELIA MUNOZ
MACRA I, 1969, 290 × 180
Woven by the artist

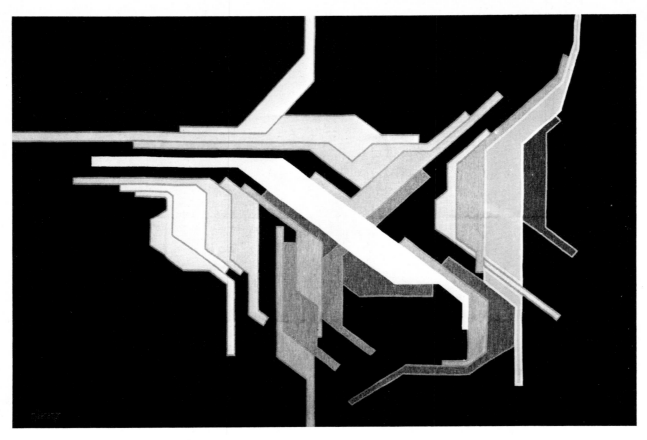

YVES MILLECAMPS — SIRIUS, 1969, 200 × 300 — Atelier Pinton, Aubusson

JOSEP GRAU-GARRIGA — SUN AND RAIN, 1967, 205 × 267 — Alfombras y Tapices Aymat, Barcelona

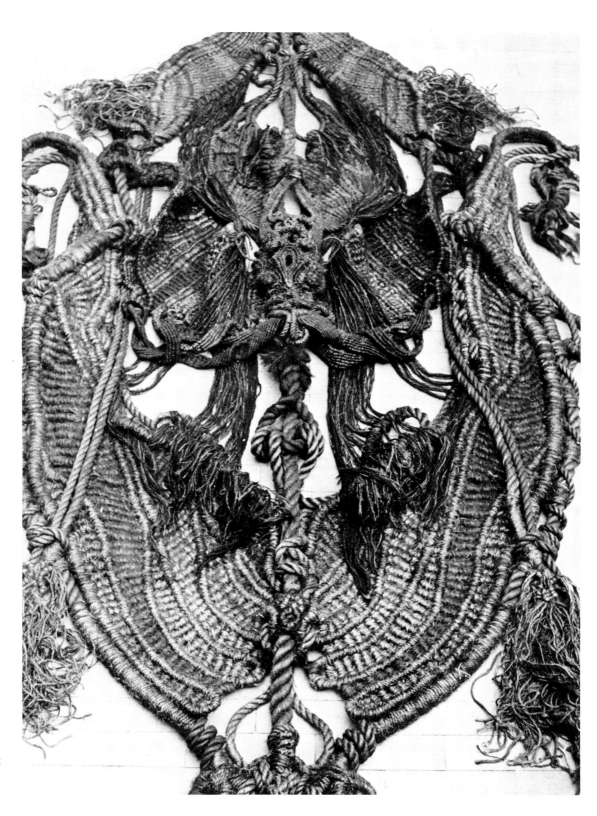

NEDA AL-HILALI
SUN SPELL (DETAIL), 1970-71
550 × 183
Woven by the artist

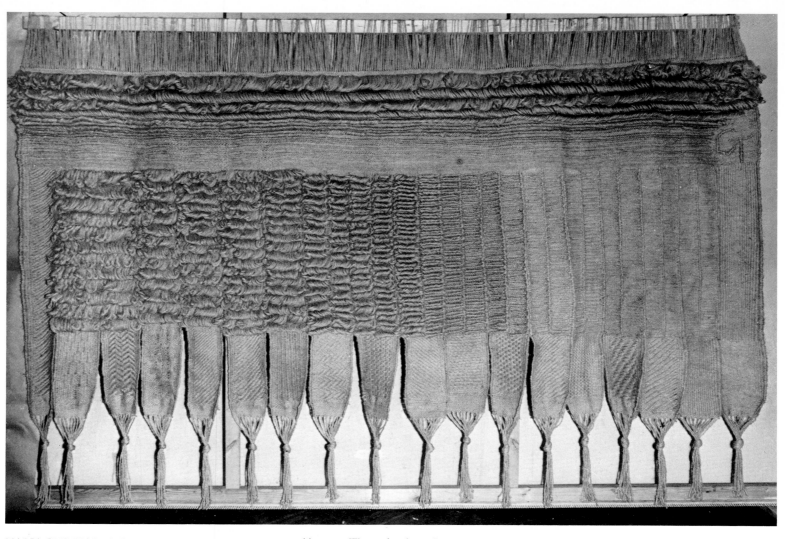

MARIA CHOJNACKA-GONTARSKA — SOUND, 1970, 227 × 330 — Woven by the artist

MEGGIE DIRKS — WHITE, 1970, 250 × 425 — Woven by the artist

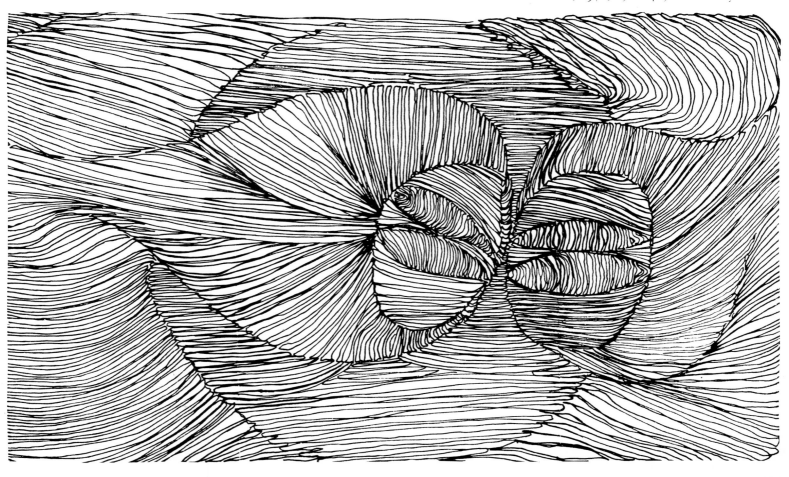

ANNE-MARIE MATTER
No. 32, 1970, 200 × 300
Woven by the artist

SANDOR TOTH
RHYTHM, 1971, 350 × 150
Woven by the artist

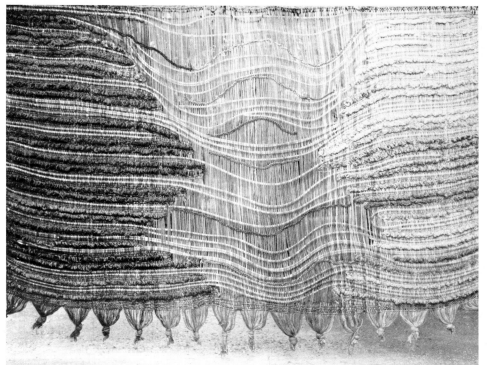

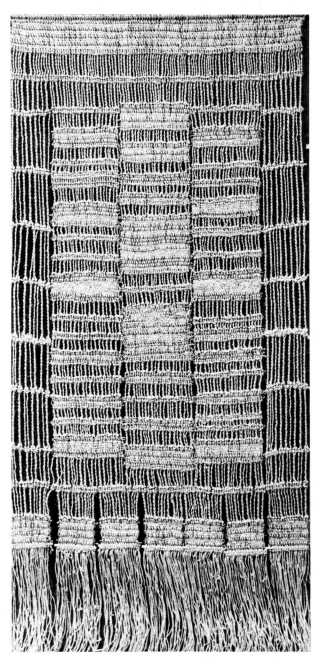

AURELIA MUÑOZ
PERSONNAGE, 1970-71
170 × 85
Woven by the artist

INGE VAHLE
VERSTECKE IN BABEL, 1970-71
295 × 350
Woven by the artist

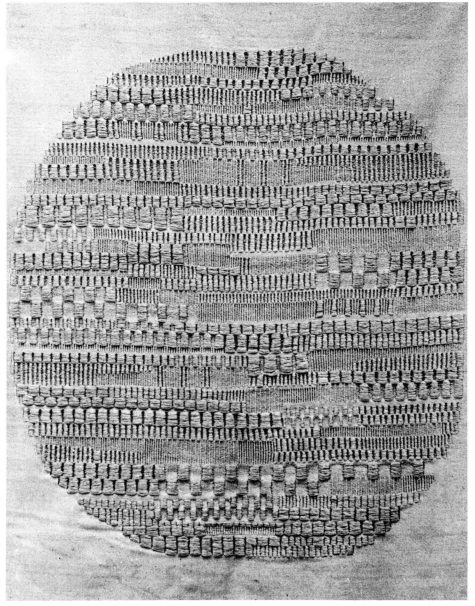

KLARA CSAGOLY
VOLLKOMMENHEIT, 1970
260 × 195
Woven by Edith Hanula, Budapest

BIENNIAL VI

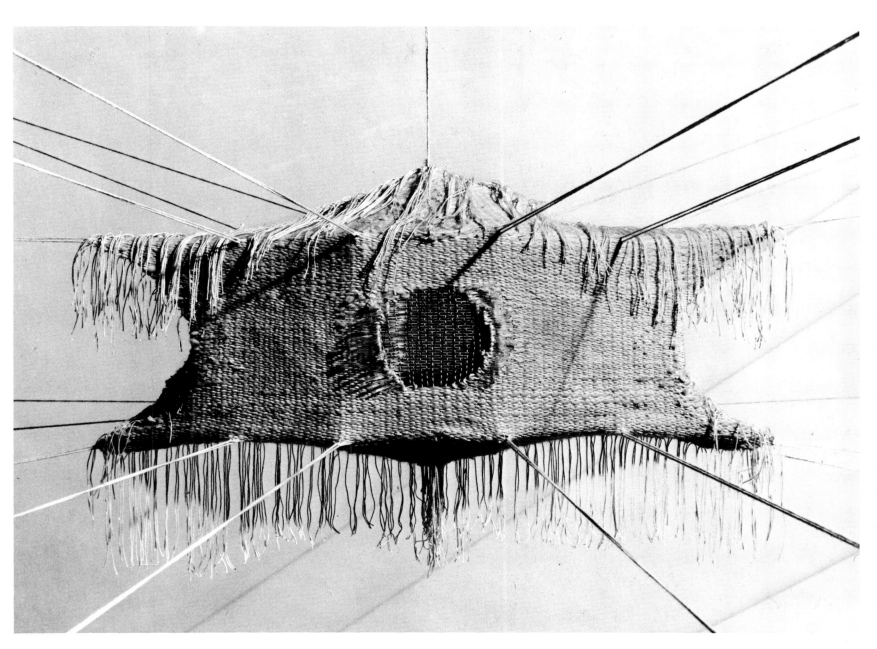

MARC BANKOWSKY — NACELLE, 1973, 300 × 700 × 300 — Woven by the artist

CHINAYA NAKAGAWA — ROOM DIVIDER
1972, 220 × 135
Woven by the artist

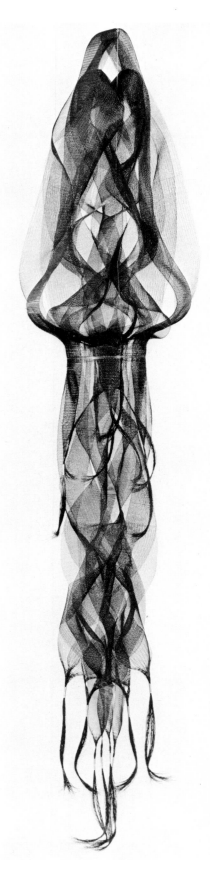

BERYL ANDERSON
THE FIRE TREE, 1972, 300 × 60 × 65 (3 times)
Woven by the artist

DANIEL GRAFFIN
A TRIANGULAR AFFAIR
1973, 600 × 640 × 50
Woven by the artist

◁ KAY SEKIMACHI
NOBORI, 1971, 229 × 48 × 48
Woven by the artist

RITZI AND PETER JACOBI
TRANSYLVANIA, 1973, 400 × 500
Woven by the artists

MICHIKO SAKUMA
A NEW PLANET (DETAIL)
1972-73, 30 × 300 × 400
Woven by the artist

URSZULA PLEWKA-SCHMIDT
ORGANIC STRUCTURE, 1973
500 × 300 × 200
Woven by the artist

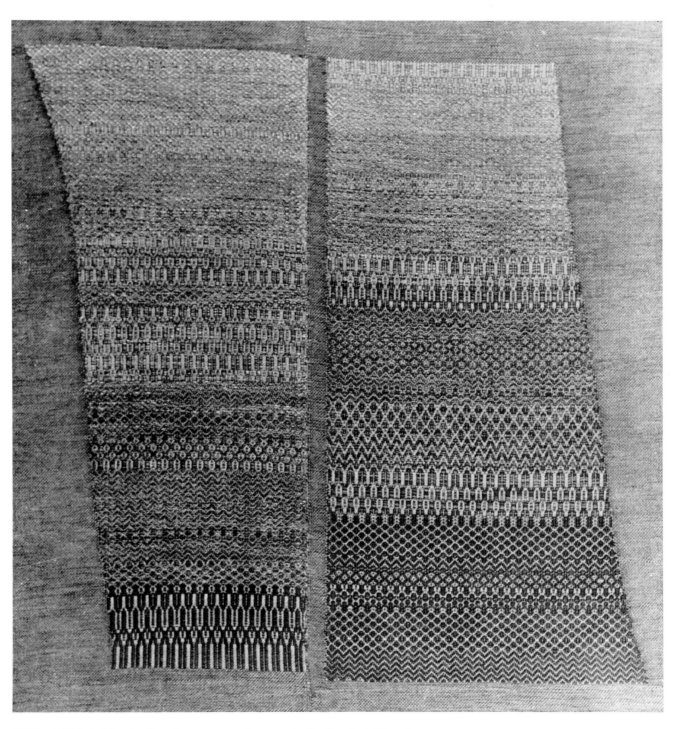

RENATA BONFANTI — ALGERIA, 1975, 250 × 200 — Atelier Bonfanti, Mussolente

FRANÇOISE GROSSEN — FIVE RIVERS, 1974, 225 × 244
Woven by the artist

RUTA BOGUSTOVA — MUSIC, 1973-74, 250 × 260 × 100
Woven by the artist

LIA COOK — SPACE DYED (DETAIL), 1975, 244 × 366 × 30
Woven by the artist

SHERRI SMITH — CORDILLERA, 1974, 244 × 244
Woven by the artist

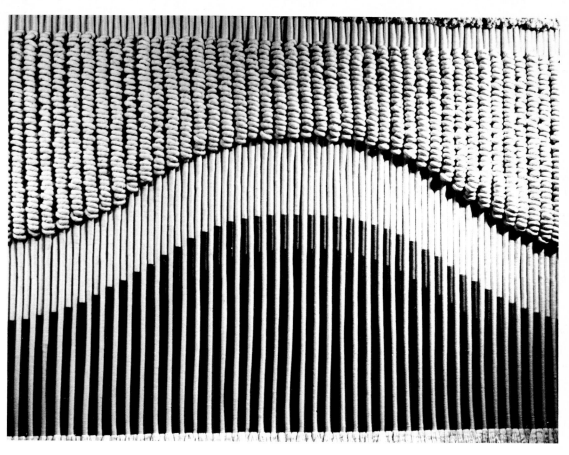

RYSZARD KWIECIEN – KASTOPLOT "PM", 1974
355 × 170
Woven by the artist

MIHOKO MATSUMOTO
MORNING GLOW R-3, 1975, 190 × 230
Woven by the artist

AKIKO SHIMANUKI – UNKNOWN GARDEN, 1975, 285 × 164 (2 pieces)
Woven by the artist

DEBBE MOSS – FOREST, 1972-73, 305 × 244 × 244
Woven by the artist

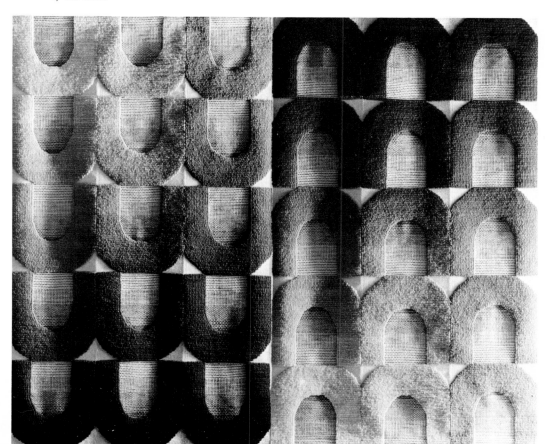

JAGODA BUIC
BLACK VARIABLE, 1974-75
350 × 600 × 100
Woven by the artist

GERHARDT KNODEL
PARHELIC PATH, 1974
540 × 1200 × 240
Woven by the artist

184

BIENNIAL VIII

AKIO HAMATANI – IN WITH LUCK, OUT WITH THE DEMON (DETAIL), 1976, 600 × 300

Woven by the artist

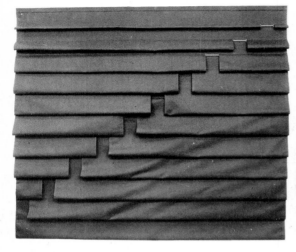 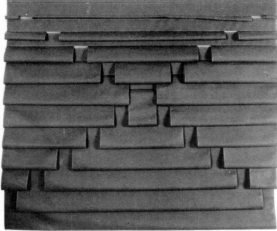 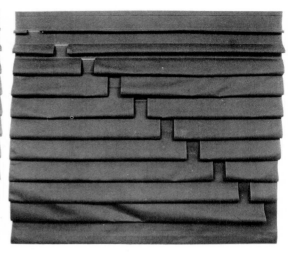

ROLF BRENNER – ZIPPER LX, X, XI, 1976, 180 × 200
Woven by the artist

FRANCES HELEN GREGOR – TOTEM No. 3, 1976, (10 times)
Woven by the artist

YOICHI ONAGI – A RED GLOVE, 1976, 220 × 90 × 270
Woven by the artist

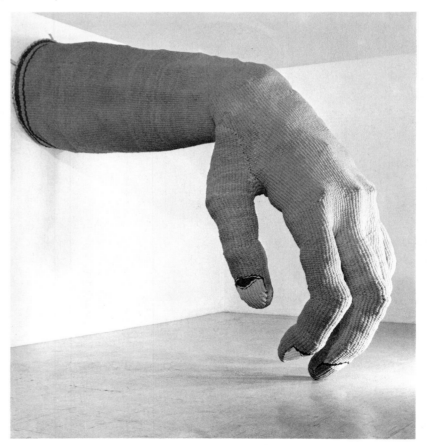

STEFAN POLAWSKI — THE MEETING, HELSINKI 1975, 1976, 180 × 304 — Woven by the artist

TETSUO KUSAMA — NO TITLE, 1977 — Woven by the artist

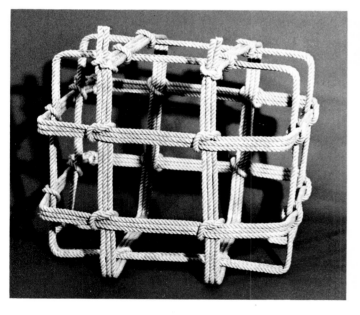

MORINO SACHIKO — ROPED AIR, 1976, 147 × 157
Woven by the artist

187

POLLY HOPE
INSIDE OUTSIDE
MARCH 25 IN GREECE
350 × 260 (twice)
Woven by the artist

188

THE
WEAVER'S ART

FRANÇOIS TABARD

Master Weaver at Aubusson

With the Collaboration of Jacques Brachet, Weaving Instructor at Sèvres

SHORT INTRODUCTION TO AN AGE-OLD CRAFT

Low-warp loom illustrating the old system of tautening the warp threads by means of a lever applied to the back roller only. This was a dangerous method because if the ropes snapped the weavers could be injured or even killed by the lever. The different parts of the loom are identified as follows: *a)* stay-rope holding the front roller to the loom; *c)* lever; *d)* rope for winding up the back roller; *e)* pins to hold the rope to the lever; *f)* iron pin on the front roller to receive the stay-rope; *g)* rollers; *h)* wood block to prevent the front roller from shifting. Today's looms are appreciably different from this one, which was in use at the Gobelins Manufactory during the 18th century.

All over the world, wonderful rock-paintings thousands of years old prove conclusively that prehistoric man knew how to decorate the walls of his home, even with the rudimentary means at his disposal. Some of his paintings and drawings have remained sheltered from the elements and are still as fresh today as when he laid down his primitive brush with a grunt of satisfaction. Unfortunately, the same is not true of the other accomplishments cultivated by ingenious men during the long darkness of the prehistoric period. But the cave dwellings were finally superseded by lakeside villages built on piles and, in the peat-covered remains of these homes, scraps of decorative woven fabrics have been discovered. Though not a treasure trove, the find nevertheless proves that weaving was known and practised even in those far-off ages.

Where and when did some industrious soul first hit on the idea of setting up two beams (vertically or horizontally) supporting two rollers and a whole series of warp threads, and then weaving another thread through this warp, right up to the selvedge and back again? Nobody knows, but on that day the art of weaving was invented and the fundamental process of tapestry-making was laid down for good. Ancient writings and remnants of fabric prove that weaving was practised at a very early date by the Egyptians, Hebrews and Greeks, and a painting found in the necropolis of Beni-Hassan (dating from around 3000 B.C.) is of the greatest interest, because it shows a high-warp loom very similar to those now in use at the Gobelins. It clearly illustrates the vertical warp threads stretched between two rollers, with the short rods which separate the even threads and the uneven threads into two series (the "back" and the "front" series, from the point of view of the weaver). It also depicts the heddles, or loops of thread passed round each warp thread of the "back" series, which enable the whole series to be pulled through to the front. The painting even shows the weaver's familiar comb with which he rams down the weft thread after it has made two or three journeys across the width of the warp threads and back again. In Latin literature an excellent description is supplied by Ovid who writes in the *Metamorphoses* (VI, 53-58): "Thereupon Minerva and Arachnae each set up her loom and stretched the smooth warp threads. The loom was completed by the crossbeam (roller) and the threads separated by the reed (the modern separating-rod). Now through the gap goes the shuttle bearing the weft thread, which is unreeled by nimble fingers, and beaten down by the teeth of the comb once it has crossed the warp."

Excavations and research work by archaeologists and historians have brought to light many tissues, some from China, others from Peru. But the finest, most interesting and most numerous are the Coptic tissues found in Egypt. These date from the first century A.D. and their structure is identical to that of present-day tapestries.

Very few crafts have weathered the centuries without undergoing at least some technical modifications, even if the basic methods, tools and movements employed have remained unchanged. It matters little whether the forerunner of the low-warp loom—probably of Eastern origin—came before or after the high-warp loom—used at a very early date in Egypt. Despite differences in the assembly

This engraving shows the interior of a high-warp workshop belonging to the Royal Gobelins Manufactory in the 17th century. The following key corresponds to the letters on the engraving: *a)* warp threads concealing the weavers; *b)* small board to avoid working against the light; *c)* large board to protect the tapestry already woven; *d)* top and bottom rollers, bearing respectively the spare warp thread and the woven tapestry; *e)* levers maintaining the tension of the warp thread; *f)* uprights, or side-beams; *g)* young man bringing a fresh supply of loaded shuttles to the weavers; *h)* workman cleaning a completed piece of work; *i)* workman winding up the lower roller; *l)* workmen winding up the top roller; *m)* workman fetching more shuttles; *n)* child carrying skeins of wool; *o)* woman winding skeins on to shuttles; *p)* spinning wheel; *q)* struts supporting the looms.

of the machine, the principle is always the same and the results achieved are identical. The only alterations worth mentioning are in the system used to obtain the tension of the warp threads.

A very clear illustration of the loom on which Penelope wove as she waited for Ulysses' return is given on an ancient vase unearthed at Chiusi and dating from 300 B.C. Here the loom is of the high-warp variety and the tension is obtained by means of weights attached to each warp thread. Later, in both high- and low-warp looms, the tension was obtained by rotating the roller carrying the unused warp thread, while the other roller, bearing the woven tapestry, was immobilized by strong ropes. The roller was rotated by means of a wooden lever, ropes and sheer muscle force (see reproductions from Diderot's Encyclopaedia on pages 190 and 192, showing the old method of "winding up" with the lever). However, there was always a danger of the ropes snapping and the workmen being injured, and the system was therefore improved. The lever was connected to the roller by means of an iron "sleeve" and the ropes were manoeuvred through a winch

fixed to the "side-beam", the other roller being immobilized by means of a ratchet-toothed collar encircling it and interplaying with a catch on the side-beam. A few of these old "bar-looms" remain at Aubusson. The system was subsequently modernized and the vital warp tension obtained in a different way. The distance between the two rollers was now increased by moving one of them laterally away from the other but without rotating it. This method is described further on in the section dealing with the "screw-loom".

Whatever the types of loom used over the centuries, however, tapestry textures have varied little. Like any other woven tissue, tapestry is composed of a warp and a weft. The warp, which is nothing but a skeleton structure, disappears completely beneath the body of the fabric. All that can be seen in a finished tapestry is the weft, made up of the different coloured threads forming the decorative scheme. However, the weft threads are not taken systematically right across the width of the warp, as in other tissues, but only across that part of the warp corresponding to the coloured area indicated in the section of the cartoon being woven. In other words, tapestries are woven in patches and several rows of the same colour are woven consecutively.

By virtue of its purely manual technique and basic independence of any purely mechanical aid, tapestry fulfills all the conditions required for the production of an original work of art. It is born of the collaboration between the artist who creates the cartoon and the weaver who translates the cartoon into textile matter—not with the cold precision of a machine but with his own personal understanding and his skill at bringing into play all the resources of his craft. This is one of the essential differences between true tapestry and the numerous other decorative fabrics produced at various periods of history on more or less mechanical looms which can work fast and produce many copies of the same composition, or, if need be, endless exact repetitions of the same motif.

We cannot always tell from descriptions of tapestries found in old texts whether these works are in fact true tapestries. Sometimes, embroidered work on an ordinary, plain fabric, and even brocaded stuffs, are incorrectly included under this description.

The surviving Coptic tapestries and the very earliest mediaeval works are true tapestries. But one of the most famous "tapestries" in history, the "Bayeux Tapestry", representing the Norman Conquest of England, is not technically speaking a tapestry at all, but an embroidery worked on a previously-woven cloth. During later centuries, the term "tapestry", usually accompanied by the name of the place of origin (e.g. Flemish, Aubusson, Gobelins or Beauvais tapestry) was quite clear and unambiguous. Today, however, the word is often wrongly used to describe all kinds of fabrics used for wall decoration, and in order to avoid the risk of confusion the term should always be qualified in one of the following ways: high-warp tapestry, low-warp tapestry, cross-stitch embroidery (or needle-work), machine-woven tapestry, printed tapestry or painted tapestry.

Of all the patterned fabrics devised by man over the centuries, tapestry, rich and luxurious, is in a category of its own. Its history is inseparable from that of society as a whole—in France at any rate—and it provides one of the most faithful records of the tastes, interests and modes of living of generation upon generation of purchasers. Precisely by reason of its close links with the history of civilization, the craft has known periods of mixed fortunes; it has risen to the heights of grandeur and has sunk at times into the fens of decadence. But it has always triumphed eventually over its financial or aesthetic problems, to flourish again.

Now, after a long period of decline, tapestry has made a dazzling come-back. Restored to its true functions, it brings a surge of colour, of warmth and of life to the severe and denuded architectural lines of the modern home. In public buildings, national monuments, embassies, churches and the halls of government, tapestry's monumental character and righful place have been rediscovered. The greatest museums and collections in the world have been enriched with tapestries recently by contemporary artists.

There is no shadow of doubt that a new era in the history of tapestry has begun. The revival started at Aubusson, and there also it grew and gained strength. And if today, as in the past, tapestry workshops are springing up or coming back to life in many other countries, credit must be given to Aubusson and to its generations of weavers who have preserved the traditions of this wonderful art intact throughout the centuries. We shall, in the following pages, try to analyse and define the rules of this technical tradition.

The detailed illustrations reproduced here show exactly how the warp threads were tautened in the high-warp loom. Fig. 1 shows two workmen, *a)*, winding up the top roller with the lever *b)*. Fig. 2 shows the mechanism employed: *a)* arrangement of the warp threads on the upper roller; *b)* large iron pin inserted into the holes in the roller and receiving the looped end of the rope; *c)* looped end of the rope used for winding up the roller; *d)* hole made in the roller to receive the pin; *e)* groove into which is fitted the iron bar securing the warp threads. Fig. 3 shows *a)* a workman rotating the lower roller in order to wind on to it the length of the tapestry which has already been woven; *b)* lower lever; *c)* upper lever released to allow lower roller to be turned. This type of loom is no longer in existence.

GLOSSARY OF THE PRINCIPAL TERMS USED IN TAPESTRY-MAKING

This system used for winding skeins of wool on spools has remained unchanged for several centuries. The engraving, reproduced from Diderot's and Alembert's famous Encyclopaedia, shows (left) the spool being turned by the spinning-wheel and, (right) the wool-winder which carries the skeins of wool.

Arras (place name). — Town in the department of Pas-de-Calais, France, where high-warp tapestry-weaving was practised during the 14th and 15th centuries. The craft was originally brought from Paris and the town rapidly became celebrated for the beauty of its work. The word "arras" is often used in old English texts as a synonym for tapestry.

Aubusson (place name). — Town in the department of La Creuse, France, where the art of low-warp tapestry-weaving has been practised for centuries. The origin of the craft at Aubusson cannot be traced with certainty. It is definitely known to have been practised there in the 14th century but according to tradition it dates back even further to the 13th century.

Bench, n. *(Low-warp weaving).* — Wooden plank used as a seat.

Band, n. — Narrow band often used for edging the beginning and end of tapestries. The band serves two purposes: it clearly outlines the tapestry and it receives the hooks or rings by which the tapestry is hung on the wall.

Bar, n. — 1. Iron rod used to secure the two extremities of the warp into the grooves of the rollers. 2. See Lever.

Bar-loom, n. — Old type of loom in which the warp tension was obtained by rotating the top roller (in *high-warp weaving*), or the back roller (in *low-warp weaving*) by means of the bar, or lever.

Beauvais, (Manufactory). — Royal tapestry manufactory founded by Colbert in 1664, now a National Manufactory. Following the destruction of its premises, the Beauvais Manufactory has since the 1939-45 war been installed in premises belonging to the National Gobelins Manufactory at Paris. Beauvais tapestries are woven on low warp-looms.

Bobbin, n. *(Low-warp weaving).* — Tool made of turned wood and loaded with wool or silk, used to pass the weft in between the two series of warp threads.

Boiling-point, n. — Dyeing at boiling-point means that the temperature of the dye-bath exceeds 100° C.

Border, n. — Decorative motif of varying importance framing certain tapestries.

Calibre, n. — Number indicating the exact thickness of a thread in terms of thousands of metres spun from 1 kilogram of the raw material. For example, the numbers 12, 16, 20 or 24 indicate that 12,000, 16,000 20,000 or 24,000 metres of the initial thread were spun from 1 kilogram of the wool or cotton in question. For wool and silk, the calibre number is preceded by another figure indicating the number of strands assembled in the thread. For example, 2/20 wool means that the thread is made up of two twisted strands of an original thread of 20,000 metres to the kilogram; 3/18 means 3 twisted strands of an original thread of 18,000 metres to the kilogram. For cotton, the calibre is indicated by the first figure and the number of strands by the second. For example, 12/18 cotton means an assembly of 18 strand of an original thread of 12,000 metres to the kilogram.

Canvas, n. *(Low-warp weaving).* — Thick canvas made of cotton, linen or hemp which may be fixed to each end of the front roller to protect the tapestry which is already woven and wound on to this roller.

Cartoon, n. — Full-scale plan on the basis of which the weaver executes the tapestry. The cartoon can be painted, numbered, or photographic.

Catch, n. *(High- and low-warp weaving).* — Small piece of steel swivelling around a pin and interlocking with the ratchet-toothed collar encircling the end of the roller, thus enabling the latter to be immobilized.

"Chevillon", n. Fr. — Wooden stick used, together with the spar (q.v.), for wringing out the skeins of wool after dyeing.

Clamps, n. *(High- and low-warp weaving).* — Small iron fasteners placed in the grooves of the rollers and used to fix into position the iron bars securing the ends of the warp.

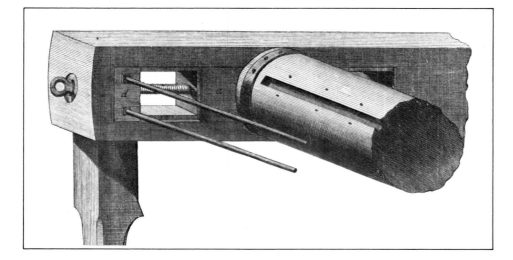

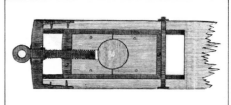

This engraving shows the relative positions of the roller, the side-beam and the slide-block. The worm-screw (see detail above) enables the roller to be moved laterally, without rotation, to increase the tension of the warp threads.

Collar, n. — Iron band encircling and strengthening each end of the rollers.

Colouring agent, n. — Dyestuff used for colouring wools and silks. In the old days colouring agents were of vegetable origin—madder, indigo, woad, logwood, orchil, etc., or even of animal origin—i.e. cochineal. Nowadays the dyes used are synthetically produced; most of them are by-products of the carbides contained in coal tar.

Colourist, n. — Name given to specialists responsible for sampling and matching and for supervising the dyeing process. The colourist must have a well-trained and sensitive eye able to appreciate and pin-point the slightest variations of colour.

Comb, n. — Weaver's tool, usually of box-wood, for beating down the double passages of weft thread into the warp.

"Corde", n. Fr. — Group of 4 or 5 skeins of wool, weighing about 550 grams, or just over 1lb.

Cords, n. *(Low-warp weaving).* — Short cords linking the section-rod to the heddle-bar.

Crossing, n. — 1. Gap made between the even and uneven series of threads enabling the bobbin or the shuttle, loaded with the weft thread, to be passed through. 2. Process by which the edges of two adjacent colour areas parallel to the warp can be joined together during weaving. This crossing technique eliminates the need for "relay" joins (q.v.).

Crosswise design, n. — Shape woven in the direction of the weft.

Cushion, n. *(Low-warp weaving).* — 1. Cylindrical-shaped pad about 2 ft. long by 10-12 in. across, placed by the weaver, when working, between the front roller and his thorax. The cushion serves two purposes; it softens the contact between the weaver and the roller, and it wedges the weaver into his place between the bench and the roller. 2. An oblong cushion measuring about 10 in. by 20 in., placed on the bench to make the weaver's position more comfortable.

Door-pieces, n. — See "Portières".

Dose, n. — Quantity of dye added to a dye-bath.

Double bracket, n. — Two wooden arms fixed above the dye-bath. From these, by means of the "lissoirs" (q.v.), the skeins of wool can be suspended as they are taken out of the bath.

Double passage, n. — Result of two passages of the weft thread between the warp threads. Superimposed double passages rammed down with the comb constitute the substance of the tapestry.

Drawing-board, n. *(Low-warp weaving).* — Board placed a few inches below the warp threads and against the front roller, on which the cartoon rests.

"Driadi", n. Fr. — Knotted stitch worked on two warp threads during weaving to strengthen and stabilize an oblique or curved line.

Dropping, v. — When the weaver is working on a "progression" in an unpatterned area, he has to "drop" threads, i.e. at each double passage he abandons one warp thread at each end of his working face. The superimposed double passages therefore become shorter and shorter and the woven area takes on the aspect of an isosceles trapeze.

Drum, n. — Cage-shaped reel used for unwinding skeins.

Dupion, n. — Raw silk of fine quality taken from double cocoons—i.e. spun by two silk-worms for one single cocoon.

Dyer's weed, n. — See Weld.

Edging, n. — Before beginning the actual weaving of the tapestry, a few passages are made of the same cotton thread as was used for the warp. Pulled very tight, this edging holds the warp threads parallel once they have been evened up by the weaver.

"Entrefenêtres", n. Fr. — Small strips woven specially to fit over or between windows.

Even, v. — To equalize the spaces between the warp threads with the aid of the pricker (q.v.), after the warp threads have first been mounted on the loom, or after one turn (q.v.) of the rollers.

Felletin, (place name). — Sister-town to Aubusson where low-warp tapestries are also woven.

Flat patch, n. — Part of a tapestry woven uniformly without relief modelling.

Floss, n. — Silk thread of second-best quality taken from the outer layer of the silk-worm's cocoon.

Fluff, n. — Accumulation of short wool fibres appearing on the surface of new tapestries and giving them a velvety aspect. The fluff disappears gradually after a certain amount of brushing and wear.

Freeing, n. — The final phase when the weaving is completed and the tapestry is freed from the loom by cutting the spare warp threads.

Gobelins, (Manufactory). — Royal tapestry manufactory founded under Louis XIV and now a National Manufactory, specializing in high-warp weaving.

Graduation, n. — Gradual transition from a dark tone to a light tone of the same colour, through intermediate values.

Grain, n. — Aspect of the tapestry determined by the fineness or otherwise of the warp threads.

Groove, n. — Long furrow hollowed out of each roller into which fits the iron bar securing the warp threads.

"Hachure", n. Fr. — Spike-shaped interpenetration of two colours, woven in the direction of the weft. Hachures are used to obtain colour shading and relief modelling.

Hatching, n. — Interpenetration of colours, akin to the hatching technique used in engraving.

Heddles, n. — *Low-warp weaving*: Short loops which encircle each warp thread on the loom. All the even-numbered threads are encircled by the same series of heddles, and all the uneven-numbered threads encircled by another series. Each series of heddles is linked through the heddle-bar to the section-rod which, lowered by pressure on the treadle, pulls down half of the warp threads over a width of 1 ft. 4 in. *High-warp weaving*: Only the back series of warp threads are equipped with heddles, the two series of threads being held apart by the separating rod. The heddles, fixed to the heddle-rods, are manipulated by hand and enable the warp threads from the back series to be brought through in front of the front, or fixed series.

Heddle-bar, n. 1. *(Low-warp weaving).* — Wooden rod to which are attached the heddles controlling half of the threads in a section of warp, and which is in turn linked by cords to the section-rod. 2. *(High-warp weaving).* — Piece of wood fixed above the weaver's head, parallel to the rollers, and supporting the heddles.

Heighten, v. — In dyeing, to increase progressively the density of a colour.

High-warp weaving, n. — The high-warp loom is characterized by the fact that the warp threads are stretched vertically. The heddles, placed over the weaver's head, are manipulated by hand, and the cartoon is set up behind the weaver.

High-warp weaver, n. — Weaver practising high-warp weaving.

Jack, n. *(Low-warp weaving).* — Accessory made of wood and metal, resembling a pair of scales. The arms of these scales are linked, above, to the section-rods and, below, to the treadles. The jack rides in the trough of the transom.

Ladle, n. — Kind of long wooden-handled copper ladle used to dilute the dye and introduce it into the dye-bath. Also used to stir the solution in the dye-bath.

Lay, v. — *(Low-warp weaving).* — To place the cartoon carefully into position on the drawingboard underneath the warp threads.

Lever, n. *(Low-warp weaving).* — Used in the old "bar-loom". Cylindrical piece of wood about 6 ft. long and 5-6 in. in diameter used to rotate the back roller, thus giving the necessary tension to the warp threads. The lever was made of oak and fixed at one end to the back roller by means of the "sleeve". The other end received the cable which ran through a winch.

"Lissoir", n. Fr. — Wooden bar resting on the edges of the vat by means of which the skeins of wool are suspended and moved about in the dyebath.

Low-warp weaving, v. — Weaving carried out on a loom in which the warp threads lie horizontally. The heddles are arranged underneath the warp threads and controlled by treadles.

Low-warp weaver, n. — Weaver practising low-warp weaving.

Madder, n. — Perennial herb yielding a red dye.

Marche, (place name). — Old province of France including the present department of La Creuse in which Aubusson and Felletin, with their low-warp industries, are situated.

Model, n. — Scaled-down draft often preceding the preparation of the full-scale cartoon.

Monochrome, adj. — Part of a tapestry in which the motifs are worked in varying shades of the same colour.

Mottle, n. — Result obtained in weaving by mixing on the same bobbin or shuttle several threads of widely differing colours or shades of one colour. Mottled mixtures enable many visual effects to be achieved; and they can be used to shade down from a dark tone to a light tone. For instance, the transition from black to white can be achieved by using the following successive combinations: 4 black threads; 3 black threads and 1 white; 2 black threads and 2 white; 1 black thread and 3 white; 4 white threads. The transition from pure black to pure white thus passes through three different greys.

Passage, n. — Interweaving of a weft thread between the two series of warp threads by means of the shuttle *(high-warp weaving)* or bobbin *(low-warp weaving)*. The two passages, completed after the warp threads have been crossed twice, make a double passage.

Pastel, n. — Plant yielding a blue dye.

Pin-head design, n. — Result of a weaving process which produces a tiny two-colour check.

"Piqué", n. — Weave in which threads of two widely different colours or shades are mixed on one shuttle or bobbin.

Plaits, n. — The prepared sections of warp thread which are plaited as they come off the warping machine.

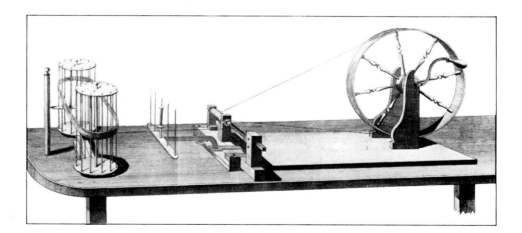

Another centuries-old type of spinning-wheel is used for loading wool on to shuttles and bobbins. It comprises a wheel turned by a handle, a rack which can receive several bobbins and a cage-like wool-winder.

Portee, n. — A portee comprises 12 warp threads. The fineness of a tapestry's texture is designated by the number of portees to the section—which is 1 ft. 4 in. of warp. For example, a 20-portee tapestry has 20 times 12 threads, i.e. 240 threads, over 1 ft. 4 in. of warp, which comes to 15 threads to the inch.

"Portières", n. Fr. — Small tapestry strips woven specially to fit over doors.

Positioning line, n. — Pencil line drawn on the cartoon perpendicular to the edge on which weaving commences, enabling the weaver to position the cartoon correctly. The positioning line must run exactly parallel to one warp thread.

Pricker, n. —Iron instrument used to even out the warp threads.

Progression, n. — Part of a tapestry under execution which is more advanced than the rest. A progression may be required either by the design of the cartoon, or else to prepare the way for working on the verges.

Pull, n. *(High-warp weaving)*. — Manual traction on the heddles resulting in the second crossing of the warp threads.

Rack, n. — Kind of wooden shelf fixed to the wall of the matching-room and bearing horizontal rows of short metal pins set at an angle. The pins are about 4 in. apart and receive the spools loaded with wool. This method of arranging the loaded spools according to their colour family enables the colourist to find a required tone with ease.

Rake, n. — Thick wooden rule planted with nails and used to help in setting up the warp thread on the loom.

Range (of colours), n. — Series of shades, from dark to light, of the same colour.

Relays, n. — Break in continuity of a tapestry when the edges of two adjacent shapes are parallel to the warp and the weaver has not used the crossing technique. When the tapestry is finished, the relays must be sewn together.

Repair work, n. — Operation enabling worn, destroyed or accidentally cut parts of a tapestry to be reconstituted. Repairs are carried out by needlewomen working at low looms, and consist of reconstituting, first, worn or cut warp threads and then the tissue itself.

Rippling, n. — Kind of waffled effect sometimes appearing in a finished tapestry and due to unequal tension on the warp threads during weaving. The most tightly stretched threads will contract more than the remainder, so producing rippling.

Rod, n. — 1. Separating-rod *(High-warp weaving)*. — A wooden rod used to separate the warp threads into two series, the "front" and "back" series. 2. Section-rod *(Low-warp weaving)*. — A wooden rod 20 in. long attached to the heddle-bar controlling a section of warp, i.e. 40 cm. width of warp.

Rollers, n. — Wooden or metallic cylinders whose axes rest in the side-beams. In *low-warp weaving* the two rollers are in an almost horizontal plane. On to the "back" roller—the further away from the weaver—is rolled the unused warp thread, while on to the "front" roller is wound the tapestry as it is woven. In *high-warp weaving* the two rollers are placed one vertically above the other, the top roller carrying the unused warp and the bottom roller receiving the tapestry.

Rolls, n. — Cardboard tubes used in place of spools, on to which cotton for the warp is wound after spinning.

Rosary, n. — Sample range of wools or silks corresponding to the different colours or shades chosen for the execution of a particular cartoon, strung together in little skeins resembling the beads of a rosary. For a numbered cartoon each little skein must bear a number or a sign corresponding to those used in the cartoon. For each cartoon, three rosaries are usually made; one is given to the artist, one to the weaver as a guide to the colours to be used during weaving, and the other is filed away for future reference.

Sampling, v. — Operation preceding weaving, consisting of choosing the dyed wools or silks corresponding to the different colours of the cartoon to be woven; the concrete result of the sampling is the rosary.

Scraper, n. *(Low-warp weaving)*. — Kind of small flat comb made of wood or metal with hooked teeth. It is used to insert the weft thread into the warp and pull it down against the already woven fabric after one passage of the bobbin.

Section, n. *(Low-warp weaving)*. — Unit of warp thread taking up a width of 1 ft. 4 in. The width of a low-warp loom is usually indicated by the number of workable sections—e.g. a 10-section loom can produce tapestries 4½ yards wide.

Selvedges, n. — Extreme edges of a tapestry. A distinction is made between the warp selvedge, which runs up the edge of the warp, and the weft selvedge, which finishes off the work at the beginning and end of the weaving process.

Separate, v. — During the preparatory warping process, to criss-cross the warp threads between the finger and thumb so that the even-numbered threads are separated from the uneven-numbered ones. The threads are then slipped off the fingers and on to the pegs of the warping machine.

Sequence, n. — See Set.

Series, n. — 1. The whole of the even-numbered threads, or the whole of the uneven-numbered threads, or else all of these threads together. 2. See Set.

Set, n. — A certain number of tapestries, hung side by side or near each other, dealing with the same subject or composed so as to form a homogeneous whole. Two examples are the Angers *Apocalypse*, and Jean Lurçat's *Song of the World*.

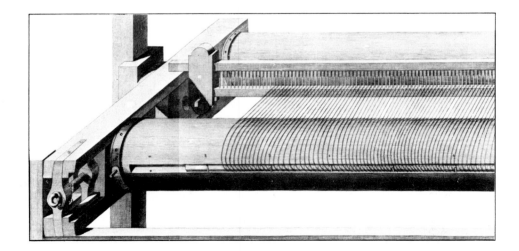

The rake is an accessory instrument used to help in mounting the warp threads on the loom. The threads are passed between the teeth of the rake and so are kept separate from each other during the tricky and all-important process of mounting the warp. (See page 215, figs. 1 and 2).

Sewing, v. — Operation of closing up the relay joins of a tapestry, after weaving, with appropriately-coloured linen threads. The work is facilitated by mounting the tapestry on a small, low loom and subjecting it to a moderate degree of tension.

Shrinkage, n. — The warp threads, tightly stretched between the rollers, contract when the tapestry is taken off the loom. This causes an appreciable shortening of the tapestry in the direction of the warp, and a much smaller contraction in the direction of the weft, known as shrinkage.

Shuttle, n. *(High-warp weaving)*. — Tool made of turned wood and loaded with wool or silk, used to thread the weft in between the two series of warp threads.

Side-beams, n. — Strong wooden beams forming the sides of the loom and supporting the axes of the rollers.

Sleeve, n. — In the old bar-looms, an iron accessory consisting of two rings fixed to the roller and through which the lever could be pushed.

Slide-blocks, n. — Apparatus whose essential component is a worm-screw, placed in each side-beam and enabling the back roller (in *low-warp weaving*) or the bottom roller (in *high-warp weaving*) to be moved further away from the front or the top roller respectively.

Spar, n. — Piece of wood shaped like a truncated cone, about 2 ft. long and used, together with the "chevillon", to wring out the skeins after dyeing or to twist them for storage in the stock-house.

Spare, n. — The length of warp thread left between the end of the tapestry and the reserve roller.

Stay, n. — Iron bar used in big looms to prevent the rollers from flexing under the pull of the warp threads. The stay is fixed down the middle of the loom between, and at right angles to, the rollers, thus keeping them parallel.

Strand, n. — Term used to describe the elements making up a thread.

Stripes, n. — 1. Crosswise stripes are obtained by double passages or a succession of double passages, regularly or irregularly spaced on their background. 2. Upward stripes are obtained by means of adjacent passages of each colour; they are necesarily regular and of the same minimum thickness as one warp thread.

Strut, n. *(Low-warp weaving)*. — Sort of buttress used to stabilize the legs of the loom.

Suite, n. — See Set.

Texture, n. — State of arrangement of threads in a woven fabric.

Thread (linen), n. — A fairly fine thread (No. 100) used to sew up "relay" joins.

Thrown (cotton), adj. — Cotton thread used for the warp, obtained by twisting several initial threads in a given direction, and then assembling them by twisting them all together in the opposite direction.

Transit shade, n. — Intermediate between two colours, obtained either by the use of a third colour or else by "hachures".

Transom, n. *(Low-warp weaving)*. — Wooden member supporting the jack. The transom is fixed parallel to the rollers below and about 20 in. away from the warp threads, and roughly mid-way along the length of the loom. Each end of the transom rests in a metal stirrup which is fixed to the side-beam.

Treadle, n. — *(Low-warp weaving)*. — Wooden pedals linked to the section-rods and heddlebars via the jack. By pressing down alternately on the two treadles the weaver can lower first one and then the other series of warp threads.

Treadling, v. *(Low-warp weaving)*. — Separating the two series of threads by depressing the treadle with the foot.

Trough, n. — *(Low-warp weaving)*. — Hollowed-out part of the transom in which rides the jack.

Turn, v. — 1. To wind a portion of the tapestry on to the front roller (in *low-warp weaving*) or the bottom roller (in *high-warp weaving*). A corresponding length of unused warp must at the same time be wound off the reserve roller. 2. To weave outside and around the contour of a motif.

Twist (cotton), n. — Cotton thread used for the warp, obtained by spinning several threads and twisting them together, and then twisting together two, three, four or more of these assembled threads. The result is an extremely strong and resistant thread.

Upward design, n. — Shape woven in the direction of the warp threads.

Vat, n. — Rectangular tank in which dyeing operations are carried out.

Verge, n. *(Low-warp weaving)*. — Kind of "no man's-land" of warp thread where two sections meet. To work up the verges the treadles must be specially harnessed so as to control simultaneously the appropriate warp threads of the two adjoining sections.

Warp, n. — The whole series of threads stretched between the two rollers, horizontally in the low-warp loom, vertically in the high-warp loom. It used to be made of linen or wool but is nowadays usually of cotton.

Warping, v. — Assembling the sheaves of separated warp thread on the warping machine.

Warp-mending, n. — In repair work, the reconstitution of worn or cut warp threads.

During the 18th century, the transom and the jacks were suspended above the warp threads. Nowadays they are placed underneath the warp. This arrangement does not in any way alter their function but offers the advantage of giving the weaver a freer field of action.

Weft, n. — Threads passed between the warp threads and completely encasing the latter. In the finished tapestry, only the weft remains visible.

Weld, n. — Plant used to obtain a yellow dye.

Wheel, n. — 1. Kind of spinning wheel used to wind off the skeins on to spools. 2. Kind of spinning wheel used to wind off the spools on to the bobbins.

Winch, n. *(Low-warp weaving)*. — In the old bar-looms, a small wooden winch on a support fixed to one of the side-beams. Working in conjunction with the lever and a cable this mechanism enabled the back roller to be rotated in order to increase the tension on the warp threads.

Window-pieces, n. — See "Entrefenêtres".

Wind-up, v. — In the old bar-looms, to stretch and taughten the warp thread by rotating the roller with the aid of the lever and ropes.

Woad, n. — See Pastel.

Yellow-weed, n. — See Weld.

BRIEF DESCRIPTION OF THE HIGH-WARP LOOM

Not a three-handed weaver but an illustration of three actions repeated in high-warp weaving: a) with his left hand the weaver pulls on the heddles to bring the back threads through to the front, while his right hand passes the shuttle; b) after each passage the wool is beaten down with the tip of the shuttle. c) Small heddle-bar; d) separating-rod keeping the front and back series of threads separate; e) heddles; f) warp; g) woven tapestry; h) shuttles of different coloured wools.

A radical improvement, carried out in the 18th century, replaced the old system of tautening the warp by a new system which was at the same time more efficient, more smoothly operated and less dangerous. Details: a) warp thread; b) side-beams; c) upright used for supporting the heddle-bar; d) separating-rod; e) and f) slide-block which, working with a worm screw, moved the lower roller laterally away from the upper roller, so increasing the warp tension; g) workman turning the handle so as to lower the bottom roller and tauten the warp. This new method replaced the old rotatory system (see page 192) which has now been completely abandoned.

The high-warp loom (see pages 191 and 192) is composed of two horizontal rollers, placed vertically one above the other and approximately 1.50 m. (5 ft.) apart. The rollers revolve around their axes which are supported by two strong uprights, standing vertically on either side of the loom and called "side-beams". Each end of each roller is encircled by a ratchet-toothed collar which interplays with a catch fixed to the side-beam. Each end of the axis of the lower roller rests in a socket provided in a movable block inserted in the side-beam—the "slide-block" (letter e, page 198). A worm-screw and a system of gears enable the two slide-blocks to be moved up or down simply by turning a handle, and this vertical movement tautens or slackens the prepared warp threads. Each of the two rollers has a groove running from one end to the other and into this groove fits an iron bar of the same length, held in place by small iron clamps. This iron bar, when fixed into position, secures the ends of the warp threads to the roller. The top roller holds the reserve of warp threads which is wound off as required, the lower roller receiving the tapestry as it is woven.

Next, the warp is divided into two "series" by means of a thin wooden rod—the separating rod (letter f, page 199). All the even-numbered threads are placed in front of this rod and remain free, while the uneven-numbered threads remain at the back and are each encircled by a cotton loop or heddle (e). The heddles are brought through the gaps in the front series of warp threads and attached to the heddle bar which spans the width of the loom at a distance of about 50 cm. (19 ½ in.) in front of the warp threads. It is fixed at each end to the side beams.

The outstanding features of the high-warp loom as compared with the low-warp loom are as follows: a) The warp threads are stretched vertically between the rollers; b) The warp is kept permanently "crossed" by the separating rods; c) Only the back threads are equipped with heddles; d) The loom has no treadles and so the traction on the heddles is effected by hand and not by foot. The high-warp weaver works with his hands alone; highwarp weaving is slower than low-warp weaving where the separating operation is performed by the feet.

Pl. IX.

Fig. 1.

High-warp weaver at work: *a)* pulling the heddles with the left hand and holding the shuttle with the right, ready to make one passage of the weft; *b)* the large heddle-bar, a beam which serves to support the heddle-bars proper; *c)* heddle-bars bearing the heddles each of which controls one warp thread belonging to the back series; *d)* ropes supporting the heddle-bars; *e)* heddles; *f)* separating rod used to separate the warp threads into two series, back and front; *g)* separating string; *h)* chain or cord used to maintain apart the back and front series of threads; *i)* large iron bracket supporting the heddle-bars; *l)* board raised to avoid working against the light; *m)* woven tapestry; *n)* shuttles of different coloured wools; *o)* comb used for packing down the weft threads after two or three double passages.

STUDY OF
THE LOW-WARP LOOM

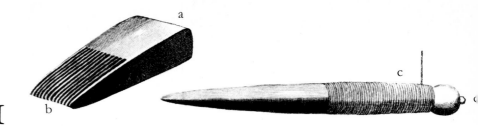

The low-warp loom (see cross-section on page 201), consists basically of two parallel rollers held in an almost horizontal plane by the two side-beams.

The distance between the axes of the two rollers is about 1.15 m. (45 in.). The one which is further away from the weaver is called the "back roller" and carries the reserve warp threads (1), while the "front roller", nearer to the weaver, receives the tapestry as it is woven (2). From each end of each roller protrudes a steel axis and around the roller's circumference at each end is a steel ratchet-toothed collar (3). Steel catches (4) are fixed to the sidebeam and when lowered into position interplay with the ratchets, preventing the rollers from unwinding in an inward direction. The axis of the front roller rests in sockets in the side-beams placed roughly 40 cm. (1 ft. 4 in.) from the front of the loom, and the axis of the back roller rests in metal carriages which slide along runners in the side-beams. A worm-screw enables these carriages to be

The weaver's comb, a) is used to beat the weft threads firmly down after two or three double passages; previously made of box-wood, these combs are now of plastic. The blade-shaped teeth b) are extremely strong. In high-warp weaving, the wool is carried on shuttles c); the tip of the shuttle is used to press down the weft after each passage; the other end d) is rounded to keep the wool in place.

The low-warp loom consists essentially of two rollers supported by two sturdy side-beams. The back roller (on the right of the picture) carries the unused warp thread, while the woven work is wound on to the front roller (left). The tension of the warp threads between the rollers is obtained by means of the slide-block, seen in the hollowed-out part of the side-beams, which can be given a lateral movement by means of a worm-screw. The cartoon, placed under the warp, is pinned to the drawing-board (seen to the right of the front roller). The hollowed-out member seen in the middle of the picture under the warp is the transom, and in its central trough ride the jacks. The jacks are linked below to the treadles and above to the heddle-bars and enable the weaver to alternately cross the even and uneven warp threads. The loom is firmly fixed to the floor.

moved towards the rear of the loom and the catch immobilizing the back roller is fixed to the carriage. The whole unit—carriage, runners, catch and worm-screw, constitutes the "slide-block" (5), incorporated in the rear part of each side-beam and serving to regulate the tension of the warp threads.

As in the high-warp loom, each roller has a longitudinal groove into which fits an iron bar held in place with clamps, and the looped ends of the warp threads are held on to the rollers by means of these iron bars. The rollers were often made of oak in the old days but are now usually made of pine. Their diameter depends on the width of the loom and can vary from 15 cm. (6 in.) for small looms carrying two or three "sections" of warp (0.80 m. or 1.20 m. width of warp—2 ft. 8 in. or 4 ft.) to 40 cm. (1 ft. 4 in.) for big looms carrying 20 sections (8 m.—26 ft. 8 in. of warp). A medium-sized loom with 10 sections (4 m. of warp—13 ft. 4 in.) will have rollers 20-25 cm. (8 in.—10 in.) thick. The warp is divided into sections. Each "section" is a slice of warp 40 cm. (1 ft. 4 in.) wide. The side-beams are made of thick pieces of wood (6) supported by strong square legs (7). As mentioned above, the side-beams serve to support the axes of the rollers—directly in the case of the front-roller; indirectly, through the slide-blocks, in the case of the back roller. The side-beams also support the wooden bench (8) at the front of the loom; as well as the "drawing-board" (9) which is held up against the front roller, underneath the warp. The "transom" (10) runs across the width of the loom under the warp and has a deep trough from one end to the other, into which fits the "jack" (11) linked to the section rods and the treadles.

Although there is no hard and fast rule, the most usual dimensions of the side-beams are the following: overall length 1.90 m.- 2 m. (6 ft. 7 in.-6ft. 7 in.); height from the ground 1 m. (3 ft. 3 in.) at the front, 1.20 m. (4 ft.) at the back. The bench is 70 cm. high (2 ft. 3 ½ in.), the distance between the axes of the two rollers is roughly 1.20 m. (4 ft.) and the transom is suspended 60 cm. (2 ft.) above the ground.

The side-beams are usually constructed of hard wood—either oak or beech—and the dimensions of the pieces of wood used vary according to the size of the loom. For small looms carrying 2 to 4 sections, the legs are usually 5 cm. × 5 cm. (2 in. × 2 in.) square and the side-beams are 25 cm. (10 in.) wide by 5 cm. (2 in.) thick. For big looms the feet are 10 cm. × 10 cm. (4 in. × 4 in.) and the beams measure 40 cm. wide by 10 cm. thick.

The loom is fixed to the floor by means of iron plates screwed to the feet of the loom and to the floor. The loom must also be braced by round iron struts with flattened ends. One end of each is screwed to the floor, about a yard away from the leg of the loom, and the other end is screwed to the leg itself, about a yard above the floor, The whole system—leg, floor and strut—forms a right-angled triangle whose hypotenuse is the strut. In the biggest

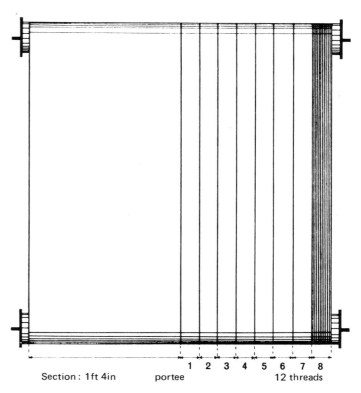

Section : 1ft 4in   portee   1 2 3 4 5 6 7 8   12 threads

The above diagram explains why a tapestry is always defined in the trade by its number of portees or units of 12 warp threads. The warp is divided into sections, always measuring 1 ft. 4 in. along the roller (in the diagram the roller carries two sections, or 2 ft. 8 in.). From the right-hand section it can be seen that this is an 8-portee tapestry, with 8 × 12 threads giving 96 threads to 1 ft. 4 in.

Description of the low-warp loom:
1. Back, or reserve roller; 2. Front, tapestry-bearing roller; 3. Ratchet-toothed collar; 4. Catches preventing the rollers from unwinding inwards; 5. Slide-block enabling the warp threads to be tautened by moving the back roller laterally away from the front roller; 6. Side-beams; 7. Leg; 8. Bench or seat for the weaver; 9. Drawing-board; 10. Transom; 11. Jack in the trough of the transom; 12. Heddles for even-numbered threads; 13. Heddles for uneven-numbered threads; 14. Heddle-bar; 15. Section-rod; 16. Cords linking the heddle-bar to the section-rod; 17. Chain coupling the arm of the jack to the treadle. 18. Treadle.

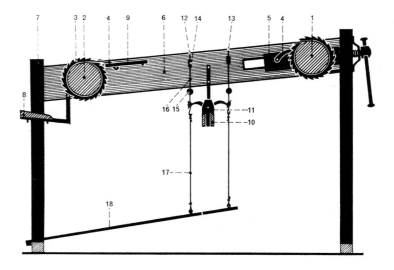

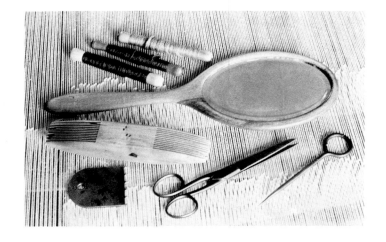

The low-warp weaver's tools laid out on the warp. In the top left corner are the bobbins, each loaded with a different coloured wool. The mirror is slipped under the warp threads to check the appearance of the right side during weaving. The box-wood comb is used to pack down the weft thread after two or three double passages and the scraper is used for the same purpose after a single passage. The pricker is used to even up the spaces between threads, especially when the warp is being mounted on the loom.

looms the two side-beams must also be linked by another iron rod which meets them at right angles and prevents any bowing movement.

MECHANISM

The warp is now tighly stretched between the two rollers and looks like a smooth level sheet. In each section, all the even-numbered threads are encircled, each by its own particular heddle (or loop), and this whole series of heddles (12) hangs down under the warp and is fixed round the corresponding heddle-bar; the process is repeated for the uneven-numbered warp threads which are linked by their own series of heddles (13) to their own heddle-bar. Each heddle-bar (14) holds a series of heddles corresponding to 1 ft. 4 in. of warp thread, and can therefore be used to lower half of the threads in one section of warp. The heddle-bars are linked with "section rods" (15) which are slung below them by strong cords (16). In the center of the section-rod is a hook which slips round one of the arms of the jack (11) (which is itself resting on the transom (10)). The uneven warp threads are linked, through the same process, to the other arm of the jack. Each arm of the jack is connected by ropes or chains (17) to one of the treadles (18). In this way, one end of the treadles is always suspended by its chain, while the other end rests on the ground. When the weaver presses down one of the treadles with his foot, one arm of the jack comes down in a see-saw movement and lowers half of the warp threads in the section (for example, the even series). This creates the gap for the bobbin to be taken through. Then the weaver depresses the other treadle, which lets the even threads resume their place and lowers the uneven threads for the second passage of the bobbin.

Underneath a low-warp loom (left). The photograph clearly shows the mechanism by which the even and uneven threads are alternately lowered by the weaver. In the lower foreground are the two treadles, each of which is coupled by a chain to one of the arms of the jack, which is itself set in the trough of the transom. Higher up the arms of the jack are seen linked to the section-rods, which are in turn attached to the heddle-bars. Each section-rod thus controls half of the threads in the section—either the even half or the uneven half. By depressing the treadles the weaver is able to cross the warp threads and make a gap to take the bobbin through.

TEXTURES—
AND HOW TO VARY THEM

Although the warp disappears completely into the body of the tapestry, its essential role being to support the weft, it nevertheless exerts a direct influence on the look of the tapestry since it determines the texture or "grain". The thicker the warp thread, the coarser the "grain" and the more noticeable the "ribs" of the tapestry. This statement, however, should not be taken as meaning that the thickness of the warp threads can be chosen arbitrarily simply in order to obtain a coarse or a fine texture. Other purely technical considerations come into play and the cartoon-painter must be acquainted with them before he begins on his cartoon.

First of all, the thickness of the warp threads determines the distance between these threads. In this way, a coarse thread will result in a density of, for example, three threads to the centimetre (10 portees (q.v.) per section of 40 cm.) while a very fine thread will give, say, nine threads to the centimetre (30 portees per section of 40 cm.). The calibre of warp threads is also correlated to that of the weft, and to obtain a normal texture, thick warp calls for thick weft, while fine warp requires fine weft.

Fineness of texture is not sought as an end in itself, either by the cartoon-painter or by the weaver. But the calibre of the warp and weft threads—on which the tapestry's fineness depends—must be chosen according to the simplicity or otherwise of the cartoon.

If the tapestry is a big one, intended to cover a large wall area, and if the cartoon is broadly painted without too much small detail, then the coarsest possible texture should be chosen. On the other hand, an intricate design intended for a small-sized tapestry will demand the use of a finer texture.

A fairly coarse texture which catches the light well and shows off the beauty of the wool gives tapestry its true character; the cartoon-painter should, therefore, bear this fact in mind and design his cartoon accordingly. However, the choice of texture is important not only from the aesthetic, but also from the financial point of view. A fine texture takes longer to weave and so is more expensive, and since tapestry is in any event a relatively costly fabric,

this point should not be overlooked—particularly so as for once financial and aesthetic considerations fall into perfect harmony!

This essential question of texture, therefore, has to be taken into consideration from the very outset, when the cartoon is being designed. And because the warp is the determining element in the fineness of the texture, its nature should be clearly understood.

The warp is divided into a certain number of "sections", each considered as a unit and each taking up a width of warp threads corresponding to 40 cm. (1 ft. 4 in.). The warp threads, divided into two series (even and uneven) can be alternately lowered and raised by means of the treadles acting through the heddle-bars.

The section is composed of a certain number of "portees", each portee invariably containing 12 warp threads. In technical terms, the "fineness" of a tapestry is traditionally designated by the number of portees making up a section of the warp. For example, a tapestry with twenty portees has twenty times twelve threads to forty centimetres, which comes out to six threads to the centimetre.

A very wide range of textures is available, varying from eight portees or 2 ½ threads per centimetre, up to 33 portees, or ten threads per centimetre. The most commonly used textures range from about ten portees to thirty portees i.e.

10 portees, i.e. 120 threads per section	viz. 3 threads per cm.
13 portees, i.e. 156 threads per section	viz. 4 threads per cm.
16 portees, i.e. 192 threads per section	viz. 4 $8/10$ threads per cm.
18 portees, i.e. 216 threads per section	viz. 5 $4/10$ threads per cm.
20 portees, i.e. 240 threads per section	viz. 6 $4/10$ threads per cm.
22 portees, i.e. 264 threads per section	viz. 6 $6/10$ threads per cm.
25 portees, i.e. 300 threads per section	viz. 7 $5/10$ threads per cm.
27 portees, i.e. 324 threads per section	viz. 8 $1/10$ threads per cm.
30 portees, i.e. 360 threads per section	viz. 9 threads per cm.

Very coarse textures of eight and ten portees, in which only the simplest and broadest designs can be correctly rendered, are used mainly for carpet-making, rarely for wall tapestries. Sixteen portees is the texture most often used for weaving cartoons by contemporary designers, and thirteen portees is also perfectly suitable for large-scale

A. 10-portee tapestry, i.e. 120 threads per section (40 cm.—1 ft. 4 in.), or 3 threads per cm. (7 ½ per inch). Texture used for floor carpeting.

B. 15-portee tapestry, i.e. 180 threads per section, or 4 ½ threads per cm. (11 per inch). Texture often used for tapestries with simple designs.

C. 18-portee tapestry, i.e. 216 threads per section, or 5 4/10 threads per cm. (13 ½ per inch). Texture used for cartoons with small details.

D. 20-portee tapestry, i.e. 240 threads per section, or 6 4/10 threads per cm. (16 per inch). The same remark applies as for 18-portee tapestries.

To appreciate the different textures now being used in tapestry making, the reader must consider the unit of warp thread known as a section (40 cm. or 1 ft. 4 in.). Each section consists of a certain number of portees, each portee comprising 12 warp threads. The more portees there are in a section, the more threads there will be per 40 cm. and *ipso facto* the finer the tapestry's texture will be. This is why the texture of a tapestry is usually indicated by the number of portees per section. Four examples are given (left).

hangings if the cartoon is sufficiently simple. However, intricate designs full of small detail may require textures of 18 to 20 portees. Fine textures of twenty-two to thirty portees are never used except for reproductions of 17th- and 18th-century works, for chair covers and for certain imitations of paintings.

Warp threads are normally made of thrown or twisted cotton, spun to the thicknesses appropriate to the different textures

12/18 for 8-10 portees	24/8 for 22 portees
12/12 for 13 portees	34/9 for 25 portees
12/9 for 13 portees	14/6 for 27 portees
24/12 for 18 portees	16/6 for 30 portees
24/10 for 20 portees	24/6 for 33 portees

The first indicates the calibre in terms of thousands of metres to the kilogram of the initial thread; the second indicates the number of strands. 12/18 means that there are eighteen strands of a thread of 12,000 metres to the kilogram. (For wool and silk weft threads the two figures are given in the reverse order.)

Cotton, which is both strong and supple, is undoubtedly the most suitable material for warp thread. Linen, which has all the necessary strength, lacks elasticity. It is, therefore, heartily disliked by tapestry-weavers and very rarely used. Using wool for warp threads has been virtually abandoned, for two reasons. First, although both strong and supple, wool customarily was subject to attack by moths. Second, the warp threads, which must be tightly twisted, sometimes contracted unevenly producing a rippled effect.

The second element of the texture (the weft), however, is usually made of wool. Silk, which was often used in the old days in conjunction with wool, is rarely employed nowadays for contemporary tapestries. However, if judiciously used, it can in certain cases give an interesting effect of contrast.

Weft wool, originally spun by hand, was later replaced by machine-spun wool, which is more even. Nowadays, the wool used for tapestries is generally worsted yarn from

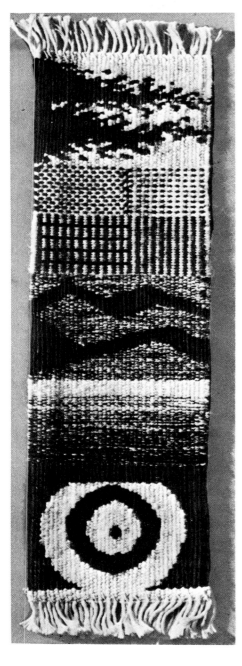

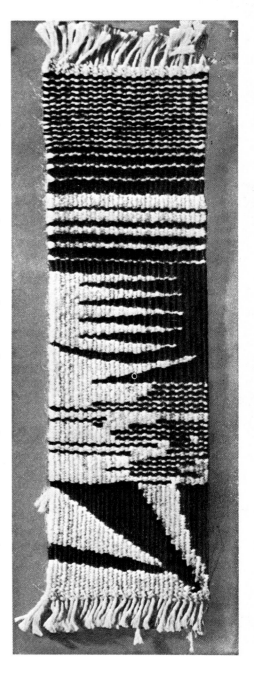

← Shapes with broken edges

50-50 stripes →

← Diagonal and straight pinheads

Stripes used for shading down →

← "Grid" stripes and ordinary
stripes, going up the warp.

Regular hachures →

← Shapes on mottled background

Irregular hachures →

← Mottle used for shading down

Hatching →

← Curved shapes

Slanting lines →

either Australia or New Zealand. Finely spun, it produces an extremely strong strand, a certain number of which are assembled to make the thickness of weft thread required by the chosen texture of the tapestry.

For example, 2/20 wool (in other words 2 strands of an original thread of 20,000 metres to the kilogram) can be used in the following combinations: 6 strands for a 13-portee tapestry, 5 strands for 16 portees, 4 strands for 18-20 portees, 3 strands for 22-25 portees, 2 strands for 27 portees, and 1 single strand for 30 portees. This system of assembling relatively fine strands of wool of the same calibre simplifies the question of supplies, since the same shades of the same wool can be used for every texture by adjusting the number of strands accordingly. Furthermore, strands of different colours can in this way be mixed so as to produce intermediate shades of the initial colours, or to obtain certain visual effects. The same process, of course, can be applied to finer threads such as 2/30 or 2/40 or coarser threads like 2/18, 1/14, etc.

The different qualities of silk, of varying lustre, which are used in tapestry are called fancy silk, floss, dupion or Chinese silk.

THE CARTOON

The foundation stone for the creation of any tapestry is, of course, the full-scale model, or cartoon, prepared by the artist.

A tapestry cartoon is not a picture and the cartoonist is not free to utilize all the resources and means of expression which are open to the pictorial artist. A cartoon-painter worthy of the name must discipline his art to meet the requirements of a particular technique, of a particular raw material and, naturally, of the tapestry's particular destination—mural decoration.

The shapes used in a cartoon must be precisely drawn, the boundaries of the different zones of colour clearly outlined and the change-over from one colour to another, or the interpenetration of intermediate shades, indicated by hatching or zigzag edges, which the weaver will interpret by means of spike-shaped "hachures".

When preparing his cartoon, the artist must, as already stated, bear in mind the texture of the finished tapestry, as this will limit the fineness of the forms designed. He must also consider the direction of the weave, because this will influence to a certain extent the general lines of the cartoon and will be the deciding factor in the weaver's choice of hachures, stripes or other means with which to interpret the design. For example, let us take the thinnest possible form, a straight line. If this has to be woven in the direction of the warp, it obviously cannot be thinner than one of the warp threads up which it will be worked, and this, in a texture of 16 portees, will give a thickness of 2 millimetres. If the line slants slightly across the warp, it will have to be woven in "steps" up successive warp threads and will finally consist of a series of short, juxtaposed vertical lines, jumping from one thread to another. In point of fact, however, weaving on one single warp thread is slow and bristles with difficulties; in practice a minimum of two threads are used for upward lines, giving a thickness of 4 millimetres, and always resulting in a "staggered" effect for slanting lines. By contrast, a contour woven along the direction of the weft presents no difficulty and one single passage of the welt thread will give a line less than 1 millimetre thick (still for a texture of 16 portees); while lines slanting fairly obliquely across the warp can be rendered with the greatest precesion and without apparent breaks.

It will be seen from the foregoing that the cartoon-painter should know;

1) That the outlines of his cartoon will be most easily and accurately translated into tapestry, if composed in the direction of the weft.

2) That the lines and shapes of his running cartoon in the direction of the warp will have staggered edges and that their minimum width will be limited to that of two warp threads.

3) That hachures, stripes and hatching indicated in his cartoon can only be worked in the direction of the weft.

To start his tapestry, the weaver usually turns the cartoon on to either its right or left side and works across it. In other words, in the finished tapestry, the warp will be horizontal and the weft vertical, and so all the hatchings, hachures and stripes must be indicated vertically on the cartoon.

However, if the majority of shapes and lines in the cartoon are horizontal, the weaving will proceed from the bottom upwards; thus the warp of the finished work will be vertical and the weft horizontal, but this will mean that all the hatchings, hachures and stripes must be placed horizontally in the cartoon.

The cartoon may be painted either in oils (but any effects of lustre or of impasto must be strictly avoided) or, pre-

◁ (Left) Fragment of a cartoon painted in gouache. Shapes used in tapestry design must be clearly set down, different zones of colour firmly outlined, and interpenetrations of tone indicated by hatching or zig-zag edges, which the weaver will interpret by means of hachures. The final texture of the tapestry must be borne in mind when the cartoon is being designed. Above all the painter must try to understand the weaver's working methods in order to express himself freely within—and despite—the limits inherent in weaving. A cartoon is a tool entrusted to the master-weaver; with it he must turn the designer's idea into a tangible and permanent work of art.

In his château of Saint-Céré, Jean Lurçat (above) works on a cartoon which is half gouached, half numbered. The numbered cartoon, perfected by Lurçat, avoids the danger of misinterpretation of colour by the weaver, because each number corresponds to one single well-defined colour. Of course, the same number does not correspond to the same colour for every artist who uses this method, but each artist must conform to his own system. In this way, Jean Lurçat has for the last thirty years used the same range of blues, numbered 50, 51, 52, 53 and 54, from the lightest to the darkest. The rosary of samples bears corresponding numbers.

207

This detail from a cartoon representing a game of Blind Man's Buff, after Fragonard, shows just how much the technique of cartoon-designing has changed during the history of tapestry-making. During the 18th century, the cartoon-painter produced a painted canvas which the weaver copied in every minute detail to make a tapestry as similar to the original painting as possible.

The system of the numbered cartoon is clearly illustrated in the detail below. Each number corresponds to a skein in the rosary or string of samples of the different coloured wools to be used during weaving. In this way the weaver cannot misinterpret either the shapes or the colours of the cartoon.

ferably, in gouache. It may also be drawn with great precision and the colours indicated by a number or a conventional sign corresponding to a dye previously selected from a certain range of wools (this method of the numbered cartoon is employed by Jean Lurçat). The numbered cartoon is efficient in that it forces the artist to set down the exact outlines of what he wants—every shape and every shade of colour being clearly circumscribed. It also guarantees against any misinterpretation of colour by the weaver, because every number corresponds to a specific dye; and it saves the artist the time and trouble of actually painting his cartoon.

One more method is also sometimes used—the photographic cartoon. Starting from a small-scale ("maquette" or "petit patron"), a photograph is taken and enlarged to the size of the future tapestry. This process considerably reduces the artist's work, but it has certain limitations. One is that the composition must be fairly simple. The other is that the model be exact down to the minutest detail. In practice, it is almost always necessary to make certain alterations or corrections of the shapes enlarged by this photographic process. Photographic cartoons are usually numbered or, if the tapestry is sufficiently small, the weaver can use the cartoon for the design and refer to the model ("maquette") for the colours.

On low-warp looms, the weaving is done from the back, so that the design of the cartoon will be inverted in the tapestry, which will look like the cartoon seen in a mirror. The artist must remember this point and the disadvantages which it can entail for his composition, especially for any caption or signature included. The latter will of course have to be written back to front and from right to left on his cartoon. However, if the artist has forgotten to take this inversion into account when preparing his cartoon, it is still possible to mend matters by making a tracing and turning it back to front. This tracing will guide the weavers for the design and the original cartoon will be hung behind them as a colour reference. But this is an irksome procedure, first because the tracing takes time and secondly because the weavers are considerably slowed down in their work, having continually to turn round and consult the cartoon for the colours. In high-warp weaving the tapestry is executed the same way round as the cartoon.

Another important point for cartoonists is to take into account the effect of shrinkage. Once the tapestry is off the loom a certain contraction of warp and weft threads occurs, resulting in an appreciable shortening in the direction of the warp and a much less noticeable shrinkage in the direction of the weft. Temperature, humidity, degree of tension of the warp and other factors influence this, so that the amount of shrinkage is never constant. On an average, however, the shortening of the warp threads is somewhere around 3-3 ½ cm. per metre (1-1 ¼ in. per yard), while for the weft it is no more than 1 cm. per metre (⅓ in. per yard).

DYEING

Before the weaver begins to prepare his loom the all-important dyeing of the wool and silk takes place. If the colours indicated in the cartoon can be correctly matched in wool, then the transposition of the artist's work into tapestry form is already halfway to success. And if the dyes used are resistant to the effects of light, then the colours—after the inevitable initial modifications over a certain period of time—will settle down for posterity into a pleasing and age-long harmony.

The great strides made in the art of dyeing have meant that vegetable dyestuffs—which for many years were the only colouring agents used—have now been largely abandoned. It is true that, some years back, the Gobelins National Manufactory reorganized a workshop specializing in the use of vegetable dyes, but their tests seem to have gone no further than the experimental stage. Virtually all the textile materials used in modern tapestry-making are dyed with the aid of synthetic products.

Manufacturers of synthetic dyestuffs, both in France and abroad, now offer a vast range of products, and all are subjected to a ruthless process of elimination. Each dye undergoes a laboratory study which determines its coefficient of resistance to the various wear factors it will encounter (light, washing, rubbing, etc.). Only those dyes which are most resistant to light—i.e. having coefficients of 6, 7, 8 or 9—should be used for tapestry.

Unhappily, there are a certain number of vivid and particularly beautiful colours which do not resist light. Ephemeral as the sunset, they must reluctantly but resolutely be banished, for time inevitably transforms them into lifeless twilight greys. Many of the more practised cartoon-painters by now have a certain experience in this field and take care to avoid using too-fragile colours. But new artists coming to tapestry-designing for the first time should beware of the danger lurking behind the use of certain innocent-seeming tones. The best thing is to consult a weaver or a dyer before embarking on a cartoon. Dyers work in several ways. Most often the master weaver gives them samples of wool to match the artist's colours or the sample will be taken from the standard range of colours employed by a particular artist. Sometimes the artist will provide a piece of paper or canvas on which are painted samples of each colour used so that the dyer can work from them direct.

The dyer has to use all his skill to produce a shade as close as possible to the sample, whether he is copying in wool a colour already existing in wool or taking a colour expressed in one medium and transposing it into another medium.

He must take into account the fact that, as a general rule, all dyes lose a little of their brilliance after a relatively short exposure to light before finally becoming stable. Moreover, after the completion of the weaving process, their intensity is slightly diminished because of the optical effect of the shadow created by the grain of the tapestry. For both of these reasons, dyers must usually heighten all their colours in advance.

Dyeing is usually carried out on the spot by dye-works attached to the weaving centers (Gobelins and certain private factories at Aubusson and Felletin) or by specialized dye-works which take in orders from several different factories.

The equipment of these dyers is generally quite primitive, because the great variety of colours and the relatively small amounts of each required do not justify large-scale mechanization. Modern "mass-production" techniques cannot economically be applied to such small quantities. Furthermore, when the dyeing is done by hand it is easier to check the fibres constantly during the course of dyeing and alter the composition of the dye-bath if the dye is not "taking" properly.

The different operations are performed in rectangular copper or stainless steel tanks, known as "barques" or "vats" roughly 60-65 cm. (2 ft.-2 ft. 2 in.) deep by 40-60 cm. (1 ft. 4 in.-2 ft.) wide and at least 50 cm. (1 ft. 8 in.) long. The bath is heated progressively to more than 100° C. The skeins of wool, grouped into "cordes" of four or five (weighing about 500 gr. or roughly 1 lb.) are hung over "lissoirs"—wooden bars placed with their ends resting on the edges of the vat enabling the skeins to be moved about in the bath to ensure an even and through impregnation. Though various dyeing processes exist, each one suitable to one of the various types of dye, acid colouring agents are most frequently used for

dyeing tapestry wools. Right at the beginning of the operation, highly concentrated "Mittin FF" (a Geigy product:
there are equivalents in Great Britain made on a penta-
chlorphenol base) is mixed into the bath to immunize the
wool against attack from insects.

To the dyebaths are added 10%-15% of sodium sulphate
and either 2%-4% of sulphuric acid or 5%-15% of sodium
bisulphite. The dyeing takes a bit more than an hour at
just over boiling point. With some colour agents the
wool is plunged directly into the hot bath, or even at
boiling point, while with others the wool is put in at
50°-60° C. The solution (containing only half the acid) is
brought slowly to boil and the rest of the acid is added
only after a half hour's boiling.

The dye required is placed customarily in the "cassin"—a
long wooden-handled copper ladle—then carefully diluted
with water and vigorously stirred into the bath to ensure
its equal distribution. Once the dye has been stirred in,
the skeins, hanging from their "lissoirs," are plunged
vertically into the dye-bath and must be constantly turned
around the "lissoir," each end of the skein alternating
inside or outside the bath. The dye is added to the bath
in successive doses, the first much lighter in shade than
the final tone aimed at. The colour is intensified by repeated doses and occasionally small quantities of different
dyes are added to modify or switch the colour.

Before the addition of each new colour dose, the skeins
are taken out of the dye-bath and hung up—still on their
"lissoirs"—over a "double bracket" made of wood, and
the dyer compares their colour with his sample and decides
how much more dye is needed. Then the skeins are put
back in the bath and the long turning process is repeated.
Once the dyeing is finished, the skeins are dipped into a
slightly acid bath and then rinsed in abundant cold water.
The dyer then wrings them out by twisting them tightly
between a "spar" and a "chevillon" (see illustration, top
left) and finally hangs them up to dry in the fresh air.

Dyeing operations are carried out in copper or stainless steel vats
in which the dyeing solution is heated rapidly to over 100° C. The
wooden bar used by the dyer to hang the skeins in the vat is known
as a lissoir. The skeins are constantly turned around the lissoir and
the colouring agent is added to the dye-bath in repeated small doses.
Before the addition of each dose of dye the skeins are taken out of
the bath and compared with the sample. They are then replaced
in the bath for a fresh dose of colour. At the end of the process the
skeins are passed through an acid bath, rinsed in cold water, wrung
out (above, left) and dried.

WINDING SPOOLS AND BOBBINS

Unchanged over the centuries and admirable in its simplicity is this device used for winding wool on to spools as and when required. The skein of wool is placed over a winder (right), and through the action of a driving-belt the wheel (left) turns the spool (centre) on to which the wool is wound. These spools, once wound, are placed on the storage-rack seen in the background.

After drying the dyed wool is stored in the stock-room, a well-lit room with special wall compartments in which the maximum number of twisted skeins can be stored in the minimum amount of space. In each compartment the different shades, from light to dark, of the same colour range are usually grouped. It is then a simple matter to find any given colour at a moment's notice.

When wool is needed it is selected from the stock-room and wound on to spools. This operation is usually carried out in a large "matching-room", which has one wall completely glazed in order to let in the maximum amount of natural light.

The other walls are lined with racks which receive the loaded spools. Spooling is still done with a primitive kind of spinning wheel. It consists of a large wooden wheel about 65 cm. (2 ft. 2 in.) in diameter which is hand-turned by means of a handle and connected by a "driving-belt" made of string to a little grooved pulley. This pulley is fixed to a steel shaft which receives the spool and which is rotated rapidly through the action of the wheel. The skein to be wound is slipped over two parallel cage-shaped drums which revolve around their axes and whose distance apart can be adjusted. The skein is stretched between these drums and can be wound off with ease (see illustrations, right).

For the weaving process, the strands of wool must now be assembled in the numbers required by the thickness of texture chosen, and wound on to the bobbins. These are slim, hollow reels of turned wood, 12 cm. (4¾ in.) long, swelling out and rounded off at the ends (see illustration, lower right).

The wheel used for winding the bobbins is similar to the one described above for the spools, the only difference being in the arrangement of the shaft on to which the bobbin is fixed. The number of spools used corresponds to the number of strands required by the weft thread. They are placed one above the other on thin metal rods around which they revolve, the rods themselves being supported by a wooden frame similar to that used for unwinding the skeins. The wool must be very tightly and evenly wound on to the bobbins so as not to create any ridges which might catch on the warp threads during weaving.

After spooling, the wool is wound onto the slender bobbins used by the low-warp weaver. The weft thread so prepared consists of an assembly of several strands (four in our picture) which will give the weft the thickness corresponding to the texture decided upon. With a weft thread of four strands, the tapestry will have a 22-25 portée texture. Such fineness is very rare nowadays.

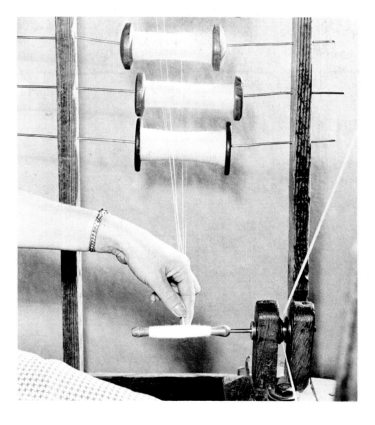

SAMPLING

Sampling, or the choice of different dyed wools corresponding to the colours indicated on the cartoon, results in the creation of the rosary, which is given to the weaver to guide him in his use of the different coloured wools. If the weaver is working from a numbered cartoon the skeins of the rosary are also numbered.

"Sampling" is the selection of all the wools corresponding to the different colours on any given cartoon which is to be woven. This is a delicate and crucial process, for it determines how closely the tapestry will resemble the artist's work, at least as regards colour. It demands an experienced and extremely sensitive eye, capable of discerning very subtle differences in shade.

The choice of a particular wool, made by a professional "colourist", is determined, naturally, by the exactness of its colour and depth of shade. But its relationship with neighbouring colours must also be taken into consideration, because a colour which looks "right" when seen by itself may look quite different (and "wrong") beside another colour. So, as the sampling proceeds, the wools chosen must be continually compared with each other and occasionally changed, where necessary.

The person responsible for sampling is known as the "colourist" and he chooses from from the bobbins of wool grouped on the wall racks according to their colour family and shade. If the colour sought is not there, it may still be found in the stock-room.

The thickness of texture chosen for the weaving of a cartoon determines the number of strands of wool in each colour thread. This mixing of a certain number of strands on the same bobbin enables even the most difficult-to-match shade to be reproduced in wool for, while no single colour may be exact, a mixture of several strands of widely differing shades may produce just the right visual effect. If judiciously used, mixtures of very dissimilar colours or shades can also yield special contrast effects such as "piqués" or "mottles".

Once the sampling is finished, small skeins of each colour selected are made and strung together to form a "rosary" (see illustration, left). Usually three copies of the rosary are made; the first is submitted to the artist for his approval and comments, the second is given to the weaver to guide him during weaving and the third is filed in the archives after being ticketed and indexed. If the cartoon is not painted but numbered, each little skein bears a number corresponding to a specified colour from a range of dyed wools previously chosen in agreement with the cartoon-painter.

PREPARATION
OF THE HEDDLES

Two series of heddles are needed for one section of warp thread; one series for the even threads and one for the uneven threads. Each series has, therefore, half as many heddles as there are threads in the whole section. The heddles, consisting of loops about 10 cm. (4 in.) long and made of strong cotton twist, must be regularly spaced so as to take up exactly 40 cm. (1 ft. 4 in.). They must then be linked and aligned by two threads of cotton twist whose ends can be fixed into small slots at the ends of the heddle-bars. In this way the whole series of heddles can be quickly connected to the section-rods.

To make the heddles, a small and very simple apparatus is used. One element is a small bench. Vertically placed at each end is a runner. The two runners can receive two square movable wooden bars which are secured to them by means of metal pins. When in use, the two horizontal bars are placed in a vertical plane one above the other a few inches apart.

Taken together, the two bars have eight sides and each of these sides is marked off into divisions corresponding to different numbers of weaving portees (10, 13, 16, 18, 20, etc.). With these eight different measuring faces the apparatus can therefore be used for the preparation of heddles for eight different textures.

Two strands of cotton twist are stretched along the upper surface of the top bar (this surface being the one marked with the appropriate divisions for the texture chosen). The operator takes a bobbin loaded with cotton twist and makes one loop around the two bars (lower right); the thread is pulled tight and fastened with a single knot to the horizontal threads (top right). One heddle is thus made.

Before making a second loop, the operator makes a series of knots similar to the first and designed to fill in the space between the heddles so that 6 successive heddles will occupy exactly one of the divisions corresponding to a portee. By the time the last heddle has been made, the whole series measures exactly 40 cm. and the thread is then fastened off before being cut. The bars are freed by removing the pins holding them to the runners and the series of heddles can be taken off ready for mounting on the heddle-bars as previously indicated.

The operator, shown here preparing heddles, has just made one loop around the two auxiliary bars and is finishing off the thread by making a single knot round the two threads which are stretched along the upper surface of the top bar (above). Afterwards she starts on a new heddle by making another loop around the two bars (below), then pulls the thread tight and fastens it off as before (above). Once the heddles are completed the bars are taken away. The double thread which was stretched along the upper bar is later fixed to the ends of the heddle-bars and each heddle is passed over the appropriate warp thread.

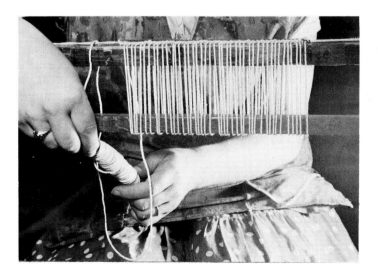

WARPING
THE THREAD

This operation, which precedes the mounting of the warp on the loom, consists of assembling into sheaves of a predetermined length the cotton threads which will finally become the homogeneous sheet of warp comprising the framework of the tapestry.

The warping machine used here consists of a square drum which revolves round a vertical axis, and a rack with 12 horizontal axes around which turn 12 bobbins loaded with cotton. Set between the rack and the drum is a vertical plank pierced by two superimposed rows of 6 holes, through each of which is passed one of the 12 threads. The threads are fairly taut and the passage through the holes ensures that they stay separate from one another. The sheaves must be precisely so prepared that the warp is separated up thread by thread and also portee by portee. With the aid of the thumb and forefinger and a slight backward and forward rotatory movement of the wrist (fig. 1), the threads are separated and then slipped on to the drum where two wooden pegs (fig. 2) replace the fingers and allow the hand to be withdrawn. The drum is then rotated and the 12 threads are wound like a tape around it. When the predetermined length of warp has been so wound on to the drum, the whole sheaf of 12 threads is taken in a figure eight movement around two more pegs (fig. 3), thus realizing the second requirement of separation portee by portee. The drum then reverses its direction of rotation and the threads are wound back to the first pair of pegs, where the thread-by-thread separation is repeated. The whole operation continues until the number of portees required, i.e. 10, 13, 16 or 18, has been obtained. Each complete rotation of the drum in either direction results in the creation of one portee.

Small cords are next slipped through the threads, in place of the pegs, and tied in such a way as to maintain the separation of the warp, both thread by thread at the one end and portee by portee at the other. This prepared unit of warp which, on the loom, becomes a "section", is then taken off the drum and plaited to prevent the threads becoming entangled. Fastened off and twisted up, this unit is called a "plait." The number of plaits made up corresponds to the number of sections required by the tapestry.

Warping the thread means separating the whole length of warp—thread by thread (all the even threads together, all the uneven threads together)—and portee by portee. Thread-by-thread separation is achieved by means of the thumb and forefinger (fig. 1) and a rotatory wrist movement. It is maintained by two pegs (fig. 2). At the other end of the warp each portee is separated from the rest by a figure-eight movement round two more pegs (fig. 3). The process is repeated in the reverse direction and so on until all the thread is prepared.

Warping the thread is the work of a specialist who hands over to the weaver the plaits of warp thread ready for mounting on the loom. From that moment until the tapestry is freed from the loom the work is the responsibility of the weaver—or team of weavers. The first step in mounting the warp consists of fixing it to the back roller by slipping the looped ends over the iron bar. The portees are spaced along the bar equidistant from one another and separated by the rake (figs. 1 and 2). They are arranged so as to take up exactly the width of one section (1 ft. 4 in.). Once the iron bar has been clamped into its groove in the back roller, the warp is almost completely wound on to this roller. At the other end of the warp the thread-by-thread separation is maintained by two tightly-stretched cords and the weaver cuts through the end of each sheaf of threads so as to be able to pass the threads through the heddles (fig. 3).

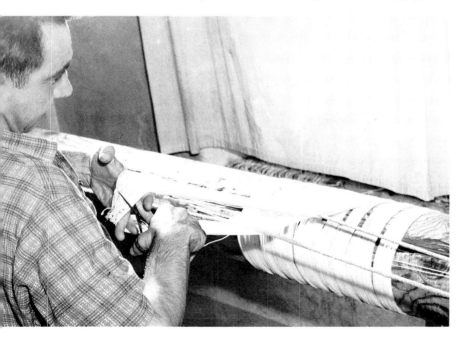

MOUNTING THE WARP

The loops at that end of the plait which is separated portee by portee are slipped over the iron "bar" of the back roller (fig. 1).

The portees are spaced out at equal distances along the bar in such a way that all the portees belonging to one section fill up 40 cm. on the roller (fig. 2); at the same time the portees are passed between the teeth of the "rake" (a temporary device only used for mounting the warp) and here also they are so arranged as to take up a width of 40 cm. (fig. 2).

Once the bar has been clamped into the "groove" made for this purpose in the roller, the whole of the warp is rolled on to this back roller. On arriving at the other end of the plait, which is separated thread by thread, the small cord used to maintain this separation is replaced by a rope, as thick as a little finger and tighly stretched between the two side-beams of the loom (fig. 3).

The rake, which has now fulfilled its mission of guiding the warp threads, is taken away.

Next, all the loops are cut (fig. 3) and the threads are slipped one by one into the heddles. All the even-numbered threads go into one series of heddles and all the uneven-numbered threads go into a second series. This task is carried out by two operators facing each other. One of these workers picks out the threads and gives it to the second, who passes it through the corresponding heddle (see fig. 1 on page 216).

The threads are now grouped 8 or 12 at a time and tied into a large knot, all the knots being evenly aligned (fig. 2, page 216).

The closed ends so formed are then threaded over the iron "bar" of the front roller (fig. 3, page 216) and spaced out in such a way as to occupy a width of 40 cm. along the rod, which is then clamped into its groove (fig. 4, page 216).

Finally, the threads are evened out with the "pricker", on both front and back rollers, so that the resulting series of warp threads occupies 40 cm. per section, with every thread equidistant from its neighbour (fig. 5, page 216). Mounting the warp is a delicate task which may take as long as two days.

To position the heddles, two operators work face to face. One of them picks out the warp threads one by one and passes them to the other who slips them through the corresponding heddles (fig. 1). Next, the ends of the threads are knotted in such a way that all the knots are evenly aligned (fig. 2). Then the weaver passes the iron bar of the front roller through the loops thus made (fig. 3) and evens out the loops over the width of one section (fig. 4). The iron bar is clamped into its groove and the worker then takes the pricker to even up the spaces between the individual warp threads (fig. 5). In practice, mounting the warp is carried out by a team of weavers. Four workers will take about sixteen hours to mount a sheet of warp thread 4 ½ yards wide (10 sections), but to this must be added the work of other weavers who help to position the heddles—1920 of them for a 10-section, 16-portee tapestry.

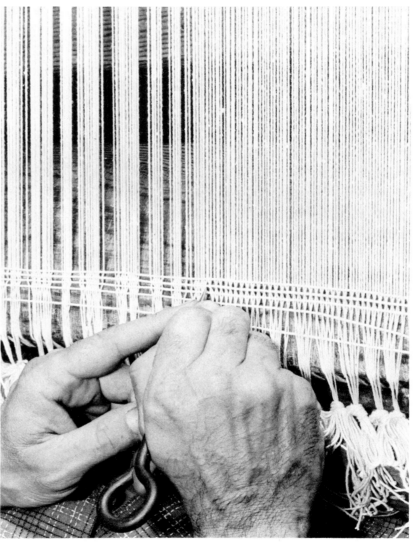

LOW-WARP WEAVING

The warp has now been mounted on the loom with the threads evenly spaced and the necessary tension obtained by manoeuvring the worm-screws at the rear of each side-beam. The weaver has next to put the cartoon into position by sliding it under the warp on to the drawing-board. The cartoon must be set in place with great care, the line marking its edge being exactly at right angles to the warp. Now the weaver harnesses the treadles. Squeezing under the loom (right), he sets the "jack" in the trough of the transom level with the section on which he is about to work. By means of the "cords" he links the heddle-bars to the section-rods, themselves harnessed by their central hooks to the jack. Lastly, each arm of the jack is coupled to the appropriate treadle by a rope or chain.

The beginning and end of a tapestry are traditionally marked by a thin band which can be left as an edging to the tapestry if the cartoonist has made allowance for it. If not, it can be turned back after the weaving is finished. So the weaving begins with this band.

When the weaver presses down on the treadle he lowers one series of warp threads. Taking in his right hand a bobbin loaded with wool, he slips it in between the two series, at the same time inserting his left hand into the gap at the other end of the section. Passing the bobbin from his right hand to his left hand, he draws it out through the left-hand gap (fig. 1, page 218), allowing the thread to unravel at the same time. The weft thread, which is now in a slightly oblique position across the warp, is held fairly taut, but not rigid, by the left hand. With his right hand the weaver pushes the weft thread into the warp and close up against the fabric already woven, by means of the "scraper." As the scraper advances, the left hand lets out the amount of thread required to enable the weft to take on the slightly wavy shape imposed by its passage round the warp threads (fig. 2, page 218). This first operation is called a "passage". Then the weaver depresses the second treadle to produce the second "crossing" of the warp threads, and repeats the whole process in the opposite direction, reversing the role of the two hands. These two passages are a "double passage" and from countless superimposed double passages the tapestry gradually takes shape. When the weaver has completed three or

When the warp is finally mounted on the loom, the treadles must then be harnessed. The weaver crawls under the loom and sets the jack in the trough immediately below the section he is going to work on. The heddle-bars are next linked to the section-rods and the section-rods are placed just over the appropriate arm of the jack. The jack is coupled to the treadles and so one treadle controls all the even threads in a section; the other controls all the uneven threads.

four double passages, he packs the weft down hard with the aid of the "comb" (fig. 3, page 218). The weft, in fact, must completely encase the warp which remains absolutely invisible in the body of the tapestry.

For weaving the band, or any other unpatterned area, the passages must be of the maximum length consonant with the correct execution of the movements described above, but not exceeding 40 cm.—i.e. the width of the section. In actual practice, for an unpatterned area extending over a certain number of sections, the width at the beginning of the weaving process is deliberately restricted to roughly 30 cm. Apart from the selvedges at left and right, where the weft in any case has to stop at the same warp thread, the weaver proceeds in a series of "progressions" by abandoning or "dropping" one thread at each end of his working area after each double passage. The superimposed double passages therefore become shorter and shorter and the woven surface looks like an isosceles trapeze in the middle of the section. Once the limit of the band or of the colour area is reached, the weaver must harness his treadles to the adjoining section and repeat the operation. After this, he re-arranges the section-rods, jack and treadles so as to be able to work on the "verges," that is, the part which overlaps the two sections. This unworked part also looks like an isosceles trapeze—but this time upside down (fig. 4, page 219). In each double passage, the weaver picks up the warp threads "dropped" during the earlier progressions, and so no break in continuity is left in the tapestry.

Once the band is finished, the weaver, still working alternately in the section or in the verges, tackles the actual motifs of the cartoon itself, peering through the warp threads at the shapes and colours indicated (in the case of a painted cartoon) or at the shapes and numbers marked (in the case of a numbered cartoon).

When the weaver is working on small shapes which only require double passages up to an inch or so long, he does not use the scraper but simply pulls the weft into the warp with his fingernail (fig. 2, page 219). In such cases the weaver generally leaves his left hand flat on the warp and picks up on his thumb at each "treadling" action a number of threads corresponding exactly to the shape being woven, while the right hand works alone at passing the weft and pressing it home with the nail. Some weavers achieve a skill, bordering on virtuosity, in this technique.

After having depressed one treadle, and with it one series of warp threads, the weaver takes in his right hand a bobbin loaded with weft thread and passes it between the two series (fig. 1). Immediately after this passage the weft is pressed snugly into the warp by means of the scraper (fig. 2). After two or three double passages, the weft thread is packed down hard with the box-wood or ivory comb (fig. 3). During weaving, the warp threads must be kept absolutely parallel: this is harder than it sounds and a major difficulty for beginning weavers.

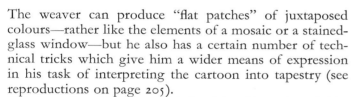

The weaver can produce "flat patches" of juxtaposed colours—rather like the elements of a mosaic or a stained-glass window—but he also has a certain number of technical tricks which give him a wider means of expression in his task of interpreting the cartoon into tapestry (see reproductions on page 205).

"Hachures", which are a kind of hatching shaped like elongated triangles, enable two or more successive colours to interpenetrate. For the tips of these "hachures" just one double passage is used and for their bases a number of double passages corresponding to the instructions on the cartoon. Weaving proceeds with the various colours which have to interpenetrate being worked simultaneously along the same horizontal "working face."

Certain kinds of colour graduation and many other effects can be achieved by using stripes of varying width spaced at varying intervals, the narrowest interval corresponding to one double passage.

The softened transition from one tone to another, and also certain intermediate colour effects, can be obtained by hatching, which is simply the interpenetration of successive double passages.

Pin-head designs can be obtained by alternating short double passages of, for example, black and white. The resulting flecks of colour can be superimposed to form a straight pin-head (or dotted pattern) or worked slant-wise to produce a diagonal effect.

Stripes going up the warp (necessarily limited in minimum

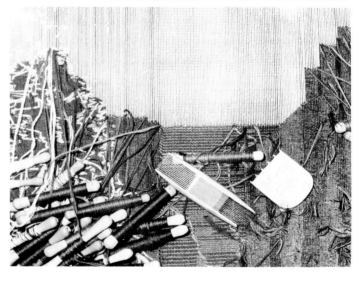

The master-weaver may put several weavers to work on the same loom, and these workers must of course synchronize their efforts as much as possible (fig. 1). When the weaver is working on small shapes, with short passages of an inch or so, he abandons the scraper and presses home the weft thread with his fingernail (fig. 2). Occasionally the line of junction between two shapes is exactly parallel to the warp; in this case, to avoid a gap (known as a relay) the weaver crosses over the bobbins carrying the two colours (fig. 3). To avoid breaks between the sections, the weavers work up in a series of steps or progressions (fig. 4).

width to the thickness of one warp thread) are obtained by alternating the colours concerned. A grid effect can be achieved by the same technique as for up-warp stripes, but inserting at regular intervals a horizontal stripe made up of an odd number of passages (3 for instance) of either colour. The use of "mottles" can produce many different visual effects and also gentle colour graduations.

When the contour separating two shapes is exactly parallel to the warp, the resulting break is called a "relay." "Crossing" is a process which enables these two shapes to be joined together during weaving. At the end of each double passage up to the line of junction, the weaver interlaces, or crosses, the bobbins carrying the two colours, which are thus joined by a loop, before proceeding to the next double passage (fig. 3, page 219).

Weaving alternatively in the section and in the verges necessitates, as we have seen, working up in progressions. The same technique may be required by the very design of the cartoon and by the distribution of zones of varying degrees of intricacy on the cartoon (fig. 4, page 219).

The only direct view that the low-warp weaver ever has of his tapestry is of the reverse, or the wrong side. However, so that he can have an idea of what he is doing, he is usually provided with a hand mirror. Parting the warp threads, he slips the mirror obliquely between the tapestry and the cartoon from time to time to check his work (fig. 2, page 220).

As soon as a few inches of tapestry have been woven, the cartoon—which was originally fixed to the drawing-board—is freed from the board and pinned directly to the tapestry. Up to the end of weaving the cartoon must remain closely fastened against the tapestry, though it is not wound on to the roller with the tapestry.

When the weavers have produced about a foot of tapestry, the fabric must be wound on to the front roller and a corresponding length of virgin warp thread unwound from the back roller. The cartoon is carefully pinned along a line about an inch behind the working face and all the other pins are taken out. The warp is slackened by manoeuvring the worm-screws controlling the slideblocks, the catches of the back roller are lifted and the completed portion of tapestry is wound on to the front roller. As soon as the heddle-bars have been slid back along the warp to their normal position the warp is re-stretched and the space between the threads on the back roller is evened up. This whole operation is known as a "turn." After the last "turn," which marks the end of the weaving, the tapestry is completely unwound and checked to make sure that the left-hand and the right-hand edges are of exactly the same length. If necessary, a small correction is made before the end band is woven. The warp is then slackened and cut a few inches from the end of the tapestry, which is unwound from the front roller and freed from the loom by cutting the warp close to the iron bar holding it to the roller (see page 223). This final operation is known as "freeing" from the loom.

The cartoon is pinned underneath the warp threads but the weaver can only see the wrong side of his work (fig. 1). He can check the appearance of the right side—but only in piece-meal fashion—by using a hand mirror which he slips under the warp (fig. 2).

HIGH-WARP WEAVING

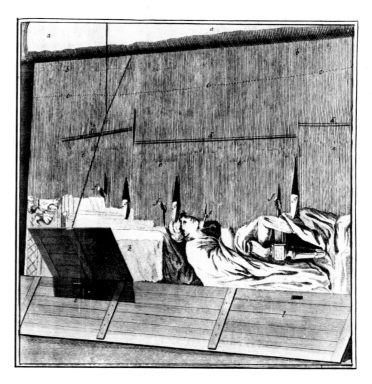

This engraving shows the arrangement of a half-finished tapestry on a high-warp loom, seen from the front: *a)* a piece of serge protects the warp threads wound on to the top roller; *b)* string to maintain the warp threads; *c)* chain or cord used to maintain apart the back and front series of threads; *d)* separating-rods; *e)* heddles; *f)* shuttle; *g)* comb; *h)* serge protecting the woven fabric; *i)* board to save the weaver from working against the light; *j)* large board to protect the tapestry already woven and wound on to the bottom roller.

The principles of high-warp and low-warp weaving are exactly the same; the same technical means of expression are used by the weavers and the final results obtained are absolutely identical. Technically speaking, there is no real difference between high-warp and low-warp tapestries. Yet there are basic differences between the two processes. In high-warp weaving, the warp is stretched vertically and the two series, of even-and uneven-numbered threads, are kept permanently separated by the separating rods. Only those warp threads belonging to the "back" series are equipped with heddles, which are brought through to the front and hung over the "heddle-bar"—a wooden beam fixed above the weaver's head and parallel to the rollers. The result of this arrangement is that the warp is permanently "crossed," the second "crossing" being obtained by hand traction on the heddles bringing the back threads through to the front. The heddles—made on the spot when the warp is mounted—are continuous over the whole width of the warp. In this way the high-warp weaver can work on any part of his tapestry without having to make any alterations in the disposition of his loom. For the weaving process, the weaver sits in front of the loom and, inserting his left hand between the two series of threads, draws towards himself the number of warp threads corresponding to the width of the shape he is working on. With his right he passes the shuttle through the gap from left to right, and taps down the weft thread not with a scraper, as in low-warp weaving, but with the pointed end of the shuttle. One passage being thus completed, he crosses the warp threads again by pulling down on the corresponding heddles, and passes his shuttle through in the opposite direction. Each new double passage is pressed home into the warp with the tip of the shuttle. When several double passages have been completed, the weaver beats them firmly down with the comb. One of the essential characteristics of high-warp weaving is the way in which the cartoon is used. Before starting on his tapestry, the weaver makes a tracing of the broad lines of the cartoon. Fixing this tracing temporarily up against the warp behind the loom, he copies off the design on to the warp threads themselves in indelible ink. This outline guides him for the measurements and principal forms of the cartoon, but for small details and colours he must refer to the cartoon itself, which is usually hung behind him. Like the low-warp weaver, he can use "hachures," stripes, mottled and pin-head designs and so on, and may also, as required by the cartoon, have to work in progressions.

It cannot be denied that high-warp weaving is slower than low-warp weaving, since in the case of the latter, the two series of threads are separated by foot-controlled treadles leaving both hands completely free to pass the bobbin and press down the weft. The high-warp weaver has the advantage of being able to check his work by means of a mirror set up in front of the loom, and of going round to the front as often as he wishes to inspect the tapestry in detail. He can see all, or a large part, of the cartoon whereas the low-warp worker only sees small fragments of his cartoon through the warp threads.

SIGNATURES AND MARKS

Whether a tapestry has been made on a high-warp or a low-warp loom, it traditionally bears the signature of the artist, the distinguishing mark of the workshop and sometimes also the year of production. Moreover, tapestries woven in the Gobelins or Beauvais National Manufactories also bear the names of the weavers responsible for the work (see page 193). Unfortunately, many old tapestries —especially Gothic ones—have no mark or signature. The different marks used enable tapestries to be authenticated, from both the aesthetic and technical points of view. In the past, however, counterfeits and copies were abundant, despite these precautions. At the present time, the artist supplies an additional guarantee in the form of a small tape or tab of material sewn to the wrong side of the tapestry and numbered and signed by himself.

MARKS OF SOME CONTEMPORARY WORKSHOPS

PINTON, FELLETIN

GOUBELY, AUBUSSON

PICAUD, AUBUSSON

TABARD, AUBUSSON

MARKS OF 15th—TO 18th—CENTURY WORKSHOPS

AUBUSSON
16th, 17th, 18th centuries

BEAUVAIS
17th, 18th centuries

AUDENARDE
late 15th century
and 16th century

BRUSSELS
16th, 17th, 18th centuries

M·R·DE FELETIN·P·M

FELLETIN
17th century

TOURNAI
15th, 16th centuries

GOBELINS
17th, 18th centuries

MORTLAKE
17th century

SIGNATURES OF SOME CONTEMPORARY CARTOON-PAINTERS

Prassinos

MARIO PRASSINOS

Adam

HENRI-GEORGES ADAM

Tourlière

MICHEL TOURLIÈRE

Lurçat

JEAN LURÇAT

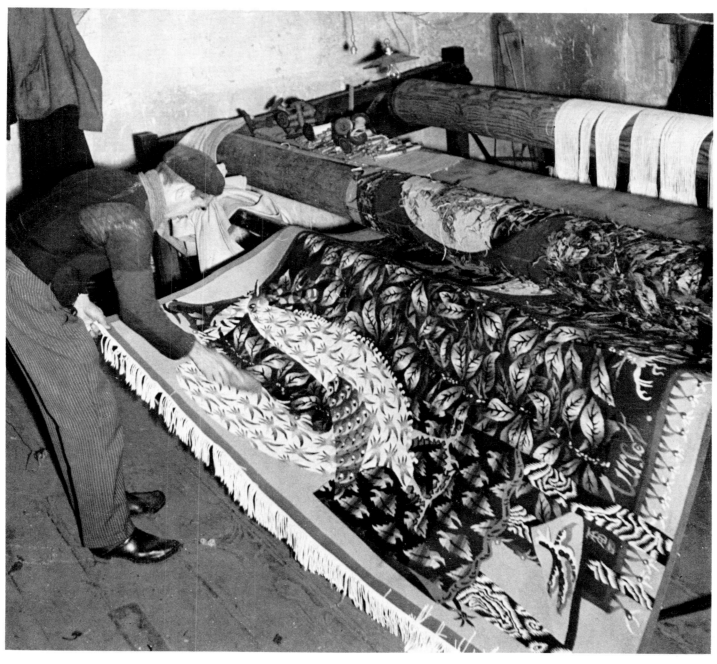

The weaver—like the painter—will not see the completed tapestry until the moment when the roller is unwound and the work cut free. This is the long-waited freeing from the loom. The tapestry is brushed and passed over to the needlewomen for the final touches.

SEWING AND IRONING

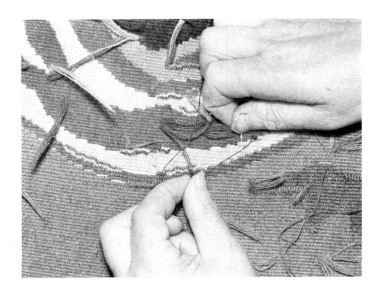

If, during weaving, the "crossing" technique, already described, is used, a certain number of "relay" joins can be avoided. However, the process of "crossing" is long and slow and cannot be used everywhere. Thus, when the tapestry is freed from the loom, it contains a large number of small slits which have to be sewn up. This work is carried out by specialized needlewomen. The tapestry is mounted wrong side upwards on small, low looms where it is subjected to a moderate degree of tension. All the existing gaps are then faggot-stitched up with linen threads matching the colours of the tapestry (see illustrations). The seam must be invisible from the right side of the tapestry.

The two ends where the warp threads have been cut are fastened off and generally turned back to form a hem. Next, the tapestry is briskly brushed to remove any fluff or fuzz which may have accumulated during weaving.

The final operation consists in ironing the work on the wrong side with a very heavy iron over a damp cloth.

When a tapestry comes off the loom, it invariably contains a large number of small slits which must be closed up before the tapestry is really finished. This is the work of trained needlewomen, working at a small loom on which the tapestry is subjected to a moderate degree of tension.

APPENDIX

BIBLIOGRAPHY

I. Bibliographies

GUIFFREY. J.
Bibliographie critique de la Tapisserie dans les différents pays de l'Europe depuis ses origines jusqu'à nos jours, in: Société des études historiques, 1904

MARQUET DE VASSELOT, J.-J. and WEIGERT, R.-A.
Bibliographie de la Tapisserie, des Tapis et de la Broderie en France — Paris, 1935

GÖBEL, H.
Wandteppiche, 3 vol. Bibliography in last vol.—Leipzig, 1923-1934

Enciclopedia universale dell Arte
Article: Arazzo, Bibliography at end of article Istituto per la collaborazione culturale—Venice-Rome, 1958

II. General Works

GUIFFREY, J.; MUNTZ, E.; PINCHART, A.
Histoire générale de la Tapisserie, 3 vol. in-fol. — Paris, 1878-1884

GUIFFREY, J.
Histoire de la Tapisserie depuis le Moyen Age jusqu'à nos Jours — Tours, 1886

HUNTER, G.-L.
Tapestries, their Origin, History and Renaissance — New York, London, Toronto, 1912

HUNTER, G.-L.
The Practical Book of Tapestries — London, Philadelphia, 1925

ACKERMANN, P.
Tapestry the Mirror of Civilisation — Oxford, 1933

GÖBEL, H.
Wandteppiche, 3 vol. — Leipzig, 1923-1934

DIGBY, G.-W.
European Tapestries and Carpets. The Concise Encyclopaedia of Antiques, vol. II, p. 32-42 — London, 1955

PLOURIN, M.-L.
Historia des Tapiz en Occidente — Barcelona, 1955

WEIGERT, R.-A.
La Tapisserie — Paris, 1956

GUIMBAUD, L.
La Tapisserie de Haute et Basse Lisse Paris, 1963

HEINZ, D.
Europäische Wandteppiche — Braunschweig, 1963

III. French Tapestry

General Works

BAZIN, G.; LURÇAT, J.; PICART LE DOUX, J.; SAINT-SAËNS, M.; DEGAND, L.; TABARD, F.
Muraille et Laine — Paris, 1946

JANNEAU, G.; FONTAINE, G.; NICLAUSSE, J.; VERLET, P.
La Tapisserie française — Paris, 1947

DEVILLE, J.
Recueil de statuts et de documents relatifs à la Corporation des tapissiers de 1258 à 1875... Paris, 1875

Studies on Gothic Tapestry

DEMOTTE
La Tapisserie gothique — Paris, 1922-1924

JUBINAL, A.
Les Anciennes Tapisseries historiées, ou collections des monuments les plus remarquables de ce genre qui nous soient restés du Moyen Age, à partir du XIe au XVIe siècle inclusivement... 2 vol. Paris, 1818-1830

PLANCHEMINAULT, R.
Les Tapisseries d'Angers — Paris, 1955

RORIMER, J.
Unicorn tapestries at the Cloisters — New York, 1962

Gobelins Manufactory

WEIGERT, R.-A.
Musée des Gobelins, les belles tentures de la manufacture royale des Gobelins 1662-1792 — Paris, 1937

Beauvais Manufactory

AJALBERT J.
Beauvais, la Manufacture nationale de Tapisserie — Paris, 1927

Aubusson Manufactory

WEIGERT, R.-A.
Cinq siècles de Tapisseries d'Aubusson
Paris, 1935

Contemporary French Tapestry

CASSOU, J.; DAMAIN, M.; MOUTARD-ULDRY, R.
La Tapisserie française et les Peintres Cartonniers — Paris, 1957

IV. Flemish and Brussels Tapestry

WAUTERS
Tapisseries bruxelloises—Brussels, 1878

SOIL DE MORIAMÉ, E.-J.
Les Tapisseries de Tournai — Tournai, 1892

CRICK-KUNTZIGER, M.
Les Tapisseries de l'Hôtel de Ville de Bruxelles—Antwerp, 1944

HULST R.-A. D'
Tapisseries flamandes—Brussels, 1960

V. Various Countries

CRUZADA VILLAAMIL, D.-G.
Los tapices de Goya — Madrid, 1870

THOMSON, W.-G.
Tapestry Weaving in England — New York, 1914

KURTH, B.
Die deutschen Bildteppiche des Mittelalters
Vienna, 1926

PAGACZEWSKI J.
Gobeliny Polskie, Tapestry in Poland
Cracow, 1929

MARILLER, H.-C.
English Tapestries of the Eighteenth Century — London, 1930

YSSELSTEYN, G.-T. VAN
Geschiedenis der Tapijweverijen in de Noordelijke Nederland — Leyde, 1936

GEBAROWICZ, M.; MANKOWSKI, T.
Arrasy Zygmunta Augusta, The Tapestry Collection of King Sigismond-August (Rocznic Krakowski vol. 29) —Cracow, 1937

MARILLIER, H.-C.
The Tapestries at Hampton Court Palace
London, 1951

MANKOWSKI, T.
Tkaniny i hafty polskie XVI-XVIII w.
Polish Fabrics and Embroidery of the 16th-18th Centuries—Wroclaw, 1954

BLAZKOWA, J.
Wandteppiche aus tschechoslowakischen Sammlungen — Prag, 1957

BULHAKOWA, K.; GRABOWSKI, J.; MARKIEWICZ M.; PLUTYNSKA, E.
Tkanina Polska, Polish Fabrics—Warsaw, 1959

VIALE FERRERO, M.
Arazzi italiani—Milan, 1961

VI. Catalogues and General Inventories

BARBIER DE MONTAULT, X.
Inventaire descriptif des Tapisseries de Haute Lisse conservées à Rome — Arras, 1879

RIGONI, C.
Catalogo della R. Galleria degli arazzi
Florence-Rome, 1884

BÖTTIGER, J.
Svenska Statens Samling af Wäfda Tapeter, 4 vol. — Stockholm, 1895-96

VALENCIA, J. DE
Tapices de la Corona de España — Madrid, 1903

DESTRÉE, J.; VEN, P. VAN DE
Musées royaux du Cinquantenaire: Les Tapisseries—Brussels, 1910

SANCHEZ CANTON, P.
Tapices de la Casa de Rey — Madrid, 1919

BALDASS, L.
Die Wiener Gobelinsammlung—Vienna, 1920

FENAILLE, M.
Etat général des Tapisseries de la Manufacture des Gobelins, depuis son origine jusqu'à nos jours (1600-1900) — Paris, 6 vol. in-folio, 1903-1923

HUNTER, G.-L.
Victoria and Albert Museum, catalogue of Tapestries — London, 1924

GOMEZ MARTINEZ, A.; CHILLON SAMPEDRO, B.
Los Tapices de la Catedral de Zamora
Zamora, 1925

MESSELET, J.; WEIGERT, R.-A.
Cinq Siècles de Tapisseries d'Aubusson
Paris, 1925

KENDRICK, A.-F.
Victoria and Albert Museum London, Dept. of Textiles: Catalogue of tapestries — London, 1928

RORIMER, J.
Mediaeval Tapestries, A Picture Book
New York, 1949

VIALE, M. et V.
Arazzi e tappeti antichi—Turin, 1952

TORRALBA SORIANO, F.
Los Tapices de Zaragoza — Zaragoza, 1953

CRICK-KUNTZIGER, M.
Musées royaux d'art et d'histoire, catalogue des tapisseries—Brussels, 1956

VII.

MADELEINE JARRY
La Tapisserie des Origines à nos Jours, Hachette — Paris 1968

JULIEN COFFINET
Arachné ou l'Art de la Tapisserie, Editions de la Coulouvrenière — Genève, 1971

JULIEN COFFINET, MAURICE PIANZOLA
La Tapisserie, Bonvent — Genève, 1971

DARIO BOCCARA
Les Belles Heures de la Tapisserie, Les Clefs du Temps — Zoug, 1971

ANDRÉ KUENZI
La Nouvelle Tapisserie, Bonvent — Genève 1973

MADELEINE JARRY
La Tapisserie, Art du XXe, Office du Livre Fribourg, 1974

LILY BLUMENAU
The Art and Craft of Handweaving, Crown Publishers Inc. — New York, 1962

TADEK BEUTLICH
The Technique of Woven Tapestry, Batsford — London, 1967

PETER COLLINGWOOD
The Technique of Rug Weaving, Faber London, 1968

LILY BLUMENAU
Creative Design in Wall Hanging, Crown Publishers Inc. — New York, 1972

MILDRED CONSTANTINE, JACK LENOR LARSEN
Beyond Craft: The Art Fabric, Van Nostrand Reinhold Company — New York, 1973

SHIRLEY HELD
Weaving, Holt, Rinehart and Winston New York, 1973

W. G. THOMSON, E. S. THOMSON
A History of Tapestry from the Earliest Times until the Present Day, EP Publishing Limited — Wakefield, 1973 (3rd ed.)

PRINCIPAL HISTORICAL FIGURES
MENTIONED IN THIS BOOK

Alba, Ferdinand Alvarez de Toledo (1508-1582), Duke of Alba, General under Emperor Charles V and Philip of Spain, Governor of the Low Countries from 1567 to 1573. A skilful general and ruthless politician, he remains notorious for his cruelties.

Anne de Beaujeu, (1460-1522), daughter of Louis XI. She was Regent of France from 1483 to 1491 during the minority of her brother Charles VIII.

Anne de Bretagne, Duchess of Brittany from 1488 to 1514. Through her marriages first to Charles VIII and then to Louis XII, Brittany was joined to France.

Barberini, Francesco, Cardinal, nephew of Urban VIII (Maffeo Barberini), Pope from 1623 to 1644.

Charles the Bold, (1433-1477), Duke of Burgundy from 1467 to 1477, son of Philip the Good. Violent and headstrong, he was a constant danger to the Kingdom of France. He was killed outside Nancy in a duel with René II, Duke of Lorraine.

Charles I, (1600-1649), King of England and Scotland from 1625 to 1649. Died on the scaffold.

Charles II, (1630-1685), King of England and Scotland from 1660-1685. His reign was full of incident.

Charles V, (1337-1380), King of France from 1364 to 1380, eldest son of John II. He brought peace and order to the realm, protected arts and letters. Many palaces were constructed or improved by him (Hôtel Saint-Pol, Louvre); he also accumulated an important collection of manuscripts.

Charles VI, (1368-1422), King of France from 1380 to 1422. His reign was troubled and he finally went mad while France was torn by political rivalries and the English invasion. His wife was Isabeau of Bavaria.

Charles VII, (1403-1461), King of France from 1422 to 1461, son of Charles VI and Isabeau of Bavaria. When he came to the throne much of France was occupied by the English. But Joan of Arc rallied the patriotism of her countrymen and, at the end of Charles' reign, only Calais remained in English hands.

Charles VIII, (1470-1498) King of France from 1483 to 1498, was the first French king to claim a right to the crown of Naples. His expedition into Italy revealed to the French the existence of a civilization which was more refined than their own. The influence of the Renaissance in France dates from this period.

Charles V, (1500-1558), Holy Roman Emperor from 1519 to 1556. He held sway over the Austrian Empire, the kingdom of Spain and the lands of the Holy Empire. For thirty years he was the implacable enemy of Francis I of France.

Christine de Pisan, (1364-1430), French authoress who wrote a panegyric on King Charles V under the title "Livre des faicts et bonnes mœurs du Roi Charles V."

Clemence of Hungary (died in 1328), daughter of Charles Martel, King of Hungary. She became the second wife of Louis X the Headstrong, King of France from 1314 to 1316.

Clement VI (Pierre Roger), Pope from 1342 to 1352. He resided at Avignon, protected Petrarch and patronized the arts.

Colbert, Jean-Baptiste (1619-1683), minister to Louis XIV, was responsible for the establishment of the Royal Gobelins Manufactory.

Diane de Poitiers (1499-1566), Duchess of the Valentinois country. Enjoyed a certain political influence through her liaison with King Henry II, celebrated for her beauty and her interest in the arts.

Este (House of), illustrious family of Italian princes, protected poets Arioste and Tasso. The Estes' court at Ferrara was one of the focal points of the Renaissance.

Fouquet, Nicolas (1615-1680), Superintendant of Finances of the Kongdom of France at the beginning of Louis XIV's reign. Protected La Fontaine and Molière, constructed the Château of Vaux. Imprisoned for embezzlement in 1664, he died in the fortress of Pignerol.

Ferdinand V (1452-1516), King of Aragon, Sicily and Naples. Under his reign Christopher Columbus discovered America.

Ferdinand, Infante of Portugal (1402-1443). Died a prisoner of the King of Fez following an ill-fated expedition against Ceuta.

Francis I (1494-1547), King of France from 1515 to 1547. A brilliant and courageous king, he protected literature and the arts (Leonardo da Vinci, Benvenuto Cellini) and founded the College of France.

François de Lorraine, Duc de Guise (1519-1563) a skilful warrior and shrewd politician.

Frederick II (1515-1576); Palatine elector. An avowed Calvinist, he played a prominent role in the organization of this church in Germany.

Gonzaga, family of princes reigning over Mantua from 1328 to 1709.

Henry II (1519-1559), King of France from 1547 to 1559, the son of Francis I and husband of Catherine de' Medici, he was, like his father, a discerning protector of arts and letters.

Henry IV (1553-1610), King of France from 1589 to 1610. He reunited France after the earlier religous wars.

Henry VI (1421-1471), King of England from 1422 to 1471. During the 100 Years' War he was crowned King of France at Notre-Dame de Paris on Charles VI's death.

Isabeau de Bavière (1371-1435), Queen of France, wife of Charles VI. Through the 1420 Treaty of Troyes she surrendered the greater part of France to the English.

James I (1566-1625), King of Scotland from 1567 to 1625, became also King of England in 1603.

Jean, Duc de Berry (1340-1416), son of King John II of France. Played a mediatory role between the houses of Burgundy and Orleans. Patron of the arts and letters, amateur and collector.

John the Fearless (1371-1419), Duke of Burgundy from 1404 to 1419, assassinated on the bridge of Montereau by Charles VII's advisers. John the Fearless was the father of Duke Philip III the Good.

Julius II (Giuliano della Rovere, 1443-1513), Pope from 1503 to 1513. Protector of Bramante, Michelangelo and Raphaël, he was responsible for the construction of Saint Peter's, Rome.

Leo X (Giovanni de' Medici, 1475-1521), Pope from 1513 to 1521, protector of letters and the arts.

Louis I (1339-1384), Duke of Anjou, Count of Provence, second son of King John II. Crowned King of Naples and Sicily in 1382 but was unable to maintain his hold on the throne.

Louis X, the Headstrong (1289-1316), son of Philip the Fair, King of France from 1314 to 1316.

Louis XII (1462-1515), King of France from 1498 until his death. Under his reign the wars in Italy encouraged the development of the Renaissance in France.

Louis XIII (1601-1643), King of France from 1610 to 1643. He chose as his chief minister the illustrious Cardinal Richelieu.

Louis XIV (1638-1715), King of France from 1643 to 1715, protector of the arts and letters. His reign was a glorious one and he deserved his nickname of "Le Roi Soleil" (The Sun King).

Louis XV (1710-1774), King of France from 1715 to 1774.

Mahaut d'Artois (died in 1329), became Countess of Artois in 1302 on the death of her father Robert II d'Artois.

Marguerite of Anjou (1429-1482), wife of King Henry VI of England, celebrated for her courage during the Wars of the Roses (1455-1485).

Margaret of York (1446-1503), Duchess of Burgundy, wife of Charles the Bold.

Medicis, family of princes reigning over Florence. Its most famous members were Cosimo I (1389-1464) and Lorenzo the Magnificent (1449-1492), a patron of poets and artists and himself a poet.

Napoleon (Napoleon Bonaparte, 1769-1821), Emperor of the French from 1804 to 1814. Contemporary France and Europe still to this day bear the stamp of his genius.

Nicholas V (Tomaso Parentucelli), Pope from 1447 to 1455.

Philip II (1527-1598), King of Spain from 1527 to 1598, son of Charles V. His reign was full of difficulties. Constructed the Escorial palace and monastery (1563-1584).

Philip II the Bold (1342-1404) Duke of Burgundy, son of King John II. Philip II founded the second Burgundian dynasty and was also an art-lover.

Philip III the Rash (1225-1285), King of France from 1270 to 1285, son of Saint Louis (Louis IX) and Marguerite de Provence.

Philip V (1683-1746) King of Spain from 1700 to 1746, grandson of Louis XIV.

Philip the Good (1396-1467), Duke of Burgundy from 1419 to 1467, one of the most powerful of 15th-century European rulers, and responsible for the greatness of the House of Burgundy.

René I of Anjou (1409-1480), last Duke of Anjou. Celebrated for his love of literature and the arts. Upon his death Anjou was united with France.

Renée de France (1510-1575), daughter of Louis XII, Duchess of Ferrara.

Rolin, Jean (1408-1483), Cardinal, son of Chancellor Nicolas Rolin.

Rolin, Nicolas (1376-1461), Chancellor of Burgundy under Philip the Good. Protector of literature and the arts, he founded Beaune Hospice.

Salins, Guigone de, wife of Chancellor Nicolas Rolin.

Sixtus IV (Francesco della Rovere, 1414-1484) Pope from 1471 to 1484, responsible for the Sistine Chapel and the enlargement of the Vatican library.

Sully, Maximilien de Béthune (1559-1641), Duke of Sully, counsellor and minister to Henry IV.

Urban VIII (Maffeo Barberini, 1568-1644), Pope from 1623 to 1644. Encouraged literature and art but under his pontificate Galileo was punished for "heresy".

INDEX OF COLOR PLATES

Gothic Tapestry

Classical Tapestry

Contemporary Tapestry

INDEX OF BLACK AND WHITE ILLUSTRATIONS

Catalog I

Catalog II

Catalog III

PHOTOGRAPHY

Alinari, Florence: 106-107
Caisse Nationale des Monuments Historiques, Paris: 56-57, 108-109
Citam, Lausanne: 155-188
Yves Debraine, Lausanne: 37-39, 41-42, 46-48, 94-95, 98-99, 100, 137-149, 200, 202, 204-206, 210-220, 224
Edita, Lausanne: 190-199, 201, 207, 221-222
Lacerda Foundation Caramulo: 102-103
André Held, Ecublens: 150-152

Metropolitan Museum, New York: 40, 43, 45, 54-55
Mobilier National, Paris: 110
Musée des Arts Décoratifs, Paris: 58
Musée d'Histoire, Berne: 52-53, 58
Wawel Museum, Cracow: 104-105
Scala, Florence, 89, 90-91, 92-93, 97
Victoria and Albert Museum, London: 50-51
Dina Vierny, Paris: 110

The publisher acknowledges with thanks the assistance of those Museum curators, churchmen, artists, collectors and gallery directors who have assisted in the preparation of this book, and in particular the Centre International de la Tapisserie Ancienne et Moderne (CITAM), in Lausanne.

This book was created by
Edita S.A., Lausanne

Photolithography: Actual S.A. Bienne
Printed by GEA, Milan
Bound by Maurice Busenhart, Lausanne

IMPRIMÉ EN ITALIE